POVERTY, U. S. A.

THE HISTORICAL RECORD

ADVISORY EDITOR: David J. Rothman

Professor of History, Columbia University

WAGE EARNERS' BUDGETS

LOUISE BOLARD MORE

Arno Press & The New York Times
NEW YORK   1971

Reprint Edition 1971 by Arno Press Inc.

Reprinted from a copy in
The Newark Public Library

LC# 73—137178
ISBN 0—405—03116—5

POVERTY, U.S.A.: THE HISTORICAL RECORD
ISBN for complete set: 0-405-03090-8

Manufactured in the United States of America

WAGE-EARNERS' BUDGETS

A STUDY OF STANDARDS AND COST OF LIVING IN NEW YORK CITY

BY

LOUISE BOLARD MORE

WITH A PREFACE BY

FRANKLIN H. GIDDINGS

Professor of Sociology in Columbia University

NEW YORK

HENRY HOLT AND COMPANY

1907

PREFACE

THE study of living conditions here offered on behalf of the Greenwich House Committee on Social Investigations differs in a number of important respects from studies of standards of living in workingmen's families with which the public is already familiar.

It is, to begin with, an investigation of wage-earning families in the heart of that American city in which, partly because of its size and wealth, and partly because of the limitations of Manhattan Island, the struggle for existence is most intense. In the second place its results have been obtained by methods more thorough, painstaking, and critical than it has usually been possible hitherto to use. Statistical work, as we have known it, has had the great merit of dealing with large numbers in which small errors are to a great extent self-eliminated by mutual cancellation, but it has left much to be desired on the side of exact knowledge of the concrete facts numerically expressed. Of the figures set down in Mrs. More's tables it can be said that every one stands for something not only certainly known, but also critically scrutinized and weighed before being added to the general sum of information.

This critical thoroughness has been rendered possible by the limitations of the inquiry, and by the character of the relations subsisting between the investigator and the families whose economic status has been recorded. The tables comprise statistical data pertaining to two hundred families only. The results therefore are at best only representative, possibly only indicative of the Social Economy of Wage-earners. They make no claim to completeness. Their value turns entirely upon the scientific validity of the selection made. Nothing is easier than to choose from a given population so many hundreds or so many thousands of individuals or of families whose circumstances duly set down in arithmetical terms shall constitute a picture of economic life thoroughly biased and misleading. Thrift can be demonstrated, or the "existing social order" can be indicted for infamous cruelty to any extent desired, by the method of statistical selection. When, therefore, an inquiry, instead of covering all possible instances in a given population, is necessarily and confessedly based upon selected units, it is imperative from the standpoints alike of science and of common honesty that the selections shall be made by a strictly objective test, and that the nature of the test shall be explicitly made known to all who read and venture to use the results.

In the present study, the two hundred families finally chosen were sorted out by a method as sound as could possibly be discovered, and having the great merit that whatever co-efficient of error it introduces is obviously an error of understatement. The two hundred families making up the final list were those that proved to be able and willing to coöperate with the investigator intelligently and patiently in keeping simple accounts and in making careful, verifiable statements. This of course means that these two hundred families were in point of intelligence and character somewhat above the average of the class in which their economic lot is cast, and dwelling in the neighborhood in which the inquiry centers. Such families, whatever their circumstances, "get on" somewhat better than others. Consequently, if Mrs. More's picture of the life of these families shows much hardship and a never-ceasing struggle to keep above that line below which poverty begins, we may be very sure that it is not an exaggerated portrayal of the social-economic life of the self-sustaining working people of New York City to-day.

PREFACE

The undeniable success which has rewarded Mrs. More's experiment in making friendly personal acquaintance contribute to scientific inquiry is another distinguishing and most gratifying feature of this investigation. The poor rightfully resent most of the amateur and frankly impertinent attempts of self-appointed "sociologists" to investigate them, but they are nearly always entirely willing to coöperate.in any serious study of economic conditions when its nature and value are understood and they are assured that their private concerns will be regarded with delicacy and respect. Mrs. More has completed an investigation of great value through strictly coöperative work. The results here offered could not have been achieved without the cordial assistance of all of the families whose struggles and circumstances are set forth.

FRANKLIN H. GIDDINGS.

COLUMBIA UNIVERSITY,
April 20, 1907.

CONTENTS

CHAPTER I

vii

Comparison of Average Income and Expenditure in Native and Foreign Families—Distribution of Incomes of Various Amounts in Native and Foreign Families—Influence of Racial Characteristics on Various Expenditures, Food, Rent, Clothing, Light and Fuel, Insurance, and Sundries—Comparison of Average Expenditures of German and Irish Families having an Income between $1000. and $1200.

Comparative Size of Native and Foreign Families—Comparison of Income and Expenditure in Families of Same Size, of Different Nativity—Summary of Table IV in Regard to Incomes and Expenditures.

The Various Sources of Income, from the Husband, Wife, Children, and Other Sources—Tables A and B. Number and Per Cent of Families having an Income from Various Sources by Nativity of Head of Family—Incomes from Husbands, Wives, Children, Boarders and Lodgers, and "Other Sources," in Different Foreign Nativities and in Native Families—Tables C and D. Average Amount and Per Cent of Income from Various Sources for all Families by Nativity of Head of Family—Table E. Average Amount of Income from Various Sources, for all Families having an Income from the Specified Source, by Nativity of Head of Family.

Comparison of Families in which Expenditures for "Sundries" Extend from Less than 5 Per Cent of the Total Expenditure to more than 40 Per Cent—Proportion of "Sundries" Expended for Spending-money, Drink, etc., in all Families.

Comparison of Number of Native and Foreign Families having Various Sundry Expenditures—Comparison of Amount of Expenditures for Various Purposes—Average Expenditures for Various "Sundries" in all Families.

CONTENTS

CHAPTER V

CHAPTER VI

CHAPTER VII

WAGE-EARNERS' BUDGETS

WAGE-EARNERS' BUDGETS

*A STUDY OF STANDARDS AND COST OF LIVING
IN NEW YORK CITY*

CHAPTER I

THE INVESTIGATION: ITS OBJECT AND METHODS

THE investigations of Le Play, Engel, Booth, and Rowntree have given us important and valuable data on the subject of the incomes and cost of living of wage-earners in France, Germany, and England, and recently the Department of Labor has made a similar study,[1] in an even more extensive way, of the wage-earners of the United States. None of these investigations has had the peculiar advantage which the Social Settlement offers for an intimate and personal neighborhood study of the lives of the people in their daily social, economic, and industrial relations. To make use of the great opportunity for scientific research on th s subject which is open to the residents of a Social Settlement, situated in the heart of a crowded tenement quarter, the Greenwich House Committee on Social Investigations[2] was

[1] Eighteenth Annual Report of U. S. Department of Labor.

[2] Edwin R. A. Seligman, Chairman; Franz Boas, Edward T. Devine, Livingston Farrand, Franklin H. Giddings, Henry R. Seager; V. G. Simkhovitch, S ecretary.

formed in the spring of 1903. Its object was the establishment of a resident Fellowship at Greenwich House, a Social Settlement on the lower West Side of New York City. The general purpose of the Fellowship is the investigation of various social and economic aspects of city life.

"The standard of living among different races and occupations in the neighborhood of Greenwich House" was Object of the chosen as the first subject for investigation. Investigation. This study, the results of which are given in the following report, was begun in November, 1903, and lasted almost two years, being practically completed by September, 1905. The writer held the Fellowship, and during the first year made a personal inquiry into the standards and cost of living of 100 families. The results of this year's investigation were considered so suggestive and so descriptive of the life of the neighborhood, that the Committee decided to carry the inquiry still further in order that a more comprehensive and representative report could be made covering the experience of 200 workingmen's families. During the second year, the Fellow was assisted by Miss Elizabeth Lennox, who became a resident at Greenwich House for the purpose of completing the investigation.

From the facts collected during these two years, it has been possible to formulate some statistics showing, for a definite and not too extensive territory, the incomes and necessary and usual expenses of workingmen's families of various size and of different nationalities.

The cordial relationships formed by a constant neighborly intercourse between the residents of Greenwich House and Means of Obtain- the people of the neighborhood made possible ing Information. such a thorough and personal inquiry. The families were carefully selected for their ability to give the desired information and for their willingness to coöperate.

Frequent visits were made to each family during the time it was under observation, and every opportunity for neigh-

Personal Friend-ship. borly helpfulness was eagerly seized. Sick children were taken to the Hospital or Dispensary, many children were sent to the country through the various Fresh-air Agencies, employment was found for boys, and girls were placed in a Trade School. Genuine and mutual friendships resulted from the services which the investigators, as Settlement residents, were enabled to render. The object of the investigation was then generally explained, briefly and simply, to the mother of the family. When possible, the husband's interest in the work was also aroused. The value of the response depended invariably upon the intelligence and reliability of the wife, who is the manager and dispenser of the family income. The information received was regarded as purely confidential. In only a few cases was there any distrust of the purpose of the investigation or a refusal to give the desired facts.

The coöperation of charity and church visitors, teachers in Kindergartens, nurses, and other district workers was

District Workers. obtained. These persons come in close touch with the lives of the people, and their introductions to families who were reliable and willing to give their experience to the investigators were very helpful.

Another means of collecting information was through a Cooking Class, which the writer conducted weekly at Green-

Cooking Class. which House. Eighteen women came regularly and enthusiastically to this class. Here a friendly discussion of the prices paid for food in the neighborhood, methods of marketing and of cooking, the nutritive value of different foods, the essentials of an adequate diet, and the general cost of living, proved of great value in determining the standards of these women in their housekeeping. The class afforded an opportunity for a further discussion of these subjects in friendly calls at the homes of the members.

The Fellow was asked upon several occasions to address Mothers' Meetings in the neighborhood on the subject of Public Explana- the investigation, and in this way gained the tion. interest and coöperation of a number of intelligent housewives, who were willing to assist her with their experience.

The facts obtained in these various ways were recorded in schedules, which were made adaptable for statistical use and at the same time comprehensive enough to give Schedules. See Sample Schedule, a picture of the home life and standard of livpages 126-129. ing of each family. In detail, these schedules show the size of each family, its nationality, home surroundings and number of rooms occupied, wages of its contributing members and the estimated total income, the expenditures for all purposes, and the attitude of the family toward dress, recreation, the pawnshop, the installment system, church, or funeral expenses. Any other interesting and pertinent facts in the life of each family were carefully noted.

Household budgets were kept by 50 families for periods varying from one week to one year. These little account books, which were given out by the investi- Budgets. gators, itemized the income and expenditures of each family during the weeks they were kept. They form the basis of a more detailed study of the cost of various commodities, especially of food, during the two years covered by the investigation. The schedules which are supplemented by these household budgets are naturally the most reliable and significant.

In all these ways of collecting information, the investigators had a manifest advantage over the census-taker or collector of statistics. A mere canvass from house to house in the neighborhood would be entirely inadequate for such a study as this. The value of this investigation depends upon the friendship of the families studied, a knowledge of each family's home life and its reputation in the neighborhood, an almost daily intercourse with many of the families for long periods of time, and an intimate understanding of the needs and life of the neighborhood.

The families investigated have been called in general "wage-earners' families", but in a few instances the families *Character of the* of petty shopkeepers have been included, *Families.* because their incomes put them in this class, and their standard of living was in every respect the same. *Wage-earners and* In fact, it seemed desirable to secure the *Small Shopkeepers.* schedules of a number of such families in the neighborhood in order to contrast them with those of the families of workingmen.

As many families as possible above the so-called "dependent class" were included. The very poor are not repre- *Above the "De-* sentative of the normal workingman's family, *pendent Class".* and their struggle is rehearsed in the records of all charitable societies, yet the experience of some of them should enter into the total averages, in a study of a neighborhood of which they are a component part. Most of the families in this investigation are ordinarily self-supporting and require assistance only at critical times, when it is most frequently supplied by friends and relatives. The average wage-earner's family in this neighborhood is constantly on the verge of dependence, and would become dependent on friends or charity at any time of long-continued industrial depression, illness, or unemployment. The "margin of surplus" of the income over expenditures is very small, and it is only in exceptional cases that it is possible for a family of average size to make much provision for the future.

No arbitrary limits were set within which the incomes of the families under observation must fall. The work and surroundings of a Settlement naturally threw the investigators into contact with working-men's families of very moderate means, but in one instance the total income of a family was $2556. for the year. This was exceptional, but no more so than the lowest income of $250. a year, and both extremes represent a class in the neighborhood, and have therefore been included. In the 200 families studied, 27, or 13.5 per cent, had total incomes below $500. a year; 72, or 36 per cent, were between $500. and $800.; 44, or 22 per cent, were between $800. and $1000.; 46, or 23 per cent, between $1000. and $1500., and 11, or 5.5 per cent, had total incomes from $1500. to $2556. The writer estimates, after a careful survey, that this represents a fair proportion of the distribution of income among all the families in this neighborhood. The average income from all sources was $851.38, which is believed to be a fair average for a workingman's family in the district. On this amount some families live comfortably, others suffer privations, owing to circumstances and the nature and amount of their expenditures. In many cases, thrift and good management go far to make adequate an income generally believed insufficient for the necessities of life.

The study of a family had occasionally to be dropped because of the ignorance and shiftless methods of house-keeping of the wife, the intemperance or irregular employment of the husband, removal from the neighborhood, or exceptional circumstances which made the life of that family impracticable to study. The families as a whole represent a fair average of industry, reliability, and perseverance. A number of typical cases have been selected and a description of their family life included in the report.

From these schedules, budgets, and copious descriptive notes the following study has been made. Of special interest

Summary of
Results.

are the tabulations, classifying and arranging the various incomes and expenditures according to size and nativity of the families. These figures show, within the limitations of statistics, the standard of living and the necessary expenditures for the maintenance of this standard, and they also throw some light on the question of the amount of income requisite to enable a family to exist without outside assistance.

While it is not claimed that this study of a small group can furnish conclusive deductions for all workingmen's

Value of the
Investigation.

families, the writer nevertheless believes that the results of this investigation give a comparatively true insight into the social, economic, and industrial life of a large class of workingmen's families in any city neighborhood of similar character. A presentation of the daily lives of so many families must reveal, directly or indirectly, many facts bearing on the whole question of labor and wages, housing conditions, the rent problem, the cost of living, the economies and extravagance of the poor, their pleasures and recreations, their provisions for the future and for death, and, in outline, the whole story of the struggle for existence under the conditions of modern city life.

CHAPTER II

"GREENWICH VILLAGE"—THE NEIGHBORHOOD

No part of the City of New York has so good a claim to antiquity as Greenwich Village. Before Henry Hudson sailed up the great River, or New Amsterdam was thought of, this spot was the site of an Indian village, called Sappokanican. After the Indians were driven out by the Dutch in 1633, it finally came under English rule, about 1721, and its name was changed to Greenwich. This name still clings to the district. The village was famous in Colonial times for its healthful location, its charming river beach, the fertility of its soil, and its fragrant abundance of wild grapes, strawberries, and other fruits. So inviting a spot soon had many settlers, at first only farmers and artisans, until several epidemics drove people from the town of New York to the higher ground of the healthful little village. In 1744, Sir Peter Warren bought 300 acres near the river for his country home. During the next sixty years the village became the summer home of many wealthy New Yorkers. The road to Greenwich was the fashionable drive of the period. "Richmond Hill" was the name of the country place of Abraham Mortier, Commissary to his Majesty's forces, and here Lord Amherst was entertained. For a time this mansion was the headquarters of General Washington, after the war it was the home of Vice-

Its History.

8

president Adams, until, in 1797, Aaron Burr became its owner. This was only one of the many beautiful homes in the village.

The coming of all this fashionable society greatly stimulated the growth of the village. It became famous for its markets—Greenwich, State Prison, Jefferson, and Clinton Markets. The State Prison was built there in 1796, at the foot of the present Tenth Street, and continued in use for thirty years, until it was superseded by Sing Sing. Some idea of the low cost of living at that time in the village may be inferred from the fact that the three meals a day for the 235 persons in the prison are reported to have cost but $10.11.

The great epidemic of 1822 caused such an exodus to Greenwich from New York that its village life ceased, and it became a bustling part of a great city, and its history that of the City of New York.

The boundaries of Greenwich Village in Colonial times were a little brook called Manetta Creek, or Water, and the River. The district has practically the same extent to-day, though not so sharply defined. Broadly speaking, what has been known for many years as Greenwich is that part of New York extending from lower Fifth Avenue and West Broadway to the Hudson River, and from Fourteenth Street to Canal Street. This is the location of the district chosen for this investigation. It is the part of old New York that has retained its village features the longest. It is the last to lose its old-fashioned houses and become a tenement district. Its character has changed wonderfully in the last ten years. The old two- and three-story houses, with their quaint doorways and gabled roofs, are being rapidly torn down to make way for large tenements, or are being altered for the

Location.

Housing Conditions.

use of three or four or even more families. It is a district of extremes in housing conditions. The crowded Italian tenements on Macdougal, Thompson, and Sullivan streets are almost neighbors to fashionable Washington Square and lower Fifth Avenue. West of Sixth Avenue there are many irregular, rambling old streets, with rows of comfortable old-fashioned houses, well kept and owned for generations by the families still occupying them. These houses and this part of the present population of Greenwich Village are, of course, entirely without the province of an inquiry into the lives of the workingmen, who are rapidly becoming the most numerous inhabitants of the district. The old houses now occupied by several families are somewhat run down, but dignified even in their decay. At the other extreme are cheap tenements of the "double-decker," "dumb-bell" type, tumble-down rear houses, and several very disreputable "courts" and short streets, sometimes containing tenements scarcely fit for human habitation. The very poor frequently live in houses whose sanitary conditions and general character are as bad as can be found anywhere in New York. The whole neighborhood is in a state of transition, and its rapidly increasing population is changing the external features of the district. As yet, it is not so crowded as the lower East Side of New York, and can still retain many of its former individual characteristics.

The population is very heterogeneous and is also rapidly changing in character. It is much more typical of the entire working-class population of New York than is the Jewish East Side. Here are many Americans whose families have lived in the district for generations, who have a strong local pride in Old Greenwich, and who greatly deplore the passing of its traditions; here are the Irish and Irish-Americans, the politicians of the

Population.

Ninth Ward; and here are also to be found many French and German families, the remnants of a once large French and German quarter of the city. Until recently these nationalities largely predominated in the district. There was also a large colored quarter. Within the last few years the population has become much more cosmopolitan, and now has representatives of almost every nationality to be found in New York. For several years the Italians have come in steadily increasing numbers until now it is one of the important Italian quarters in the city. In the block in which Greenwich House is situated, though on the edge of the real Italian quarter, a neighborhood canvass (in 1904) showed there were 115 Italian families out of a total number of 296, while the census for 1900 reported no Italian families for that block. The racial feeling is often very strong. The Irish hate the Italians ("Dagos") and the negroes ("niggers"), and the North Italians despise the Sicilians. There can be no common social life nor unity of interests where there is such a diversity of nationalities. Yet, because of this mixture of native and foreign elements, Greenwich Village is notably a district in which to study the social and industrial life of workingmen's families of different races.

The occupations of the wage-earners are even more varied than is the population. There is no one highly concentrated industry as that of the garment-makers of the East Side, but a great diversity of trades and occupations. It is a district largely given over to candy, paper-box, and artificial-flower factories, and to wholesale houses. Its proximity to the North River and the docks of the great steamship lines gives occupation to many longshoremen, or dock-laborers, and to truck-drivers. Probably these occupations give employment to a larger number of men than does any other one industry. A great many clerks live here, as well as porters, waiters, carpenters, painters, plumbers, factory-workers, foremen in factories, barbers, bootblacks, bookkeepers, letter-carriers, policemen, and petty shopkeepers. All kinds of skilled and unskilled labor are represented. There is probably a larger proportion of unskilled than of skilled laborers in the district.

The personal characteristics of the working people are generally those of their nationality, and are in no respect Characteristics of exceptional to the neighborhood. Their social the People. life consists of the usual diversions—the public balls, cheap theatres, the christening parties, and the clambakes and free excursions given by local politicians in summer. The Italians have their fêtes and church festivals.

The men have the saloons, political clubs, trade-unions, or lodges for their recreation, the young people have an occasional ball or go to a cheap theatre, and in the evenings congregate on the streets and in the small parks for their pleasure, while the mothers have almost no recreation, only a dreary round of work, day after day, with occasionally a door-step gossip to vary the monotony of their lives. The Settlements and institutional churches are giving more social opportunity for the mothers and young people.

Intemperance is a flagrant evil. It is especially striking among the women, and the habit of sending children to the saloons for beer is very common. There is frequently a low ethical standard—for example, petty thieving among boys is common and is condoned, "jumping the rent" is often not considered dishonest. There is often an indifference to church ties and to religious creeds. On the other hand, one finds moral characteristics which an outsider little suspects— a spirit of charity and mutual helpfulness, a disposition to aid one poorer than one's self, to help a man when he is down, and to bear courageously and cheerfully an almost intolerable situation, and frequently a beautiful and unselfish devotion of a mother to her children. Emerson found that "in the mud and scum of things, there always, always something sings". One Settlement resident has said truly: "Much moral unloveliness may be explained by the conditions under which men live and work."

Greenwich House is admirably located for a study of all these neighborhood conditions. It is situated on a short street, only a block long, which is so set apart Greenwich House. by itself as to retain many of the aspects of a village community. The people, until the recent invasion of so many Italians, knew their neighbors, and there is still a spirit of neighborliness and interest in all the residents of "the street". There are some American families in which the parents were married on this street and have always lived here. The Irish still predominate in numbers, but the entire street is representative of the cosmopolitan elements of the neighborhood and of its varied industrial life. The residents come into very close touch with the daily life of their neighbors, and their intercourse with them is unusually friendly, natural, and responsive. The friendships formed here, and the influence of the Settlement in the neighborhood, are not confined to a single block. Members of its Clubs and Classes come from all parts of the district, and the Settlement is a recognized part of the life of the entire neighborhood.

Every neighborhood has its own characteristic features. "Old Greenwich" has its traditions, its unique housing conditions, its heterogeneous population, its Summary. diversity of occupations, and its moral characteristics and ethical standards, but for a district in which

to study the actual living conditions of the New York workingman and his family in their social, economic, and industrial
relations, it is not exceptional, and may be taken as fairly
representative of the conditions existing in many industrial
communities in our large cities.

CHAPTER III

DESCRIPTIVE ANALYSIS OF EACH FAMILY—OCCUPATION, NATIVITY, SIZE, INCOME AND EXPENDITURES

THE value of the statistical method in such a study as this depends upon the frankness with which its limitations are met and defined. To say that the facts deduced from a study of a limited number of families, even as many as 200, are typical of different nationalities or of all workingmen's families of a given size is misleading and unscientific; yet, to obtain actual statistical data touching the sources and amount of income and the objects of expenditure in representative families, and then, by tables, to present these facts clearly and logically in their relation to each other and to the whole cost of living is to throw much light on the economic life of a large class of our population.

In the first place, a descriptive analysis of each one of the 200 families was made, showing the occupation of the head of the family, his nativity and that of the wife, size of the family, total income, expenditures for various purposes, amount of surplus or deficit, and per cent of income expended. These facts are presented in the following table, which thus gives much of the material on which the later tables are based.

TABLE I

OCCUPATION, NATIVITY, SIZE OF FAMILY, INCOME, AND EXPENDITURES OF EACH ONE OF 200 FAMILIES

Occupation.	Nativity of Head of Family.	No. in Fam.	Income.†	Food.	Rent.	Cloth-ing.	Light and Fuel.	Insur-ance.	Sun-dries.	Total.	Amount of Sur-plus or Deficit.	Per Cent of Income Expended.	Nativity of Wife.
1 Hod-carrier.	English	6	775.	338.	120.	130.	58.	46.80	82.20	775.	$	100.	Irish
2 Oyster-selecter.	Irish-Amer.	9	1500.	520.	168.	560.	55.	106.60	110.40	1520.	−20.	101.3	Irish
3 Iceman.	Irish-Amer.	6	1343.	364.	225.	190.	48.		457.52	1343.	0	100.	Same
4 Truckman.	American	5	686.	286.	180.	35.*7	24.	88.24	72.76	686.	0	100.	Ger.-Amer.
5 *Washerwoman.	German	8	880.	500.	131.50	150.*7	32.	7.80	58.70	880.	0	100.	Same
6 Oysterman.	Irish-Amer.	8	744.	364.	180.	72.50*8	52.	33.80	81.70	784.	−40.	105.4	Same
7 Steamfitter's helper.	American	9	689.	179.40	144.	64.75	36.95	23.16	209.74	658.	+31.	95.5	Irish-Amer.
8 *Seamstress.	Irish-Amer.	2	260.	130.	92.75	18.	13.00	0	6.25	260.	0	100.	Scotch-Amer.
9 Glassworker.	Irish	4	1040.	520.	132.	85.	48.50	31.20	223.30	1040.	0	100.	Same
10 Truckman.	French-Am.	8	1108.	364.	216.	130.	35.	97.66	193.34	1036.	+72.	93.5	Ger.-Amer.
11 Grocer's clerk.	German	4	614.	286.	132.	62.90	36.	26.	88.	630.	−16.	102.6	Same
12 Fireman.	Irish	8	895.	481.60	108.	23.	33.	44.20	212.30	941.	−46.	105.1	Irish
13 Truckman.	Dutch-Amer.	6	560.	265.20	108.	175.	31.	41.60	91.20	560.	0	100.	Ger.-Amer.
14 Longshoreman.	Irish	10	810.	416.	138.	10.	48.		108.	885.	−75.	109.3	English
15 Casual laborer.	Irish-Amer.	3	250.	150.	84.	10.	14.80	10.40	8.80	278.	−28.	111.2	Ger.-Amer.
16 *Janitor.	Irish-Amer.	5	420.	190.	120.	50.	38.	20.80	27.20	446.	−26.	106.2	Dut.-Amer.
17 Longshoreman.	Norwegian	2	1000.	260.	186.	83.	33.	0	268.	830.	+170.	83.	(man) English
18 Letter-carrier.	American	6	1000.	364.	216.	130.	58.	104.56	127.44	1000.	0	100.	English-Am.
19 Tailor.	German	5	1214.	416.	281.	60.*3	42.70	127.88	252.42	1180.	+34.	97.2	Ger.-Amer.
20 Draftsman.	American	4	850.	364.	156.	65.	52.60	62.40	143.	843.	+7.	99.2	Irish
21 *Janitor.	Irish	8	1122.	500.	180.	110.	65.90	31.20	336.90	1173.	−51.	104.5	Same
22 Truckman.	American	7	970.	362.	129.	125.	33.44	33.80	205.76	940.	+30.	96.9	Same
23 *Housekeeper.	German	9	1450.	572.	210.	200.*6	41.	36.40	305.60	1365.	+85.	94.1	French (man)
24 Carpenter.	Scotch-Am.	6	360.	200.	109.	45.*5	31.	15.80	35.20	436.	−76.	121.1	Canadian-Am.
25 *Housekeeper.	English	6	850.	364.	120.	165.*5	45.	13.	143.	850.	0	100.	Italian (man deserted)
26 *Washerwoman.	German	5	410.	160.	90.	66.	22.56	18.20	53.80	410.	0	100.	Same
27 Porter.	English-Am.	5	670.	304.20	60.	28.	28.56	39.	130.24	670.	0	100.	English
28 *Janitor.	Irish	5	956.	416.	180.	115.	36.	86.94	143.06	977.	−21.	102.2	Same
29 Stonecutter.	Italian	6	690.	338.	108.	110.	37.40		143.60	730.	−40.	105.8	Same
30 Silversmith.	English-Am.	4	1075.	312.	185.	110.	55.	23.40	351.60	1075.	0	100.	Ger.-Amer.
31 *Washerwoman.	Irish-Amer.	5	530.	260.	120.	62.*3	30.	25.	53.	550.	−20.	103.8	Amer. (man deserted)

* Occupation of the wife who is head of the family.   † This includes income from all sources.

TABLE I—Continued

#	Occupation	Nativity of Head of Family	No. in Fam.	Income†	Food	Rent	Cloth-ing	Light and Fuel	Insur-ance	Sun-dries	Total	Amount of Sur-plus or Deficit	Per Cent of Income Expended	Nativity of Wife
32	*Housekeeper	Irish	4	725.	312.	110.	165.	25.50	8.60	103.90	725.	$ 0	100.	Same
33	Shipping clerk	American	6	756.	322.	126.	112.	82.	31.20	82.80	756.	0	100.	Irish-Amer.
34	Truckman	American	4	750.	320.	144.	100.	40.	36.04	107.46	747.50	+ 2.50	99.7	Same
35	Housekeeper	Italian	6	910.	390.	127.	115.	45.	33.80	196.45	907.25	+ 2.75	99.7	Same
36	Waiter	French	5	700.	260.	118.	72.	41.50	0	188.50	680.	+ 20.	97.1	Same
37	*Washerwoman	English	8	675.	364.	142.50	75.*6	46.	23.40	24.10	675.	0	100.	Irish (man dead)
38	Cigar-maker	Cuban-Negro	4	450.	208.	132.	40.	20.	23.40	36.60	460.	− 10.	102.2	German
39	*Housekeeper	German	5	730.	338.	157.	75.*3	42.	36.40	82.80	758.	− 28.	103.8	Same
40	Seamstress	French	2	380.	182.	120.	10.	26.	0	42.00	380.	0	100.	Same
41	In brewery	German	2	728.	300.	150.	75.	29.	47.20	51.80	653.	+ 75.	89.7	Irish
42	Longshoreman	Irish	4	675.	312.	120.	100.	42.	28.60	72.40	675.	0	100.	Same
43	Stonecutter	Irish-Amer.	2	820.	300.	120.	85.	35.	61.20	218.80	820.	0	100.	Same
44	Casual laborer	Irish-Amer.	6	980.	520.	216.	50.*4	53.50	28.60	81.90	930.	+ 50.	94.9	American
45	Printer	American	3	784.	312.	54.	150.	52.40	52.	172.20	792.60	− 8.60	101.1	Same
46	Gilder in book-bindery	Italian	8	925.	450.	136.	96.	62.35	62.40	139.75	946.50	− 21.50	102.3	English
47	Dyer	Ger.-Amer.	7	1000.	468.	240.	100.*5	46.	72.80	73.20	1000.	0	100.	American
48	Painter	English	2	900.	468.	165.	100.	65.	20.68	78.32	900.	0	100.	American
49	Barber	Italian	10	867.	400.	180.	200.	50.	0	52.00	867.	0	100.	Same
50	Postal clerk	Irish	4	1500.	676.	137.	275.*6	58.	84.40	271.60	1545.	− 45.	103.7	Same
51	Stableman	Irish	4	600.	277.	144.	40.	52.	29.25	87.25	622.50	− 22.50	103.7	Same
52	Ship-joiner	English	3	1000.	338.	106.	125.	85.	0	308.	1000.	0	100.	Same
53	Truckman	American	6	557.	260.	120.	51.	55.	15.60	89.40	577.	− 20.	103.6	Irish-Amer.
54	Elevatorman	English-Am.	8	1150.	660.40	192.	125.*6	48.	31.20	201.40	1186.	− 36.	103.1	Eng.-Greek
55	"Handy man"	American	4	611.	276.	120.	45.	28.	40.80	34.20	616.	− 5.00	100.8	Ger.-Amer.
56	Housekeeper	English-Am.	5	714.	364.	120.	70.	40.	28.60	91.40	714.	0	100.	Same
57	Automobile engineer	Swedish	4	1600.	520.	175.30	87.60	40.	7.60	319.50	1150.	+ 450.	71.9	German
58	Accountant	American	2	810.	364.	130.	100.	18.	0	138.	710.	+ 100.	87.7	Same
59	Button-maker	English	4	820.	364.	150.80	50.	36.	15.60	103.60	720.	+ 100.	85.4	Same
60	Grocer	German	6	1304.	463.	147.	78.	57.20	90.	145.80	1129.	+ 175.	86.6	Same
61	Truckman	English-Am.	8	647.	260.	147.	78.	30.90	30.72	107.38	654.	− 7.00	101.1	Irish-Amer.
62	Egg-candler	Irish-Amer.	4	792.	364.	120.	70.	60.50	46.28	59.22	792.	0	100.	Ger.-Amer.
63	Truckman	American	8	688.	364.	120.	52.50	10.	41.60	99.90	688.	0	100.	Irish
64	Glass-sign maker	American	7	700.	364.	96.	50.	25.	23.40	41.60	600.	+ 100.	87.2	Same

* Occupation of the wife who is head of the family.   † This includes income from all sources.

TABLE I—Continued

	Occupation.	Nativity of Head of Family.	No. in Fam.	Income.†	Expenditures per Year for — Food.	Rent.	Cloth-ing.	Light and Fuel.	Insur-ance.	Sun-dries.	Total.	Amount of Sur-plus or Deficit.	Per Cent of Income Expended	Nativity of Wife.
65	Elevator-man	Italian	12	1358.	512.20	216.	300.*11	89.	28.60	212.20	1358.	$ 0	100.	Same
66	Longshoreman	Italian	3	580.	247.	90.	40.	45.	13.00	150.	580.	0	100.	Same
67	Longshoreman	Italian	5	640.	260.20	90.	100.	45.	7.80	137.20	640.	0	100.	Same
68	Longshoreman	Italian	10	972.	369.20	102.	100.	51.	44.20	305.60	972.	0	100.	Same
69	Janitor	Scotch-Am.	3	660.	312.	180.	34.50	27.	44.80	36.70	635.	+25.	96.2	American
70	Pilot	Swedish	5	572.	286.	144.	70.	41.	5.60	25.40	572.	0	100.	Norwegian
71	Cabinet-maker	Italian	6	1010.	442.	144.	100.	25.	52.	172.	935.	+75.	92.6	Same
72	Baker	Swiss	6	904.	434.20	150.	75.	28.	40.80	147.	869.	+35.	96.1	Scotch
73	"Checker;" in club	Italian-Am.	4	980.	364.	150.	121.25	40.	10.40	294.35	980.	0	100.	It.-Irish-Am.
74	Truckman	Irish-Amer.	5	724.	312.	132.	40.	9.	23.40	158.60	724.	0	100.	Scotch-Amer.
75	Longshoreman	English	5	914.	500.	168.	50.	63.	29.04	157.96	914.	0	100.	Ger.-Amer.
76	Plumber	Swiss	4	680.	273.	151.	36.	37.35	83.25	99.45	680.	0	100.	Same
77	Machinist	French-Am.	2	805.	260.	184.	54.	32.	24.96	165.04	720.	+85.	89.4	German
78	Truckman	American	6	693.	234.	180.	50.	42.	25.20	161.80	693.	0	100.	German
79	Porter	Ger.-Amer.	4	652.	260.	156.	49.	50.	44.20	92.80	652.	0	100.	Same
80	Oysterman	American	7	612.	364.	130.50	30.	50.	18.20	20.30	612.	0	100.	Same
81	*Newspaper woman	Italian-Am.	4	380.	143.	144.	35.*4	25.	26.60	14.40	388.	—8.00	102.1	Same
82	Soft-drink factory	Norwegian	5	777.	314.	222.	60.*4	49.	80.40	50.60	777.	0	100.	Same
83	Captain of tugboat	Irish	10	1515.	286.	204.	65.	59.	32.30	218.70	865.	+650.	57.1	Same
84	Harness-cleaner	Irish-Amer.	7	870.	442.	156.	69.80	57.20	58.24	86.76	870.	0	100.	American
85	Porter	Amer. (negro)	3	980.	500.	228.	100.	43.	14.20	94.80	980.	0	100.	Am. (white)
86	Waiter	Jewish-Am.	5	734.	292.	180.	100.	56.50	52.44	53.06	734.	0	100.	French-Am.
87	Painter	French-Am.	8	680.	364.	144.	60.	55.	36.90	20.10	680.	0	100.	American
88	Expressman	English	4	1236.	494.	168.	185.	49.	39.10	250.90	1186.	+50.	95.9	Same
89	Stableman	Irish-Amer.	9	1054.	390.	144.	165.	44.50	52.80	258.50	1054.	0	100.	English
90	Longshoreman	Irish	4	496.	234.	128.	60.	20.	20.80	47.20	510.	—14.	102.8	Same
91	Watchman	Irish-Amer.	8	606.	260.	130.	80.	28.50	0	107.50	606.	0	100.	Irish-Amer.
92	Fireman	American	8	831.	364.	134.	100.	32.	49.40	186.40	866.	—35.	104.2	Same
93	Asst. shipping-clerk	Irish-Amer.	8	982.	436.	189.	140.	40.	89.60	87.40	982.	0	100.	Irish-Amer.
94	Butcher's helper	German	8	1047.	390.	156.	100.	49.	37.20	194.80	927.	+120.	88.5	Same
95	Coal-driver	Irish	10	575.	299.	132.	22.*9	32.	26.	85.	596.	—21.	103.7	Same
96	Comic-singer	English	5	1300.	572.	120.	110.*9	64.	62.40	371.60	1300.	0	100.	Irish-Amer.
97	Longshoreman	Irish	7	1288.	494.	150.	200.	48.	28.60	532.40	1453.	—165.	112.8	English
98	Truckman	American	7	1286.	468.	180.	50.*4	42.	78.	318.	1136.	+150.	88.3	Same

* Occupation of the wife who is head of the family.   † This includes income from all sources.

TABLE I—Continued

Occupation.	Nativity of Head of Family.	No. in Fam.†	Income.†	Food.	Rent.	Cloth-ing.	Light and Fuel.	Insur-ance.	Sun-dries.	Total.	Amount of Sur-plus or Deficit.	Per Cent of Income Expended.	Nativity of Wife.
99 Foreman of Ice Co.	Irish-Amer.	8	$1618.40	$728.	$240.	$260.	$45.	$69.80	$275.20	$1618.	$0	100.	Irish
100 Carpenter	German	8	1414.40	468.	264.	75.*6	76.	54.60	376.80	1314.40	+100.	92.9	Same
101 *Washerwoman	American	6	390.	182.	98.	32.60	30.30	20.80	26.30	390.	0	100.	Same
102 Expressman	Irish-Amer.	7	669.	343.	132.	52.	43.	40.56	88.44	699.	-30.	104.5	Same
103 Housekeeper (man)	Irish	5	397.	182.	120.	200.	32.	39.	4.00	397.	0	100.	Same
104 *Washerwoman	Irish	6	700.	410.50	168.	70.*4	47.50	0	4.00	700.	0	100.	Same
105 Hat-cutter	Irish-Amer.	5	1282.	608.40	224.	75.*5	81.	57.80	235.80	1282.	0	100.	Same
106 Bricklayer	English	6	400.	195.	84.	30.*5	20.	52.52	18.48	400.	0	100.	Irish
107 Porter	German	4	916.	520.	132.	10.*1	65.	39.	150.	916.	0	100.	Same
108 Grocer's clerk	English	7	1002.	468.	192.	45.	61.40	21.84	193.76	982.	+20.	98.	Same
109 Kitchen helper	French	3	322.	124.	111.	10.50	26.25	21.30	46.95	340.	-18.	105.6	Irish
110 Truckman	American	5	830.	384.80	192.	56.*3½	53.	26.	118.80	830.	0	100.	Irish-Amer.
111 Truckman	English-Am.	4	474.	190.	118.	41.*5½	31.28	52.	94.72	527.	-53.	111.2	Irish-Amer.
112 Fireman	Irish	6	936.	406.	120.	57.*5½	69.	52.	232.	936.	0	100.	Same
113 Porter	German	7	1144.	676.	168.	93.	49.	78.	80.	1144.	0	100.	Ger.-Amer.
114 Truckman	Irish	6	1000.	442.	200.	88.*5	39.	33.80	206.20	1009.	-9.00	109.	Irish-Amer.
115 Bookkeeper	American	10	728.	303.90	180.	46.80	43.	10.40	220.90	805.	-77.	110.6	Same
116 Foreman in factory	Irish-Amer.	6	1046.	520.	180.	140.	41.50	52.	114.	1046.	0	100.	Scotch
117 Longshoreman	Irish	5	452.	182.50	162.	27.	41.	20.80	18.20	452.	0	100.	Same
118 Janitor	Irish	7	712.	212.	159.	38.	41.	2.60	204.40	657.	+55.	92.3	American
119 Porter	Irish-Amer.	5	637.	312.	124.	28.	39.	67.60	66.40	637.	0	100.	Same
120 *Washerwoman	Irish	5	509.	286.	108.	80.	32.50	0	2.50	509.	0	100.	Same
121 Longshoreman	English	5	626.	286.	160.	40.	36.40	26.00	128.60	677.	-51.	108.1	Same
122 Waiter	Am. (negro)	4	774.	251.	256.	70.50*3	77.	0	215.50	870.	-96.	112.4	American
123 Casual laborer	Scotch-Am.	9	514.	312.	108.	36.	10.	15.60	32.40	514.	0	100.	Same
124 Brushmaker	Austrian	9	731.	312.	198.	30.	50.	49.20	91.80	731.	0	100.	American
125 *Washerwoman	Irish	8	560.	312.	158.50	35.*6	42.	18.20	24.30	590.	-30.	105.4	Same
126 Clerk in store	Irish	6	780.	364.40	219.	40.	56.	72.80	27.80	780.	0	100.	Same
127 Coal-driver	Ger.-Amer.	7	634.	286.	156.	58.	30.50	18.20	85.30	634.	0	100.	Irish-Amer.
128 Wagon washer	Irish	9	969.	563.	178.	110.*8	25.	41.60	51.40	969.	0	100.	Same
129 Asst. shipping-clerk	American	5	380.	119.50	132.	46.*5	14.25	15.60	62.65	390.	-10.	102.6	English
130 Engineer	American	6	1025.	416.	146.	70.*5	44.	36.40	445.60	1158.	-133.	113.	Irish-Amer.
131 Clerk in store	Jewish-Am.	4	619.	260.	228.	45.	45.40	23.68	17.32	619.	0	100.	Same
132 Truckman	Irish-Amer.	4	808.	358.80	168.	68.	23.40	0	135.80	754.	+54.	93.3	Italian

* Occupation of the wife who is head of the family.   † This includes income from all sources.

TABLE I—Continued

	Occupation.	Nativity of Head of Family.	No. in Fam.	Income.†	Food.	Rent.	Cloth-ing.	Light and Fuel.	Insur-ance.	Sun-dries.	Total.	Amount of Surplus or Deficit.	Per Cent of Income Expended.	Nativity of Wife.
133	Press-feeder	English-Am.	8	868.	409.	108.	100.*7	43.	26.	162.	848.	+20.	97.7	English
134	Stone-mason	Irish-Amer.	5	1039.	468.	186.	90.*41/2	41.30	33.80	139.90	959.	+80.	92.3	Irish
135	Hat factory	American	5	832.	416.	132.	46.*4	41.30	12.00	184.70	832.	—	100.7	Same
136	*Candy factory	Italian	3	366.	200.	102.	26.	29.	10.40	8.60	376.	—10.	102.7	Same
137	Clothes-presser	Italian	3	436.	160.	161.	52.	45.45		17.55	436.	0	100.	Same
138	Wagon-washer	Irish	10	1075.	598.	188.	98.20	50.	46.80	94.	1075.	0	100.	Same
139	Casual laborer	American	4	500.	234.	109.	60.	40.	26.	31.	500.	0	100.	Irish-Amer.
140	Engineer	Irish	6	952.	416.	144.	55.	52.16	60.	251.84	979.	+27.	102.8	Same
141	Barber	Italian	4	797.	271.	216.	30.*3	38.	31.20	110.80	697.	—100.	87.5	Same
142	Truckman	Irish	3	728.	364.	144.	50.50	36.	46.80	86.70	728.	0	100.	Same
143	*Janitor	American	3	428.	208.	144.	28.	33.	10.40	4.60	428.	0	100.	Italian
144	Picture-frames factory	Ger.-Amer.	5	810.	364.	120.	62.	50.	57.72	156.28	810.	0	100.	Same
145	Porter	Irish	5	520.	260.	150.	45.	35.	16.60	19.40	526.	+6.00	101.2	Same
146	*Candy store	Irish-Amer.	5	586.	286.	168.	52.	40.	33.80	6.20	586.	—	100.	French-Amer.
147	Automobile-driver	Scotch-Am.	8	1222.	657.80	162.	50.*5	57.	28.60	262.80	1218.	+4.	99.7	American
148	Waiter	Am. (negro)	2	1134.	247.50	175.	153.93	38.88	1.95	342.74	960.	+174.	84.7	Same
149	Works in oyster place	Irish-Amer.	5	565.	301.50	132.	40.	35.	31.20	25.30	565.	0	100.	Same
150	Casual laborer	Irish-Amer.	5	450.50	182.	144.	36.	20.	46.80	26.20	455.	—	100.9+	Same
151	Works in novelty fact'y	Italian	3	489.	205.	108.	32.	26.		118.	489.	—4.50	100.	Irish
152	Mason	Irish	5	1100.	561.	150.	80.*4	70.	31.20	202.80	1095.	+	99.5	Same
153	Truck foreman	German	7	780.	364.	156.	33.	28.	101.88	97.12	780.	+5.	100.	American
154	Casual laborer	Scotch-Am.	5	300.	127.	87.	34.	16.40	28.60	7.	300.	0	100.	American
155	Clerk in hotel	English	4	643.	260.	156.	67.			70.	643.	0	100.	Same
156	Freight clerk	American	4	925.	360.	176.	90.	53.	51.65	219.35	935.	—10.	101.1	Irish-Amer.
157	Truckman	Irish-Amer.	7	450.	182.	120.	75.	33.50	26.	89.65	468.65	—18.65	104.1	Same
158	Laborer in Post-office	German	9	1000.	566.80	174.	17.50*3	59.	52.	68.20	1000.	0	100.	Same
159	Truckman	American	9	790.	440.20	175.	80.	35.	57.20	64.60	800.	—10.	101.3	Same
160	Street-cleaner	Italian-Am.	4	492.	260.	132.	28.*7	35.	2.60	27.40	492.	0	100.	Same
161	*Housekeeper	Irish	4	1307.	598.	201.	94.	58.	44.20	311.80	1307.	0	100.	Ger.-Amer.
162	*Housekeeper	Irish	9	1196.	618.	186.	200.	45.80	31.20	115.	1196.	0	100.	Same
163	*Dressmaker	Irish-Amer.	5	1017.	572.	192.	75.*3	75.	26.	62.	1002.	+15.	98.5	Same
164	Switchman	Irish	7	864.	468.	168.	90.*5	53.30	36.40	48.30	864.	0	100.	Same
165	Wagon-washer	Irish	5	928.	395.20	174.	101.	56.	57.20	144.60	928.	0	100.	Same
166	*Office-cleane	American	3	479.	234.	108.	54.	16.84	6.	56.16	475.	+4.	99.2	Same

* Occupation of the wife who is head of the family.   † This includes income from all sources.

TABLE I—*Continued*

Occupation.	Nativity of Head of Family.	No. in Fam.	Income †	Expenditures per Year for							Amount of Surplus or Deficit.	Per Cent of Income Expended.	Nativity of Wife.
				Food.	Rent.	Cloth-ing.	Light and Fuel.	Insur-ance.	Sun-dries.	Total.			
167 Casual laborer	American	6	640.	390.	102.	25.	26.40	7.20	89.40	640.	0	100.	Irish
168 *Janitor	English	10	1818.	832.	195.	150.*5	36.	0	715.	1928.	−110.	106.1	Italian
169 Cl'k in wholesale house	English	4	1140.	364.	300.	140.	40.	0	276.	1120.	+20.	98.2	American
170 Pencil-box maker	American	6	1041.	390.	132.	60.	25.10	10.20	423.70	1041.	0	100.	Same
171 Carriage-caller	Irish-Amer.	3	2158.	364.	336.	400.	52.	34.	972.	2158.	0	100.	German
172 Painter	American	5	574.	312.	156.	46.	16.92	0	108.08	639.	+65.	111.3	Ger.-Amer.
173 Truckman	French	6	832.	306.80	180.	90.	35.60	30.12	176.48	819.	+13.	98.4	Ger.-Amer.
174 Bartender	Italian	8	1500.	624.	270.	170.*7	48.	0	388.	1500.	0	100.	Same
175 Bartender	German	6	1335.	364.	300.	130.	55.	42.94	443.06	1335.	0	100.	Ger.-Amer.
176 Delicatessen store	Ger.-Amer.	6	2556.	546.	300.	500.*4	37.20	43.00	539.80	1966.	+590.	76.9	Same
177 Dry-goods store	Jewish-Am.	6	986.	360.	240.	85.	58.	36.40	206.60	986.	0	100.	Same
178 Mgr. of livery stable	Ger.-Amer.	3	1450.	520.	216.	300.	42.	0	314.	1392.	+58.	96.	Same
179 Street-car conductor	American	4	867.	364.	180.	90.*5	40.	0	167.	841.	+26.	97.	Same
180 Bookkeeper	American	6	1382.	494.	300.	200.*5	75.	18.24	194.76	1282.	+100.	92.8	Same
181 Bartender	German	4	1068.	442.	300.	148.	30.67	20.80	126.53	1068.	0	100.	French
182 Porter	Italian	7	1162.	416.	216.	166.	24.90	41.60	317.50	1182.	−20.	101.7	American
183 Grocery store	American	8	644.	312.	144.	90.	19.50	31.20	47.30	644.	0	100.	English-Am.
184 Longshoreman	Scotch	8	832.	364.	120.	76.	68.20	0	203.80	832.	0	100.	Irish
185 Oysterman	Am. (negro)	3	494.	260.	72.	81.50	16.	15.60	48.90	494.	0	100.	Am. (white)
186 *Washerwoman	Irish-Amer.	4	538.	312.	96.	57.	29.51	15.60	27.89	538.	0	100.	American
187 Truckman	Irish	4	658.	286.	120.	86.	36.	23.40	129.60	681.	−23.	103.5	Irish-Amer.
188 Casual laborer	Irish	4	459.	234.	96.	40.	41.50	15.60	36.90	464.	−5.	101.1	Same
189 Works in fruit place	American	4	1534.	416.	300.	225.	44.70	21.	227.30	1234.	+300.	80.4	Same
190 Boss tinsmith	American	4	1286.	494.	300.	200.	42.25	12.	187.75	1236.	+50.	96.1	Same
191 Tailor's cutter	American	7	835.	364.	240.	35.*4	44.	52.	119.	854.	−19.	102.3	Scotch-Am.
192 Street laborer	Irish	3	713.	312.	106.	35.	75.	31.20	170.80	730.	−17.	102.4	Same
193 Truckman	Dutch-Am.	3	803.	364.	151.	75.	57.90	18.20	174.90	841.	−38.	104.7	Same
194 Machinist	American	4	558.	260.	117.	40.	30.40	0	110.60	558.	0	100.	Irish-Amer.
195 Upholsterer	Jewish-Am.	5	797.	338.	156.	30.	39.23	31.20	79.57	674.	+123.	84.6	Same
196 Musician	American	4	830.	414.	144.	50.	72.	15.60	161.40	857.	−27.	103.3	Same
197 Carpet-cleaner	Ger.-Amer.	6	645.	414.	120.	40.	35.	0	66.	675.	−30.	104.7	Swiss
198 Longshoreman	English-Am.	8	801.	312.	276.	65.*7	60.	41.60	73.40	828.	−27.	103.4	Same
199 Truckman	Irish	9	1400.	624.	384.	115.*7	72.	46.80	158.20	1400.	0	100.	Same
200 Policeman	German	5	1512.	468.	336.	85.*4	49.	26.	248.	1212.	+300.	80.2	Same

* Occupation of the wife who is head of the family.   † This includes income from all sources.

This tabulation presents in detail the industrial, racial, and financial condition of each one of the families investigated. Some important explanations are therefore necessary to show the pains taken in the collection and arrangement of the facts here given.

The starred occupations are those of the wife, in the cases in which she is the proper head of the family, in consequence of the desertion or death of the husband. There are 25 such families. In these cases "the nativity of the head of the family" given is her nativity, and that of the deceased or deserting husband is given in the last column, under the general heading "nativity of wife".

Occupations.

The various occupations of the heads of the families are shown for each one. That there is no homogeneity of industrial life in the neighborhood nor among these representative families is evident. It is impossible in this table to give the occupations of all the contributing members of the family—those of the heads of the families are typical of the others. The children are frequently skilled workers in families where the father is unskilled. The proportion of skilled and unskilled laborers by income and by nativity will be shown in a later table.[1] It will be seen that the occupations extend from hod-carriers, casual laborers, wagon-washers, stablemen, street laborers, and other forms of the lowest-paid labor, up through truckmen, longshoremen, porters, waiters, factory workers of all kinds, to the mechanic and artisan class—plumbers, carpenters, ship-joiners, and engineers. In short, there are 100 representatives of unskilled labor among the heads of families, 45 of skilled labor, and 55 who do not come under either of these forms of labor, but who are roughly called the "clerical class", including bookkeepers, clerks of all kinds, a letter-carrier, a policeman, janitors, and

[1] Table IX, p. 111, and Table IXa, p. 114.

housekeepers. A "housekeeper" is the general term here applied to the mother or father who stays at home and does the housekeeping, is supported by children or boarders, and has no other regular trade or occupation. In some cases the father was a semi-invalid and unable to do other work, and in other instances the mother, a widow, was supported by her children and kept house for them. There are no professional "housekeepers" among this number.

The multiplicity of trades and occupations represented makes it difficult to give a list of the number of persons in each one. Those having the largest number are truckmen (22), longshoremen (13), washerwomen (9), porters (8), casual laborers (7), janitors and housekeepers (16), clerks (11), factory workers of various kinds (13), and seamstresses (3). There are also seven instances where the head of the family carries on a small business of his own, i.e., two small grocery stores, a barber shop, a soft-drink factory, a candy store, a delicatessen shop, and a dry-goods store. In these cases the income given is the net income, exclusive of the expenses of the little store. "Casual laborer" is an expressive term used frequently by social writers to describe a man who has no steady employment, who works at odd jobs at odd times, and is generally a negative element industrially.

The diversity of occupations can be further analyzed by studying this table.

As no single trade absorbs the energies of the majority of the men, so no one race preponderates in numbers among these families. This table shows that **Racial Origin.** 105 heads of families were native-born Americans and 95 were foreign born; of these 35 were born in Ireland, 15 in England, 17 in Germany, 15 in Italy, 4 in France, 4 in Sweden and Norway, 2 in Switzerland, and one each in Cuba, Austria, and Scotland; in other words, eleven different nationalities were represented in this study. "First-generation Americans" (native born, but of foreign parentage) are described as German-American, Irish-American, or French-American, indicating that the head of the family himself was born in America, his father in Germany, Ireland, or France. These are all classed as "Americans" in later classifications.

Some interesting racial intermarriages may be observed by comparing the column "Nativity of head of family" with that giving the "Nativity of wife". More than half (106) have married persons of their own race or their own descent, but there are one or more instances of intermarriage among German and Dutch, English and Italian, Irish and Italian (ordinarily the most bitter racial foes), negro and white, French and German, Cuban (negro) and German, Irish and German, Swedish and German, Swiss and Scotch, French and Jewish, French and Irish, German and Italian, while the native Americans intermarry with all nationalities. This mingling and blending of different races is a characteristic phase of our American life. There are 81 cases in which one or both parents are first-generation Americans (in 43 of these families the foreign parentage was Irish), and of these, 31 married persons of their own race or descent, 24 married Americans of several generations, and the others intermarried with different races.

The number or "size of the family" includes father, mother, children, boarders (but not lodgers), and any rela-
Size of the tives or dependents who have been members Family. of the family six months or more in the year. The "size of the family" is, then, more literally the "size of the household". Transients, either visitors or boarders for a few weeks at a time, could not be included as an economic part of the family life. The small and infrequent

amounts which these persons added to the family income are included in "Income from other sources". Their expense to the family was so irregular that it could not be computed, nor separated from the whole. In case of a death in the family, the person who died was considered a member of the family if he had lived six months or more of the year investigated.

The larger the family, the larger is the income in most instances, as a large family usually implies more persons contributing to the income. The expenditure for food, light and fuel, and rent is increased by the larger number in the family (though not proportionately), while the expenditure for clothing and insurance is not necessarily increased. It is the custom for the older children to pay board to the mother, from $3.00 to $7.00 a week, according to their ability, and then clothe themselves, frequently pay their own insurance, keep their own spending-money, and, if possible, save toward getting married. These older children must be considered as "boarders", as their personal expenses do not enter into the family budget, nor is there any way of estimating them. The "size of the family" increases from two in the family to twelve, and from no children to nine. The average size of all the families in this study was 5.6,—of the native families 5.3, and of the foreign families 6. Grouping the families according to their size, the result is that 8 families, or 4 per cent, have 2 in the family; 17 families, or 8.5 per cent, consist of 3; 40 families, or 20 per cent, have 4; 39 families, or 19.5 per cent, have 5; 36 families, or 18 per cent, have 6; 22 families, or 11 per cent, have 7; 20 families, or 10 per cent, have 8; 9 families, or 4.5 per cent, have 9; 8 families, or 4 per cent, have 10, and 1 family, or one-half of one per cent, has 12 in the family. In other words, 52 per cent of all the families have 5 or less in the family, and 48 per cent have 6 or more in the family. There are in these 200 families a total of 1125 persons, including 721 children, 367 parents, 13 dependents, and 24 boarders. Eight families have no children, while the average number of children for those families having children was 3.76. The average number of parents was 1.83 to each family, making the average family by this computation 5.59. It will thus be seen that it would not make much difference in the results whether these statistics were based upon the average size of family or upon "families having no children", "families having 1 child", etc.

The following table shows the relation between the number of children and size of family:

TABLE I A

A STUDY OF THE RELATION OF THE NUMBER OF CHILDREN TO TOTAL SIZE OF FAMILY

Size of Family.	Number of Families.	Number of Children.	Number of Families.
2	8	0	8
3	17	1	14
4	40	2	46
5	39	3	33
6	36	4	39
7	22	5	26
8	20	6	17
9	9	7	9
10	8	8	7
12	1	9	1
	200		200

The largest number of families have from four to seven in the family, and from two to five children,—for example, 40 families have 4 in the family, and 46 families have 2 children, 36 families have 6 in the family, and 39 families have 4 children, and so on. In thirty-three cases either the mother or father is dead or has deserted, and accordingly there is only one parent in those families. These places are filled by 37 boarders and dependents, leaving only a fractional difference between the average size of families if computed by the number of children or by the size of the household.

The incomes vary greatly in amount, from a minimum of $250. for the year, to a maximum of $2556. No effort was made to restrict the investigation to families having incomes above or under a given amount, as the very poor and the well-to-do workingmen's families are both typical of the district. In 27 cases the total income was below $500., in 29 cases it was $1200. or more. Probably neither extreme is typical of the average workingman's "family income" in New York City, but it is reasonable and conservative to regard an income between $800. and $900. as a fair average.. An intimate knowledge of workingmen's families for several years leads the writer to feel that the average income of $851.38 for the 200 families in this investigation is a representative one. This income, which means an average all the year round of about $16.38 a week for a family between 5 and 6, is at least an interesting starting-point from which to compare the incomes and expenditures in families.

It must be remembered that the income given is the "total income from all sources" which comes into the family purse, and not the wages of the head of the family alone. An analysis of the various sources of income will be made in a later table.[1] The number of families entirely dependent upon the earnings of one person is small compared with the number whose income may include the earnings of the husband, the wife, several children, possibly some boarders or lodgers, gifts from rela-

[1] Table V p. 84 seq.

tives or friends, aid from charitable societies, insurance money in case of a death in the family,—several or all of these sources of income may enter into the total resources of that family in a year. Perhaps this income should more accurately be called the "household income", for it only represents the amount which comes into the family purse, and of which the mother, usually has the disbursement. Sometimes the man is a piece-worker and does not know just how much he has earned in the year. The wife can only estimate what he has brought home to her—the rest having been spent by the man himself, without adding anything to the family comfort or resources. In some cases the man keeps out of his wages a definite amount each week for his spending-money. Though this amount does not pass through the wife's hands, being a known quantity it can be added to the total income and also to the expenditures under the general head of "man's spending-money". In other cases grown sons and daughters or other boarders pay board and support themselves entirely, and the mother frequently does not know how much they earn nor how much they spend. The board they pay is all that enters into the "household income". It is therefore practically impossible to consider any income which does not either pass through the hands of the person who has the management of the expenditures of the family, or who knows the exact amount retained, and the purposes for which it was expended; 47 children out of a total of 721 included in this investigation have for this reason been regarded as boarders. Were this distinction not made, many complications would have resulted

Amount of Incomes.   in endeavoring to classify the amount expended for various purposes. Most of the incomes fall between $600. and $900.; 81 families have incomes within these amounts. The following table shows the number and proportion of families whose incomes are within the different groups:

TABLE I B

NUMBER AND PER CENT OF FAMILIES HAVING INCOMES WITHIN
CLASSIFIED GROUPS

Income.	Number of Families.	Per Cent of Families.	Income.	Number of Families.	Per Cent of Families.
$200–$400	11	5.5	$900–$1000	19	9.5
400– 500	16	8.	1000– 1200	28	14.
500– 600	16	8.	1200– 1500	18	9.
600– 700	29	14.5	1500 or over	11	5.5
700– 800	27	13.5			
800– 900	25	12.5	Total	200	100.

The incomes of various amounts are quite evenly distributed; no disproportionately large number of incomes comes within any one group. That is, no large proportion of these families have incomes of any one class, yet enough cases come under each group to be representative of the economic life of families within each division of income. The very small incomes of $250., $260., $360, etc.—eleven families in all having incomes of less than $400. a year—present startling figures for the outsider who does not comprehend on what a pitifully small amount it is possible for a family to exist even in New York City. It is needless to point out that such an existence must result, sometimes very quickly, in moral as well as physical deterioration. These small incomes have been estimated with exceptional care, any charity, either in money or clothing, coal or groceries given, has always been included, and in every case the investigator felt that the total amount estimated was as large as it could be made, without keeping a budget of every cent received. It is difficult to believe that families of three or four could exist in New York on such incomes, under city conditions, but these families did so, and their schedules show how they did it. They are under-fed, poorly clothed, wretchedly housed, and have the barest necessities of life. Every charitable society has instances of such extreme poverty. These families were not wholly dependent,—in most cases they had received help in one way or another, but in no large amounts.

The case of the pastor of a struggling little German church in Brooklyn, who, with his college-bred wife and two little children, lived last year on just $294. shocked those who heard it. Though this is an illustration outside this immediate district, it has several parallel cases in this investigation. He told *how* they did it: "we always had one meal a day, sometimes two, and occasionally three".

The other extreme for this neighborhood is illustrated by the 29 families whose incomes were above $1200.[1] These families usually lived in the better class tenements, were well dressed, well fed, and generally showed a surplus at the end of the year, unless exceptional circumstances had prevented any savings. They had much more than is necessary for the "maintenance of a minimum of physical efficiency" even in New York. Later tables are intended to show the distribution of expenditures for those families whose larger income gave them a surplus over what was requisite for the actual necessities of life.

The annual expenditures for each of these families for food, rent, clothing, light and fuel, insurance, and all **Expenditures.** other expenses grouped under "sundries" have been estimated with the greatest possible care and accuracy. Where no account was kept for

---

[1] The family with the largest income, $2556., kept a delicatessen store, which brought in about $100. a month net. The man also inherited some property which gave him $100. a month additional income, and they have a boarder. This family would not live in this district were it not for the store.

the entire year, the total expenditures for various purposes must naturally be estimates, but in every case a
knowledge of the family's total income and its standard
of living, the thrifty or extravagant habits of the wife, and
a familiarity with the market prices of various commodities
in the neighborhood were used to supplement and confirm
the statements of the wife and mother. If the woman was
not accurate nor reliable, or was of too low a grade of intelligence to answer the questions on the schedule intelligently,
that family was dropped, and only those cases where the
information was known to be reliable were completed.

The question of the amount paid for rent was always
the simplest to ask, for it is a fixed, definite amount which
can be verified. If the family had moved
Rent. several times within the year the amount of
rent paid in each place was included, and the full amount
of rent due for the year is always given. If it had
been dispossessed during the year, with rent unpaid, that
amount was included as if paid, and the amount that was
"skipped" was added to the income, and considered as much
an addition to the family income as if it had been honestly
earned. In cases where rent was still owing at the end of the
year, and the family still lived in that apartment, it is also
included as if paid, and the balance unpaid is set down as
a deficit or debt, as are the grocer's or butcher's bills. This
gives a uniformity in the amount paid for rent, which would
be impossible without taking these circumstances into
consideration. Usually rent and insurance are the two
obligations met first, and food and clothing are of less importance. There are exceptions to this rule, however, for
among a certain class of tenement dwellers to "jump the
rent" is not considered dishonorable by people who otherwise feel the obligation of paying their debts. The landlord

is considered a rich man, who "can stand the loss", and is an easy prey. One man had a chronic aversion to paying rent, and his family were dispossessed four times during the year. His wife was thrifty and honorable, and greatly deplored this habit.

The rents paid in this section are not so high as those in the more densely populated East Side, but are more typical for all tenement-house rents throughout the city. They have increased in the last two years, during which these statistics were taken, from 10–20 per cent. The most prominent real-estate agent in the neighborhood puts the rate of increase at about 15 per cent as a conservative estimate. The increase is from $0.50 to $2.00 a month for many of the apartments. Old tenants, however, are always favored, and frequently the landlord raises the rent for the tenants moving in, while a good tenant's rent is not changed. In other houses all apartments are impartially advanced in rent for both old and new tenants. One of the commonest causes of a rise in rent is the fact that these tenements are generally in the market and frequently have a change of owners. Each new landlord feels he must get more out of his rents than did his predecessor.

It will be seen in this table that the amount of rent paid for the year varied from $84.00 to $384.00, or from $7.00 to $32.00 a month. The case in which the rent was $54.00 a year, or $4.50 a month, for a printer's family of 3 is exceptional and not typical of the neighborhood. In this case the family lived with two relatives in an old house on Christopher Street, where the rent for two rooms on one floor and three small sleeping-rooms in the attic was only $9.00 a month. The kitchen was used in common, but all the housekeeping expenses for each family were separate. This family's share of the rent was $4.50 a month. The usual rent paid in the neighborhood was from $11.00 to $15.00 a month, or $132.00 to $180.00 a year, for a three- or four-room apartment. The average amount paid for rent was $162.26 a year, or about $13.50 a month, by these families having an average income of $851.38, and this constituted 19.4 per cent of the total expenditures.

To estimate the amount spent for food several methods were used. In 50 families accurate budgets of family

Food. expenditures were kept for various periods of time, from one week to one year. These little books always gave the food expenditures very exactly and carefully, though the other items of expense were not always so faithfully noted. When an account of the exact amount spent for food was kept for several weeks, the average amount spent for those weeks during which the budget was kept was accepted as an average week's expenditures, unless the family was larger or smaller at various times, or more was spent during sickness or less during the summer weeks, or when the head of the family was out of work, or during the weeks in which the rent was paid,—all these modifying circumstances were taken into account in estimating the total expenditure for food for the entire year. Some methodical housekeepers put aside a certain sum every week for food, and in those cases it was simple to obtain an accurate estimate. Many housekeepers said they spent less for meat in the summer, but this was counterbalanced by the ice bill, and the other items were practically the same summer and winter.

It is interesting to find that in many households in the week in which the rent is paid the allowance for food is cut down, or if a new pair of shoes or a new coat is necessary for one of the children, the food suffers. In one case of a family of four—father, mother, and two young boys—

the mother said that she usually spent $7.00 a week for food, and her account for one week showed that amount, but when questioned closely, she admitted that the weeks when the rent was paid (twice a month) the food allowance was cut down to $4.00 a week, and for six weeks when the man was out of work, they did not spend more than $4.50 a week for food. The total amount for the year, figuring on this basis, would therefore be $277., or about $5.33 a week on the average. This is an illustration of the care taken in making estimates.

The amount spent for food varies widely and should always be considered in connection with the size of the family. This expense also depends largely upon the thrift and extravagance of the mother and the steadiness and regularity of her weekly income. From $130. a year to $728., or from $2.50 to $14.00 a week for food is a wide range, but the standards and means of these different families were equally far apart. At the one extreme the total income was $260. for 4 in the family (a woman and three children); at the other the income was $1618. for 8 in the family (including three adults),—the woman was an invalid and had to have a special diet, and the family was extravagant in every way and made no effort to save. In a Norwegian family of 2, where the income was $1000., only $260., or $5.00 a week, was spent for food,—an example of thrift, good management, and careful marketing, which enabled them to have nourishing food, but no luxuries. For one who wishes to make a study of the cost of food in different families, this column is full of interest. The average amount spent for food in this investigation for 200 families, with an average income of $851.38, and an average size of 5.6, was $360.42, or about $7.00 a week. A close study of this column shows that in most families about a dollar a week for each person in the family not an infant is spent for food, except in the very poor or the more prosperous families; that is, five in a family seem to spend about $5.00 for food, 6 spend $6.00, 7 spend $7.00, etc., in cases where the income. is of moderate amount. This only applies to families having more than 3 in the family, and there are numerous exceptions to the rule. A dollar a day for food, or $7.00 a week, is generally regarded as an adequate amount for families of 5 or 6, "if we have all we need". There were several instances where the man was a waiter or a bartender, and was given his meals where he worked. In those cases the meals have been valued at $2.00 a week, and this amount added to the man's wages, and also to the family expenditure for food.

The amount spent for clothing per year was obviously the most difficult to estimate accurately. When no account had been kept of this expense, the investigator
Clothing.　　very carefully went over, item by item, each article of clothing worn by each member of the family. Thus prodded, the housewife could remember how many suits of underwear, pairs of socks, shoes, hats, overcoats, or suits of clothes her husband had bought within the year, or, more frequently, that she had bought for him, and so, in turn, for each one in the family. It was never difficult for her to remember the exact price paid for each article. The amounts spent for each member of the family were then added, a small allowance usually made for "sundries not accounted for", and the total result submitted to the mother for her approval. It was necessarily a slow and laborious method of getting at the truth, and many visits were often made before the total estimate could be reached for a family. Even with this care, there are many explanations and allowances which must be made.

Where the expense for clothing is starred in this table, the amount spent was for the number of persons indicated "Partial by the number after the star. For example, Estimates." in the washerwoman's family (No. 5), with an income of $880. and 8 in the family, $150. was spent to clothe 7 members of the family. The other member was a boarder who clothed himself and was no expense to the head of the family for clothing. There has seemed no better way to explain a difficulty which should always be noted in order to make the statement as accurate as possible.

In 43 families the clothing expenditure was not for the entire family. These families consisted of 290 persons and spent a total of $4422.50 out of the family purse to clothe 220½ persons (the fraction being due to the fact that the husband or older children were sometimes partly clothed by the mother and partly out of their spending-money).

If $4422.50 was expended to clothe 220½ persons, in the same ratio it would cost $5816.44 to clothe 290 persons, or $1393.94 more than was actually spent. If this sum were added to the total amount spent for clothing by the 200 families, the average per family (for the entire 1125 persons included as members of the families) would be $95.42 a year instead of $88.45. Making allowance for the fact that older children and boarders who clothed themselves undoubtedly spent more than the average for the other members in the family, it is safe to assume that at least $100. a year was spent for clothing for these families, whose average size was 5.6. This amount cannot be included in the total averages, since the amount spent for clothing by "boarders" does not enter into the total income.

Another difficulty found was that in the poorer families clothing was frequently given by friends, churches, or societies. The value of this clothing to the family has been computed as if it were bought for cash by the recipient and this amount added to the expense for clothing.   It

Gifts of Clothing.
is obvious that old clothing given by more prosperous friends is usually of much better quality than the cheaper ready-made goods which the housewife would otherwise have been obliged to purchase.   Its worth to her has been considered its value.   The value of this clothing has also been added to the total income under the head of "gifts".

The very common practice of buying clothing, as well as other commodities, on the "installment plan" had also

Installment System.
to be considered.   The actual price of the goods bought has been included, whether paid for within the year or not, and the amount unpaid at the end of the year is regarded as a debt or deficit, just as is back rent or an unpaid grocery or coal bill.   The article was probably worn out or consumed within the year, and hence its total value was a part of the actual cost of living for that year.   These are some of the difficulties which stood in the way of the attempt to make an absolutely accurate estimate of the cost of clothing for each family.

With these allowances and explanations, the total amount spent for clothing varied more than for any other one item,—

Amounts Expended for Clothing.
from $10.00 to $560. a year, with an average expenditure of $88.45.   In judging this expense, the regard for appearances, the general standard of living, and the various social conditions of the family should be considered, as well as the amount of income and size of family.   This will be shown more clearly in the budgets and in the descriptions of selected families which follow.*   For example, $10.00 is an entirely inadequate expenditure for clothing for a family of 4 with an income of $916.

* Chapters VI and VII.

(No. 107). In that case the expenditure was for only one
member of the family, the father, a very quiet home man,
who never went out socially, and had bought no suit, overcoat, underwear, etc., within the year. The others were
"boarders", grown sons and a daughter, who dressed themselves, and the amount they spent could not be estimated,
nor was it included as part of the income. This is, of course,
an exceptional case and should be explained, as this is not
a typical clothing expenditure for incomes of that amount.
Another case (40), where only $10.00 was expended for clothing
in a year, was that of an old French couple who had seen
more prosperous days, and had an abundance of clothing on
hand. The man was unable to do any work except assist
his wife, who was a seamstress. Her earnings and past
savings drawn from the Bank made a total income of $380.

Other families of nearly the same size and amount of
income spent very different amounts for clothing, according
to circumstances or their standard of living. Compare, for
example, No. 42 with No. 76. In the first case a family of
4 with an income of $675. spent $100. on clothing. It was
an Irish family, in which the woman was unable to do any
sewing and bought everything "ready-made". The man
was warmly dressed, the woman quietly and neatly, a boy
of 14 very poorly, and the daughter of 16, who worked in a
factory, very attractively and tastefully. This family cared
more for appearances than did the other, which was warmly
but plainly dressed. In the latter case, a Swiss family of 4,
consisting of father, mother, and two little girls, 10 and 12
years old, with an income of $680., spent only $36.00 on
clothing. The mother, with the thrift of her race, was a very
careful manager and a seamstress. She made the children's
clothes over and over. They were warmly but unattractively dressed. The man's illness had cut down an

income in former years of $906. or over to $680. in the year
of the investigation. With the larger income they had been
able to save at least $300. a year, which kept the standard
of living approximately the same. Both the man and
woman were frugal and industrious. Neither of these
families saved anything during the year investigated.

No estimate for clothing should accordingly be judged
without an understanding of the economies or extravagances
of the family and a knowledge of its standard. One woman
with an income of $1500. spent $560. on clothing for her
family of 9 (No. 2) and was able to itemize every expenditure
entering into that amount, while another with an income of
$1618. and 8 in her family (No. 99) spent only $260. for
clothing. Neither of these families made any effort to save,
but their standards of comfort differed. The extravagance
of the one family was a love of gay, cheap, and "stylish"
clothes. They spent $10.00 a week on food ($520. a year)
and were willing to live on a poor street and in an old house
where they paid $14.00 a month rent. The other family pre-
ferred to spend $14.00 a week for food ($728. a year) and to
live in a better neighborhood where their rent was $20.00 a
month, and they spent $100. for new furniture in the year.
Both families were Irish-American and had no unusual expense, such as sickness or funeral, during the year. Many
other cases could be selected to illustrate these different standards and the widely divergent amounts spent for clothing.

The expenditure for light and fuel has also been difficult
to estimate accurately. In the few instances where coal
was bought by the ton and gas-bills paid by
Light and Fuel. the month, it was easy to approximate the
total cost very closely, but in most cases coal was bought
by the pail, bushel, or 100-lb. bag just when it was needed,
and gas was burned by the "quarter-meter", a system by

which a quarter dropped in the meter burns 250 cubic feet of gas and when this amount is burned another quarter is dropped in. In most families no account was kept of the number of quarters used.

There is no item of expense in which the economy or extravagance of the wife shows more quickly than in the lighting and heating of her three or four small rooms. One woman may burn 2 bushels (at 25 cents a bushel) of coal a day in midwinter, day and night, while a careful housewife, with the same number of rooms and stoves, only uses 3 or 4 bushels a week, because she watches her fire, picks out all half-burned pieces of coal, and allows none of the heat to be wasted. Three or four rooms are usually heated by one stove in the kitchen. The other rooms are consequently cold, while the kitchen is overheated.

When coal was bought by the bushel, the housewife was asked to estimate just how much coal per week she burned each month in the year. The consensus of opinion was that for one stove for three rooms, with good management, a bushel a week (for washing and ironing) was necessary from June 1st to October 1st, when a gas or oil stove was generally used for cooking, two bushels a week during the spring and fall months (October, April, May), and from five to seven bushels a week during the winter months.

During the period of this investigation (1903–1905) coal cost 10 cents a pail, 25 cents a bushel, or $6.00–$6.50 a ton. Gas-bills averaged about $1.00 a month the year round (at $1.00 per 1000 cubic feet), when gas was used for cooking in summer. If oil was burned instead of gas, one to two gallons a week (at 12 to 14 cents a gallon) were used. Wood was seldom a large item of expense. The children usually gathered all the wood that was necessary for kindling wood, and frequently for fuel also, from buildings in process of erection or of being torn down. If there were no children to pick up this wood, and it was bought by the bundle (2 cents) or bag (10 cents), the expense for fuel is largely increased. A truckman often brought home old packing-boxes and large pieces of wood which were given to him. The families who lived near the docks frequently picked up almost all the wood and coal they needed, which accounts for the exceedingly low estimate given for some families. When wood and coal were thus picked up on the street, it was impossible to estimate the value as in the cases where clothing was given, because there was no uniformity in the amount of fuel burned and hence no standard of estimate. When coal was sent by the ton or half ton to a family, as a gift or charity, its value could then be added to the income as a gift, and also to the expenditure for fuel, as with clothing. The very poor families naturally had to economize here rather than with food, and, if they could not gather wood on the streets, frequently went to bed to keep warm! The poorest family in this study (No. 15, income $250., expenditures $278.) spent no more than $14.80 in the year for fuel and light, including a gift of a half ton of coal, for two rooms and one stove, but this amount was supplemented by fuel gathered on the streets.

At the other extreme was the family of a ship-joiner (No. 52, income $1000.) where for one stove, and occasionally two, in an apartment of four rooms, $85. was spent for light and fuel. The rooms were exceptionally dark and damp, and two lamps were kept burning day and night. For the month of April the coal-bill was $4.00,—in midwinter (4 months) it averaged $2.00 a week, and in other months from one to three bushels a week were burned. This could be estimated exactly, as the coal-dealer was paid by the week. It was burned carelessly and extravagantly.

Most of the families, however, spent from $40.00 to
$50.00 a year on light and fuel, and the average expenditure
was $42.46 a year. This seems a fair allowance to light and
heat the three or four rooms with only one stove, which the
typical apartment contains.

Most of the families had an expenditure for life-insurance.
The table shows that 174 out of 200 families, or 87 per cent,
carried some insurance. It was usually the
"industrial" or "fractional" kind, which is
frequently called "the workingman's insur-
ance". A definite amount, generally five or ten cents for
each member of the family over a year old, was paid every
week to a collector, and hence the amount for the year could
be given exactly. The statement of the mother was verified
by the insurance books. The only difficulty in computing
this expenditure was that occasionally a policy had been
allowed to lapse within the year. Then the amount given
is for the time it was carried. If a policy had been increased
during the year, this was also included. Sometimes a family
was several weeks in arrears on the payments, a friendly collector being willing to carry them along for a few weeks if
the inability to make the payments was due to sickness,
unemployment, or other unavoidable circumstances. As in
the case of back rent, this insurance is included as if paid,
in order that an exact statement could be made of the amount
carried by these families, and the amount owing is then
considered a deficit.

The prevalence of this form of expense is significant. It
is considered by the working class a form of savings. It is
an obligation which must be paid before any other. A
family is frequently willing to be dispossessed or to go without food or clothing or fuel in order to keep up the insurance.
This is due to a desire to have a "decent" or even fine

funeral and an abhorrence of pauper burial. The insurance money invariably goes to meet the expenses of the funeral or of the last illness. The larger the policy the finer the funeral. From this custom many evils arise which have created among other classes a distrust and disapproval of workingmen's insurance, but to the workingman himself it is a form of savings. The knowledge of this insurance fosters a pride which is to a certain degree creditable, a spirit of independence, and a commendable horror of pauperism. Most of the insurance was paid to the collectors of such companies as the Metropolitan, Prudential, and John Hancock.

Membership in Benefit Societies is also very common. These societies are often connected with the store or factory where a man works or with trade-unions,
Benefit Societies. lodges, or French, German, or Italian societies. If the dues of such lodges or societies are returned as benefits in times of sickness or death, they are included under expenditures for insurance. The societies require a weekly or monthly payment, from $.10 to $.50 or even more, and pay from $3.00 to $6.00 a week in case of sickness, and from $50. to $250. at death.

It will be seen by studying this table that the amount spent annually for insurance varies widely from $5.00 or
Amount for $10.00 up to $127.88. This highest amount
Insurance. was paid by a German family (No. 19). Itemized it was expended as follows:

Man: "Germania Gesellschaft"..$1.20 a month	$14.40 a year
" Prudential...............	.40 a week	20.80 "
" Hancock................	.45 "	23.80 "
" Metropolitan.............	.25 "	13.00 "
" Prudential..............	6.92 quarterly	27.68 "
Woman: Hancock..............	.25 a week	13.00 "
Three children................	.30 "	15.60 "

$127.88

This is of course an unusual amount for a workingman's family to spend. The usual amount spent for an average-sized family was $30.00 to $40.00. The average for the 200 families was $32.35, while if the average were taken for only those families who carried insurance (174), it would be $37.19, which is a more representative average. A study of this expenditure shows that in some families the amount of insurance carried is a real burden. It is far out of proportion to the amount which should be spent with some incomes. Several women said "insurance keeps us poor". The total average, however, which was spent for insurance was 3.9 per cent of the total expenditure, which does not seem an excessive proportion.

There are nine instances where the amount spent for insurance was over 10 per cent of the total expenditure. The economic condition of those families was as follows:

Marginal Number.	Nationality.	Size of Family.	Total Income.	Total Expenditure.	Expenditure for Insurance.	Per Cent of the Expenditure.
4	American	5	$686.	$686.	$88.24	12.9
18	American	6	1000.	1000.	104.56	10.5
19	German	5	1214.	1180.	127.88	10.9
76	Swiss	4	680.	680.	83.20	12.2
82	Ital.-Amer.	5	777.	777.	80.40	10.4
106	English	6	400.	400.	52.52	13.1
119	Irish-Amer.	7	637.	637.	67.60	10.6
150	Irish-Amer.	5	450.50	455.	46.80	10.3
153	German	7	780.	780.	101.88	13.1

In number 4 the large amount paid for insurance has proved a blessing, for the man has died since the investigation was made and over $3000. (of insurance) came to his widow, who was otherwise left penniless with three small children and entirely unable to support them. The man had been unable to save anything for several years, the policies were taken out when he was in business for himself, but by the greatest effort the insurance premiums were kept paid. Number 18 was a letter-carrier's family where, in addition to the regular insurance of $1.05 a week, the man belonged to the "Letter Carriers' Association", "Ready Relief" in the Post Office, a Sick Benefit of the Letter Carriers' Association, and a Sick Benefit Society at his sub-station, and the woman belonged to the "Daughters of America", all of these being societies paying benefits in case of sickness or death. For example, the "Daughters of America", on payment of $.12 a week, would pay a sick benefit of $4.00 weekly or $270. at death. This family was "insurance mad",—very few families go to such an extreme as this and the following family (No. 19), whose expenditure has already been itemized.

An interesting because exceptional case is No. 82, an Italian-American family which spent $80.40 or 10.4 per cent of the total expenditure for insurance. This family illustrates the influence of American standards and customs, for a native-born Italian seldom carries any insurance except occasionally in a lodge. When there is any carried, it is not a large proportion of the total expenditure. Only two families with small incomes ($400. to $450.50) carried an unusually high proportion of insurance; and in both cases the policies were taken out when the family had a larger income, and now it is a struggle to keep them paid up.

Among the 26 families who did not carry insurance a few families were found who were thrifty and provident, but who preferred to save their money in another way, and a few did not believe in insurance, but the larger number were very poor, or shiftless and improvident families.

All expenditures which cannot be grouped under the

"economic necessities of life", that is, rent, food, clothing, light and fuel, or insurance,—have been
grouped under the general head of "sundries".
Table VII [1] separates this amount into expenditures for
recreation, trade-unions, gifts or loans to friends or neighbors,
drink (alcoholic liquors), church, furniture, books and papers,
carfares, medical attendance, spending-money for the man
and for those older children who contribute all their earnings
to the family income, education (including kindergarten
fees, business-college expenses, music lessons and purchases
of musical instruments, pianos, violins, etc.), domestic service,
funeral expenses, and various small "miscellaneous expenses".

The expenditures for "sundries" probably reveal the
standard of living of each family more fully than does any
other expenditure, for they show what has been deemed
essential and important after providing for the necessities
of life. It has been said that "the character of a man is
shown by the way he spends his leisure"; thus here the
disposition and ambition of the family is frequently shown
by the amount spent for recreation, drink, church, books
and papers, or education. Sickness and death are often
large and unexpected drains on the family allowance for
"sundries" and form exceptions to this general rule.

It will be seen that the larger the income the larger is
the expenditure for "sundries". A family of 4 with an
income of $260. (No. 8) could only spend $6.25 on items
which are not directly concerned with the actual necessities
of life, while a family of 3 with an income of $2158. (No. 171)
could afford to spend $976. on "sundries", including $500.
for a trip to Germany for the mother and little boy (second
class) and $225. in gifts and loans to friends. The average
amount spent for "sundries" by these 200 families was

[1] Page 103.

$147.31 or 17.6 per cent of the entire expenditure, which does not seem an unreasonable amount to cover so many items of expense, when the average total expenditure was $836.25.

The surplus or deficit at the end of the year shows a condition among these families which is full of meaning. In many cases it seems entirely a question of luck whether there will be a surplus or deficit. The average housewife plans to expend her income each week as carefully as she can, but she is seldom able to prepare for a future season of unemployment or a time of sickness or death. If these crises come there is likely to be a deficit, or at best she may manage to come out even at the end of the year.

Surplus or Deficit.

It will be seen from Table I that 47 families reported a surplus, 55 families a deficit, and 98 families neither surplus nor deficit, which is the usual situation for families in the neighborhood studied. The average surplus for those families having a surplus was $104.37, and the average deficit for those families having a deficit was $34.18. This large surplus was due to a few instances of thrift and prosperity and large income, where the family was able to save considerable amounts, as much as $450. and $650.—in individual cases. The average workingman's family of moderate size can show no such prosperity, and the fact that the average family in this study has a surplus of only $15.13 at the end of the year is far more representative of the real economic condition of the tenement-house dwellers in this neighborhood. Unsteady income due to unemployment, illness, or intemperance, with regular pressing daily expenses, left this pitifully small "margin of surplus", which was all the average family had laid up for the future.

The "per cent of income expended" in the last columns

of the table shows in a more accurate and scientific way Per Cent of Income the relation of the expenditures of each family Expended. to its income. The average income was $851.38, and $836.25, or 98.2 per cent of the income, was expended. This leaves only $15.13, or 1.8 per cent of the income which was saved.

These are the more salient features in the lives of the people presented in this table. Any one who will take the trouble to read between the lines can find much more of interest and value in the facts which are here set forth.

CHAPTER IV

A STUDY OF INCOMES AND EXPENDITURES

THE statistics regarding individual families given in Table I are in sufficient detail to admit of many summaries and analyses being made. In the following tables the incomes and expenditures of these families are grouped according to nativity of head of family, size of family, and amount of income, showing the various sources of income, the amount of surplus or deficit at the end of the year, the condition of "dependent" families, and so on. These tables are supplemented by full explanatory notes, showing the significance and value of each and explaining all exceptional cases, which in many instances have modified or influenced the total results. The conclusions drawn from these tables by no means exhaust the possibilities of deduction, showing different aspects of the economic condition of these families. No attempt has been made to go back of these conditions and investigate their causes. The aim has been merely to collect reliable and accurate data in regard to actual living conditions, and from these to make some practical application of the facts brought out by each tabulation.

TABLE II

EXPENDITURES AND PER CENT OF EXPENDITURES FOR VARIOUS PURPOSES, BY CLASSIFIED INCOMES AND SIZE OF FAMILY

A. TWO IN THE FAMILY

Classified Income	Total Families	Average Income	Food	Rent	Clothing	Light and Fuel	Insurance	Sundries	Total Expenditure	Surplus or Deficit	Food	Rent	Clothing	Light and Fuel	Insurance	Sundries	Total	Per Cent of Income Expended
			Average Expenditure per Family for								Per Cent of Total Expenditure Made for							
$200–$400	1	$380.	$182.	$120.	$10.	$26.95	$0	$42.	$380.	$0	47.9	31.6	2.6	6.8	0	11.1	100	100.
600–700	1	689.	179.40	144.	64.75	36.95	23.16	209.74	658.	+31.	27.3	21.9	9.8	5.6	3.5	31.9	100	95.5
700–800	1	728.	300.	150.	75.	29.33	47.20	51.80	653.	+75.	45.9	23.	11.5	4.4	7.2	8.	100	89.7
800–900	3	811.67	308.75	144.67	66.33	28.33	28.72*	173.95	750.	+61.67	41.1	19.3	8.8	3.8	3.8*	23.2	100	92.4
1000–1200	2	1067.	253.75	180.50	118.46	35.94	.98*	305.37	895.	+172.	28.4	20.2	13.2	4.	1.*	34.1	100	83.9
Total	8	795.75	261.61	151.13	73.21	31.10	19.81*	179.51	716.37	+79.38	36.5	21.1	10.2	4.3	2.7*	25.2*	100.	90.

B. THREE IN THE FAMILY

Classified Income	Total Families	Average Income	Food	Rent	Clothing	Light and Fuel	Insurance	Sundries	Total Expenditure	Surplus or Deficit	Food	Rent	Clothing	Light and Fuel	Insurance	Sundries	Total	Per Cent of Income Expended
$200–$400	3	$312.66	$158.75	$99.	$15.50	$23.35	$14.03*	$21.45	$331.33	–18.67	47.7	29.9	4.7	7.	4.2	6.5	100	106.
400–500	4	472.50	226.75	108.	48.88	22.96	8.	56.91	471.50	+1.00	48.1	22.9	10.3	4.9	1.7*	12.1	100	99.8
500–600	1	580.	247.	90.	40.	40.	13.	150.70	580.	0	42.6	15.5	6.9	6.9	2.2	25.9	100	100.
600–700	1	660.	312.	180.	34.50	27.	44.80	36.70	635.	+25.	49.1	28.3	5.4	4.3	6.7	5.8	100	96.2
700–800	3	748.67	322.67	126.	100.17	48.30	50.41	103.98	751.53	–2.86	42.9	16.8	13.3	6.4	6.7	13.9	100	100.4
800–900	2	835.	364.	165.50	82.50	48.95	9.10*	170.95	841.	–6.	43.3	19.7	9.8	5.8	1.1*	20.3	100	100.7
1000–1200	1	1000.	338.	144.	125.	0	0	308.	1000.	0	34.	14.	12.5	8.5	0	31.	100	100.
1500+	2	1836.50	325.	270.	232.50	55.50	33.15	595.35	1511.50	+325.	21.5	17.8	15.4	3.7	2.2	39.4	100	82.3
Total	17	744.53	272.	140.71	80.70	39.28	21.62*	154.78	709.09	+35.44	38.4	19.9	11.4	5.5	3.	21.8	100.	95.3

TABLE II—Continued

C. FOUR IN THE FAMILY

Classified Income	Total Families	Average Income	Average Expenditure per Family for									Per Cent of Total Expenditure Made for							
			Food	Rent	Clothing	Light and Fuel	Insurance	Sundries	Total Expenditure	Surplus or Deficit	Food	Rent	Clothing	Light and Fuel	Insurance	Sundries	Total	Per Cent of Income Expended
$200–$400	2	$320.50	$136.50	$118.37	$26.50	$19.	$13.30*	$10.33	$324.33	$− 4.	42.1	36.5	8.2	5.9	4.1*	3.2	100.	101.2
400– 500	5	465.	214.80	119.60	34.70*	32.26	23.92	57.05	482.33	−17.33	44.5	24.8	7.2*	6.7	5.	11.8	100.	103.7
500– 600	3	532.50	268.67	107.33	52.33	41.16	13.87*	56.50	532.	0	50.5	20.2	9.8	6.3	2.6*	10.6	100.	100.
600– 700	11	636.82	273.63	151.73	64.64	45.12	29.99*	82.35	643.50	+ 6.68	42.5	23.6	10.	6.4	4.7*	12.8	100.	101.
700– 800	4	761.50	288.50	181.50	91.38	46.	18.96*	134.41	759.87	+ 1.63	38.	23.9	12.	5.9	2.5*	17.7	100.	99.8
800– 900	4	827.	375.20	154.20	58.25	52.67	23.40*	135.95	793.50	+33.50	47.3	19.5	7.3	5.8	3.	17.1	100.	95.9
900–1000	3	940.33	414.67	152.67	68.75*	41.04	33.68	221.23	943.67	− 3.24	43.9	16.2	7.3*	5.6	3.6	23.4	100.	100.4
1000–1200	5	1089.	374.40	221.60	153.60	42.25	38.77*	241.19	1070.60	+18.40	35.	20.7	14.4	3.8	3.6*	22.5	100.	98.3
1200–1500	1	1286.50	194.	300.	200.	42.35	12.	187.75	1236.	+50.	39.9	24.3	16.2	3.4		15.2	100.	96.1
1500+	2	1567.	468.	237.65	156.30		14.30	273.40	1192.	+375.	39.3	19.9	13.1	3.6	1.2	22.9	100.	76.1
Total	40	765.15	309.10	162.80	79.50*	40.16	25.56*	126.67	743.79	+21.36	41.6	21.9	10.7*	5.5	3.4*	17.	100.	97.2

D. FIVE IN THE FAMILY

Classified Income	Total Families	Average Income	Food	Rent	Clothing	Light and Fuel	Insurance	Sundries	Total Expenditure	Surplus or Deficit	Food	Rent	Clothing	Light and Fuel	Insurance	Sundries	Total	Per Cent of Income Expended
$200–$400	3	$359.	$142.83	$113.	$33.34	$20.88	$27.73	$24.55	$362.33	$− 3.33	39.4	31.2	9.2	5.8	7.6	6.8	100.	100.9
400– 500	3	426.83	177.33	113.	50.67	26.67	28.60	35.73	437.	−10.17	40.6	26.	11.6	6.1	6.5	8.2	100.	102.4
500– 600	8	553.88	286.31	138.75	52.13*	32.80	17.28*	40.61	567.88	−14.	50.4	24.4	9.2	5.8	3.1*	7.1	100.	102.5
600– 700	5	666.40	300.04	136.40	59.	37.79	40.01	97.36	670.60	−10.20	44.8	20.3	8.8	5.6	6.*	14.5	100.	101.5
700– 800	8	735.25	305.24	155.50	53.97*	48.17	26.62*	137.32	723.62	+11.63	42.	21.5	7.4*	6.2	3.7*	19.	100.	98.4
800– 900	3	824.	388.26	148.	54.67	33.67	31.91	153.06	824.	0	47.1	18.	6.6	3.6	3.9	18.6	100.	100.
900–1000	3	932.67	437.06	174.	88.67	57.73	57.73	148.54	939.67	− 7.	46.5	18.5	9.5	6.1	6.1	15.8	100.	100.8
1000–1200	3	1052.	533.67	176.	81.67*	62.10	30.33*	134.90	1018.67	+33.33	52.4	17.2	8.*	5.	3.*	13.2	100.	96.8
1200–1500	2	1248.	512.20	252.50	67.50*	61.85	92.84*	244.11	1231.	+17.	41.6	20.5	5.5*	5.7	7.6*	19.8	100.	98.6
1500+	1	1512.	468.	336.	85.	49.	26.	218.	1212.	+300.	38.6	27.7	7.	4.	2.2*	20.5	100.	80.2
Total	39	728.37	327.24	155.49	58.74*	39.95	33.12*	106.07	720.61	+ 7.76	45.4	21.6	8.2*	5.5	4.6*	14.7	100.	98.9

TABLE II—Continued

E. Six in the Family

Classified Income	Total Families	Average Income	Average Expenditure per Family for									Per Cent of Total Expenditure Made for							Per Cent of Income Expended
			Food	Rent	Clothing	Light and Fuel	Insurance	Sundries	Total Expenditure	Surplus or Deficit	Food	Rent	Clothing	Light and Fuel	Insurance	Sundries	Total	
$200–$400	2	375.	191.	103.50	38.80	30.65	18.30	30.75	413.	−38.	46.3	25.1	9.4	7.4	4.4	7.4	100.	110.1
400– 500	2	426.	188.75	123.	28.50*	30.75	36.66	18.34	426.	0	44.3	28.9	6.7*	7.2	8.6	4.3	100.	100.
500– 600	2	558.50	262.60	107.	37.	43.	28.00	90.30	568.50	−10.	46.2	18.8	6.5	7.6	4.9*	15.9	100.	101.8
600– 700	5	662.40	327.60	130.80	63.	32.06	12.72*	110.22	676.40	−14.	48.4	19.3	9.3	4.8	1.9*	16.3	100.	102.1
700– 800	6	742.50	343.15	156.17	69.50	61.42	38.53*	76.56	745.33	−2.83	46.	21.	9.3	8.2	5.2*	10.3	100.	100.4
800– 900	2	841.	335.40	150.	127.50	40.30	21.56	159.74	834.50	+6.50	40.2	18.	15.3	4.8	2.6	19.1	100.	99.2
900–1000	6	944.67	421.03	165.17	72.83*	47.61	41.93*	185.97	934.54	+10.13	45.	17.7	7.8*	5.1	4.5*	19.9	100.	98.9
1000–1200	5	1015.20	410.80	167.60	89.60*	38.22	47.39	274.99	1028.60	−13.40	40.	16.3	8.7*	3.7	4.6	26.7	100.	101.3
1200–1500	5	1362.80	441.	262.80	184.	55.44	41.93*	311.03	1296.20	+66.60	34.	20.3	14.2*	4.3	3.2*	24.	100.	95.1
1500+	1	2556.	546.	300.	500.*	37.20	43.00	539.80	1966.	+590.	27.8	15.3	25.4*	1.9	2.2	27.4	100.	76.9
Total	36	896.72	360.66	166.69	97.24*	44.70	34.62*	172.07	875.98	+20.74	41.2	19.	11.1*	5.1	4.*	19.6	100.	97.7

F. Seven in the Family

Classified Income	Total Families	Average Income	Average Expenditure per Family for									Per Cent of Total Expenditure Made for							Per Cent of Income Expended
			Food	Rent	Clothing	Light and Fuel	Insurance	Sundries	Total Expenditure	Surplus or Deficit	Food	Rent	Clothing	Light and Fuel	Insurance	Sundries	Total	
$600–$700	5	648.	333.80	132.50	44.10	34.30	37.23	72.07	654.	−6.00	51.	20.3	6.7	5.3	5.7	11.	100.	100.9
700– 800	2	740.	364.	126.	41.50	26.50	62.64	69.36	690.	+50.	52.8	18.3	6.	3.8	9.1	10.1	100.	93.2
800– 900	2	849.50	416.	204.	62.50*	48.65	44.20	83.65	859.	−9.50	48.4	23.8	7.3*	5.7	5.1	9.7	100.	101.1
900–1000	4	958.	441.50	191.25	116.25	45.36	39.57	116.57	950.50	+7.50	46.4	20.1	12.2	4.8	4.2	12.3	100.	99.2
1000–1200	5	1061.60	518.96	198.	96.80*	45.06	53.25	146.53	1061.60	0	48.9	18.7	9.1*	4.2	5.0	13.8	100.	100.
1200–1500	3	1293.67	520.	177.	114.67*	49.33	50.27	387.40	1298.67	−5.00	40.1	13.6	8.8*	3.8	3.9	29.8	100.	100.4
1500+	1	1500.	676.	180.	275.*	58.	84.40	271.60	1545.	−45.00	43.8	11.6	17.8*	3.7	5.5	17.6	100.	103.
Total	22	951.82	446.63	172.20	90.75*	43.16	48.16	149.96	950.86	+.96	47.	18.1	9.5*	4.5	5.1	15.8	100.	99.9

TABLE II—Continued

G. EIGHT IN THE FAMILY

Classified Income	Total Families	Average Income	Average Expenditure per Family for							Surplus or Deficit	Per Cent of Total Expenditure Made for							Per Cent of Income Expended
			Food	Rent	Clothing	Light and Fuel	Insurance	Sundries	Total Expenditure		Food	Rent	Clothing	Light and Fuel	Insurance	Sundries	Total	
$400–$500	1	436.	160.	161.	52.	45.45	10.	17.55	436.	0	36.7	36.9	12.9	10.4	0	4.1	100.	100.
500— 600	1	560.	312.	158.50	35.	42.	18.20	24.30	590.	— 30.	52.9	26.9	5.9*	7.1	3.1	4.1	100.	105.4
600— 700	1	675.	364.	142.50	75.	46.	23.40	24.10	675.	0	53.9	21.1	11.1*	6.8	3.5	3.6	100.	100.
700— 800	1	792.	364.	192.	70.	60.50	46.28	59.22	792.	0	45.9	24.3	8.8	7.6	5.9	7.5	100.	100.
800— 900	6	851.17	405.10	146.25	92.15*	44.77	28.16*	149.40	865.83	—14.66	46.8	16.9	10.6*	5.23*	3.2*	17.3	100.	101.7
900—1000	1	925.	450.	136.	96.	62.35	62.40	139.75	946.50	—21.50	47.5	14.4	10.1	6.6	6.6	14.8	100.	102.3
1000—1200	4	1089.75	517.60	134.25	105.*	52.85	32.70	239.10	1081.50	+8.25	47.9	12.4	9.7*	4.9	3.	22.1	100.	99.2
1200—1500	3	1290.80	539.93	198.	103.33*	60.67	40.77	296.77	1239.47	+51.33	43.6	16.	8.3*	4.9	3.3	23.9	100.	96.
1500+	2	1559.	676.	255.	215.	46.50	34.90*	331.60	1559.	0	43.4	16.3	13.8*	3.	2.2*	21.3	100.	100.
Total.....	20	992.22	456.14	165.42	102.05*	50.56	32.11*	183.56	989.84+	2.38	46.1	16.7	10.3*	5.1	3.2*	18.6	100	99.8

H. NINE IN THE FAMILY

Classified Income	Total Families	Average Income	Average Expenditure per Family for							Surplus or Deficit	Per Cent of Total Expenditure Made for							Per Cent of Income Expended
			Food	Rent	Clothing	Light and Fuel	Insurance	Sundries	Total Expenditure		Food	Rent	Clothing	Light and Fuel	Insurance	Sundries	Total	
$400–$500	1	496.	234.	128.	60.	20.	20.80	47.20	510.	—14.	45.9	25.1	11.8	3.9	4.1	9.2	100.	102.8
500— 600	1	514.	312.	108.	36.25*	10.	15.60	32.40	514.	0	60.7	21.	7.	2.1	3.	6.3	100.	100.
600— 800	2	767.	402.10	177.50	50.25*	43.50	45.60	73.15	792.	—25.	50.80	22.4	6.3*	5.5	5.8	9.2	100.	103.3
900—1000	1	969.	563.	178.	110.*	25.80	41.60	51.40	969.	0	58.1	18.4	11.3*	2.6	4.3	5.3	100.	100.
1000—1200	1	1196.	618.	186.	200.	45.80	31.20	115.	1196.	0	51.7	15.6	16.7	3.8	2.6	9.6	100.	100.
1200—1500	2	1425.	598.	297.	157.50*	56.50	41.60	231.90	1382.50	+42.50	43.2	21.5	11.4*	4.1	3.	16.8	100.	97.
1500+	1	1500.	520.	168.	560.	55.	106.60	110.40	1520.	—20.	34.2	11.1	36.9	3.6	7.	7.2	100.	101.3
Total.....	9	1006.56	471.91	190.78	153.50*	39.53	43.34	107.39	1006.45	+.11	46.9	19.	15.2*	3.9	4.3	10.7	100.	99.9+

TABLE II—Continued

I. TEN IN THE FAMILY

Classified Income	Total Families	Average Income	Average Expenditure per Family for — Food	Rent	Clothing	Light and Fuel	Insurance	Sundries	Total Expenditure	Surplus or Deficit	Per Cent of Total Expenditure Made for — Food	Rent	Clothing	Light and Fuel	Insurance	Sundries	Total	Per Cent of Income Expended
$800–$900	3	$849.	$419.33	$153.	$148.27	$51.74	$19.41	$82.25	$874.25	–$25.	48.	17.5	17.	5.9	2.2	9.4	100.	102.9
900–1000	1	972.	369.20	102.	100.	51.	44.20	305.60	972.	0	38.	10.5	10.3	5.2	4.6	31.4	100.	100.
1000–1200	2	1060.50	559.	184.	119.10*	45.	49.40	104.	1060.50	0	52.7	17.4	11.2*	4.2	4.7	9.8	100.	100.
1200–1500	1	1300.	572.	120.	110.*	64.	62.40	371.60	1300.	0	44.	9.2	8.5*	4.9	4.8	28.6	100.	100.
1500+	1	1818.	832.	195.	150.*	36.	0	715.	1928.	–110.	43.2	10.1	7.8*	1.9	0	37.	100.	106.1
Total	8	1094.75	518.65	155.50	130.38*	49.52	32.96*	230.87	1117.88	–23.13	46.4	13.9	11.7*	4.4	2.9*	20.7	100.	102.1

K. TWELVE IN THE FAMILY

Classified Income	Total Families	Average Income	Food	Rent	Clothing	Light and Fuel	Insurance	Sundries	Total Expenditure	Surplus or Deficit	Food	Rent	Clothing	Light and Fuel	Insurance	Sundries	Total	Per Cent of Income Expended
$1200–$1500	1	1358.	512.20	216.	300.*	89.*	28.60	212.20	1358.	0	37.7	15.9	22.1*	6.6	2.1	15.6	100.	100.

TABLE II—Continued

SUMMARY A. AVERAGE INCOME AND EXPENDITURES BY SIZE OF FAMILY

Number in Family	Total Families	Average Income	Average Expenditure per Family for								Per Cent of Total Expenditure Made for							Total Per Cent of Income Expended
			Food	Rent	Clothing	Light and Fuel	Insurance	Sundries	Total Expenditure	Average Surplus or Deficit	Food	Rent	Clothing	Light and Fuel	Insurance	Sundries	Total Per Cent	
Two	8	$795.75	$261.61	$151.13	$73.21	31.10	19.81*	$179.51	$716.37	+79.38	36.5	21.5	10.2	4.3	2.7*	25.2	100.	90.
Three	17	744.53	272.	140.71	80.70	39.28	21.80	154.78	709.	+35.44	38.4	19.9	11.4	5.5	3.3*	21.8	100.	95.3
Four	40	765.15	309.10	162.80	79.50*	40.16	25.56*	126.67	743.79	+21.36	41.6	29.1	10.7*	5.4	3.4*	17.	100.	97.2
Five	39	728.38	327.24	155.49	58.74*	39.95	21.61	106.07	720.61	+7.76	45.4	21.6	8.2*	5.5	4.6*	14.7	100.	98.9
Six	36	896.72	360.66	166.69	97.24*	44.70	34.62*	172.07	875.98	+20.74	41.2	19.	11.1*	5.1	5.1	19.6	100.	97.7
Seven	22	951.82	446.63	172.20	90.75*	43.16	48.16	149.96	950.86	—.96	47.	18.1	9.5*	4.5	5.1	15.8	100.	99.9
Eight	20	992.22	456.14	165.42	102.05*	50.56	32.11*	183.56	989.84	+2.38	46.1	16.7	10.3*	5.1	3.2*	18.6	100.	99.8
Nine	9	1006.56	471.91	190.78	153.50*	39.53	43.34	107.39	1006.45	—.11	46.9	19.	15.2*	3.9	4.3	10.7	100.	99.9+
Ten	8	1094.75	518.65	155.50	130.38*	49.52	32.96*	230.87	1117.88	—23.16	46.4	13.9	11.7*	4.4	2.9*	20.7	100.	102.1
Twelve	1	1358.	512.20	216.	300.*	89.	28.60	212.20	1358.	0	37.5	15.9	22.1*	6.2	2.1	15.6	100.	100.
Total	200	851.38	363.42	162.26	88.45*	42.46	32.35*	147.31	836.25	+15.13	43.4	19.4	10.6*	5.1	3.9*	17.6	100.	98.2

SUMMARY B. AVERAGE INCOME AND EXPENDITURES ACCORDING TO CLASSIFIED INCOMES

Income	Total Families	Av. Size	Average Income	Food	Rent	Clothing	Light and Fuel	Insurance	Sundries	Total Expenditure	Surplus or Deficit	Food	Rent	Clothing	Light and Fuel	Insurance	Sundries	Total Per Cent	Total Per Cent of Income Expended
$200–$400	11	4.2	$344.09	158.14	109.07	26.10	23.45	17.14*	23.83	357.73	—13.64	44.2	30.5	7.3	6.5	4.8*	6.7	100.	104.
400–500	16	4.7	454.97	205.28	119.94	43.13*	28.75	20.72*	45.10	462.92	—7.95	44.4	25.9	9.3*	6.2	4.5*	9.7	100.	101.8
500–600	26	5.2	549.88	280.79	125.16	47.44*	33.77	17.74*	55.10	560.	—10.12	50.1	22.4	8.5*	5.7	3.2*	9.8	100.	101.8
600–700	27	5.1	651.14	299.06	142.55	59.16*	37.36	30.04*	88.78	656.95	—5.81	45.5	21.7	9.*	5.6	4.6*	13.5	100.	100.9
700–800	25	5.3	746.78	326.63	156.81	68.27*	37.52	36.34*	103.84	739.41	+7.37	44.2	21.2	9.2*	5.*	4.9*	14.1	100.	99.
800–900	25	5.9	836.80	380.36	154.89	85.55*	44.51	26.10*	139.87	831.28	+5.52	45.8	18.6	10.3*	4.8	3.1*	16.8	100.	99.3
900–1000	19	6.2	946.58	433.14	165.89	88.43*	45.50	43.81	167.80	944.57	+2.01	45.8	17.6	9.4*	4.8	4.6	17.	100.	99.8
1000–1200	28	6.2	1064.11	456.20	180.72	113.04*	47.39*	37.53*	211.30	1046.18	+17.93	43.6	17.3	10.8*	4.5	3.6*	20.2	100.	98.3
1200–1500	11	7.2	1325.41	510.19	231.89	146.33*	57.73	47.48*	296.18	1289.80	+35.61	39.5	18.	11.3*	4.5	3.7*	23.	100.	97.3
1500+	11	6.1	1710.09	543.64	245.84	252.51*	47.63	38.61*	389.59	1517.82	+192.27	35.8	16.2	16.6*	3.2	2.5*	25.7	100.	88.8
Total	200	5.6	851.38	363.42	162.26	88.45*	42.46	32.35*	147.31	836.25	+15.13	43.4	19.4	10.6*	5.1	3.9*	17.6	100.	98.2

This table groups all the families according to classified incomes and size of family, and then shows the expenditures

Table II. and per cent of expenditures for various purposes for each group. For example, all families of two are grouped together and further classified according to the income, whether it is between $200.–$400., $400.–$500., up to $1500. and over; so with families of three, families of four, and so on. This classification makes it possible to study the various expenditures and their proportion to the whole, for a number of families of the same size.

Where the expenditure for clothing is starred, it is the average amount spent for clothing out of the "household income"; where the expenditure for insurance is starred, it is the average for all the families in the group, and not merely for those families (in the group) who had an expenditure for insurance. These explanations apply to all succeeding tables.

In Group A, two in the family, there is only one family with an income between $200. and $400., no families with an income between $400. and $600., one family with an income between $600. and $700., three families with incomes between $800. and $900., averaging $811.67, and so on. In all, out of 200 families, there were only eight having two in the family, and their average income was $795.75. They averaged $261.61 a year for food, $151.13 for rent, $73.21 for clothing, $31.10 for light and fuel, $19.81 for insurance (but not all families had insurance), $179.51 for sundries, and a total expenditure of $716.37, leaving a surplus of $79.38. Every family in this group had a surplus at the end of the year, except the one with the smallest income ($380.), which came out even. It is obvious that a surplus is more frequent in families with no children. Each group may be read in the same way, and then comparisons made of the amounts of different expenditures in families of various sizes. A close study of these groups suggests some interesting deductions, among which are the following: 1. In families of the same size the amount expended for food tends steadily to *increase* as the income increases, but the *percentage of expenditure* for food tends to decrease as the income increases. This is almost a self-evident proposition, but it is interesting to note how it is shown here. Where this regular progression is thrown out in this table, it is generally because there are not enough families entering into the average to make it representative, or the result is influenced by individual exceptions. For example, in Group A, the food expenditure drops to $179.40 in the family with an income of $689. Here the wife was an exceptionally good manager and very thrifty, and kept an exact budget for a year. Another apparent exception to this rule is that in small families, groups A and B, the expenditure for food increases up to a certain point where the incomes are between $800.-$900. and then, a maximum of what is necessary being attained, the average expenditure for food drops somewhat in the larger incomes. 2. In families of the same size expenditure for rent and clothing tends steadily to *increase* as the income increases. The *proportion* of rent to the total expenditure decreases, but the *proportion* expended for clothing increases as the income increases. 3. In families of the same size, both expenditure and per cent of expenditure for sundries *increase* with the income. Whenever this is not shown, there is an explanation for it. In Group A the family with an income of $728. spent less for sundries, because they preferred to save $75.; in Group B the family having an income of $660. spent less for sundries, but saved $25. In this same group the family having an income of $580. spent $150. for sundries, which is disproportionately large, because of illness

and medical attendance which cost $85. Another instance
where this expenditure was unusually high is in Group E,
because in the two families entering into the average income
between $500. and $600., one man was a hard drinker, and
the other demanded an unusual amount of spending-money.
In this group also the average for sundries, in the incomes
between $600. and $700., was raised by the cost of several
funerals. Another unusual illustration is in Group I where
the family having an income of $1818. spent $130. for drink,
and also had three deaths in the family, the funerals costing
$448. and no insurance. It is not surprising that this family
spent $715. or 37 per cent of the total expenditure for sundries.
This exceptional case naturally shows a deficit of $110., where
there would have been a surplus under ordinary circumstances.

All of these discrepancies would probably be blotted out
had the investigation included 20,000 families instead of 200.
The general deductions would remain the same, while this table
gains an added interest because of the many individual exceptions, which may usually be explained by a personal
knowledge of the individual characteristics of the families
entering into the averages.

"Summary A" reviews the incomes and expenditures for
these families according to the size of the family and the per
cent expended for each item of expense. This
Summary A.   table brings together the totals of each of the
previous groups and compares them. An inspection of this
summary shows the following tendencies:

1. In general, as the family increases in size, the income
   increases. In families where there are young children,
   boarders or lodgers may swell the income, until large
   families of seven or eight are reached, when some of
   the children are of working age and contribute to the
   "household income".

2. The expenditure for food steadily increases as the size of the family increases. The *per cent* expended tends also to increase up to seven in the family, where the increase in size is counterbalanced by the corresponding increase in income, and from this point the proportion spent for food decreases.

3. As the size of the family increases the rent *tends* to increase, more and better rooms being necessary, but it decreases in proportion to the total expenditure.

4. Clothing increases in expense also, but this cannot be shown invariably here, because of the many exceptional cases in which not all of the members of the family are clothed by the amount given.

5. The *tendency* is the same for insurance expenditures, but the averages are again upset by those families carrying no insurance.

6. The average surplus decreases as the size of the family increases, until there is an average deficit in the families having ten in the family. Exceptions are here explained by the fact that, for example, in the group having six members with an average surplus of $20.74, the larger surplus is due to two or three families in the group who had large incomes and were unusually thrifty, individual families saving as much as $100., $175., and $590. in the year. In the group having five in the family the average surplus is lowered by three families who had deficits of $65., $77., and $51.— due to unpaid rent, furniture bought "on time", or debts to neighbors.

7. As the average surplus decreases the per cent of income expended naturally increases in the larger families.

8. Note that the largest number of families consist of 4, 5, or 6 members.

"Summary B" shows these results in another way. The incomes and expenditures are grouped by classified incomes instead of by size of family. The other classifications in Groups A to K, and also Summary A, showed that as the size of the family increased the income increased. This summary shows the same fact—as the income increases the size of the family increases also. The results, as a whole, are more regular here than in Summary A.

Summary B.

1. The deduction that *all* expenditures for *all* purposes increase as the income increases, the family becoming larger at the same time, is very plainly shown here, without the exceptions which upset this progression when a smaller number of families were averaged. In the supplementary table for percentages it is shown that as the income increases the percentage expended for food, rent, and light and fuel *decreases* quite regularly, while for clothing and sundries it *increases*.

2. "Summary A" showed that the average *surplus decreased* as the size of the family increased, beginning with an average income of $795.75 for two in the family. This summary shows that the *deficit* natural to the group of smallest incomes, having an average of $344.09 for 4.2 persons in the family, *decreases* quite steadily until the group having an average income of $746.78 is reached, in which the size of the family has only increased to 5.9; then there begins to be a surplus, which remains a surplus, though not a regularly increasing one, until the income is between $1000. and $1200., from which point it increases rapidly.

3. The "per cent of income expended" *decreases* as the income increases, until the income is between $700. and $800., when it *increases* for two groups, the size of the family increasing in a larger proportion, and then

from the group between $800. and $900. it decreases again until it is only 88.8 per cent in the eleven families in which the incomes are $1500. or over, and the average size of family is 6.1.

This constant interdependence of the size of the family and the income, and of the resulting surplus or deficit, is one of the most valuable conclusions to be drawn from this table.

Other interesting comparisons can be made by combining the figures here presented in different ways. For example, this table affords an opportunity to compare the expenditures of large and small families having about the same income. Take the 25 families having an income between $800. and $900.—which is the group within which the total average income of this investigation falls.

Object of Expenditure.	Size of Family.							
	Two.	Three.	Four.	Five.	Six.	Seven.	Eight.	Ten.
	$	$	$	$	$	$	$	$
Food	308.00	364.00	375.20	388.26	335.40	416.00	405.10	419.33
Rent	144.67	165.50	154.70	148.00	150.00	204.00	146.25	153.00
Clothing	66.33	82.50	58.25	54.67	127.50	62.50*	92.15*	148.27
Light and fuel ..	28.33	48.95	46.00	48.10	40.30	48.65	44.77	51.74
Insurance	28.72*	9.10*	23.40*	31.91	21.56	44.20	28.16*	19.41
Sundries	173.95	170.95	135.95	153.06	159.74	83.65	149.40	82.25
Total av. expenditure	750.00	841.00	793.50	824.00	834.50	859.00	865.83	874.00
Total av. income	811.67	835.00	827.00	824.00	841.00	849.50	851.17	849.00

Each group of incomes may be compared in the same way.

These summaries also give the total results for the entire investigation. The total average income is $851.38, of this $836.25 was expended, including $363.42 for food, $162.26 for rent, $88.45 for clothing, $42.46 for light and fuel, $32.35 for insurance, and $147.31 for sundries, leaving an average

TABLE III

EXPENDITURES AND PER CENT OF EXPENDITURES FOR VARIOUS PURPOSES BY CLASSIFIED INCOME AND NATIVITY OF HEAD OF FAMILY

UNITED STATES

Classified Income	Total Families	Average Income	Average Expenditure per Family for						Total Expenditures	Average Surplus or Deficit	Per Cent of Total Expenditure Made for							Per Cent of Income Expended	Average Size of Family
			Food	Rent	Clothing	Light and Fuel	Insurance	Sundries			Food	Rent	Clothing	Light and Fuel	Insurance	Sundries	Total		
$200–$400	7	$331.43	$150.22	$106.68	$31.51	$20.68	$16.83	$22.22	$348.86	–$17.43	43.1	30.6	9.	5.9	4.8	6.6	100.	105.3	4.7
400–500	9	464.83	215.25	120.67	44.78	21.07	22.33	46.89	477.29	–12.46	45.1	25.3	9.4	5.7	4.7	9.8	100.	102.7	4.4
500–600	10	548.20	280.27	122.	46.82	31.78	34.63	57.51	558.70	–10.50	50.2	21.8	8.4	5.7	3.6	10.3	100.	101.9	5.3
600–700	18	654.22	303.92	149.31	49.82	34.43	34.43	83.00	655.11	–.89	46.4	22.8	7.6	5.2	5.3	12.7	100.	101.1	5.4
700–800	15	752.80	335.01	157.13	70.02	50.11	36.88	104.06	753.21	+.41	44.5	20.9	9.3	6.6	4.9	13.8	100.	101.	5.4
800–900	15	826.66	360.17	162.33	67.40	43.64	29.81	153.58	816.93	–9.73	44.1	19.9	8.3	4.5	3.6	18.8	100.	98.8	4.7
900–1000	11	971.86	414.57	197.	99.47	42.99	37.81	170.02	961.86	+10.00	43.1	20.5	10.3	4.5	3.9	17.7	100.	98.	5.9
1000–1200	11	1057.73	434.72	177.36	114.45	46.03	44.54	224.99	1042.09	+15.64	41.7	17.7	11.	4.4	4.3	21.6	100.	98.5	5.7
1200–1500	8	1310.87	512.52	221.87	156.25	54.53	36.53	277.67	1259.37	+51.50	41.7	17.6	12.4	4.3	3.	22.	100.	96.1	5.7
1500+	5	1873.36	514.80	268.00	389.00	46.88	54.88	424.94	1699.20	+174.00	30.3	15.8	22.9	2.8	3.2	25.	100.	90.7	6.
Total	105	816.61	343.34	161.72	87.61	40.09	33.03	138.36	804.15	+12.46	42.7	20.1	10.9	5.	4.1	17.2	100.	98.5	5.3
IRELAND																			
$200–$400	1	397.	182.	120.	20.	32.	39.	4.	397.	0	45.9	30.2	5.3	8.1	9.8	1.	100.	100.	5.
400–500	2	455.50	208.25	129.	33.50	41.50	18.20	27.55	458.	–2.50	45.5	28.2	7.3	9.4	4.	6.	100.	100.6	5.1
500–600	4	541.	283.75	137.13	45.50	35.37	20.31	32.80	555.25	–14.25	51.1	24.7	8.2	6.3	2.7	5.9	100.	102.8	5.7
600–700	4	634.75	322.18	126.75	76.50	39.62	23.04	99.19	646.12	–11.37	43.9	19.6	11.8	6.8	3.2	15.4	100.	101.8	4.
700–800	5	726.	451.90	152.40	69.60	49.	102.18	102.18	718.40	+7.60	44.9	21.2	9.7	6.8	3.9	12.8	100.	99.5	5.4
800–900	4	859.75	439.24	142.50	99.17	47.88	34.71	113.84	890.	–30.25	50.8	16.6	11.1	4.8	6.2	17.2	100.	103.5	8.8
900–1000	5	948.20	539.83	159.20	87.60	47.63	59.55	164.58	957.80	–9.60	45.9	16.6	9.1	4.8	3.1	17.9	100.	101.2	6.2
1000–1200	6	1088.83	539.83	164.17	110.20	53.20	34.23	196.37	1098.	–9.17	49.2	15.	10.	4.3	2.9	17.9	100.	100.8	7.7
1200–1500	3	1331.67	572.	245.	136.34	59.33	39.87	334.13	1386.67	–55.	41.2	17.7	9.8	3.7	2.5	24.1	100.	104.1	7.7
1500+	1	1500.	676.	180.	275.	58.	84.40	271.60	1545.	–45.	43.8	11.6	17.8		5.5	17.6	100.	103.	6.4
Total	35	852.83	403.89	156.04	88.66	46.99	33.68	137.95	867.22	–14.39	46.6	18.	10.2	5.4	3.9	15.9	100.	101.7	6.4

TABLE III—Continued

ENGLAND

Classified Income	Total Families	Average Income ($)	Food ($)	Rent ($)	Clothing ($)	Light and Fuel ($)	Insurance ($)	Sundries ($)	Total Expenditures ($)	Average Surplus or Deficit ($)	Food %	Rent %	Clothing %	Light and Fuel %	Insurance %	Sundries %	Total %	Per Cent of Income Expended	Average Size of Family
$200–$400	0	400.	195.	84.	30.	20.	52.52	18.48	400.	0	48.8	21.	7.5	5.	13.1	4.6	100.	100.	6.
400– 500	1																		
500– 600	0																		
600– 700	3	648.	303.34	152.83	68.33	49.80	16.47	74.23	665.	– 17.	45.6	23.	10.3	7.5	2.5	11.1	100.	102.6	5.7
700– 800	1	775.	338.	120.	130.	58.	46.80	82.20	775.	0	43.6	15.5	16.8	7.5	6.	10.6	100.	100.	6.
800– 900	2	835.	364.	135.40	107.50	40.50	14.30	123.30	785.	+ 50.	46.4	17.5	13.7	5.2	1.8	15.7	100.	94.	6.
900–1000	2	907.	484.	168.	75.	37.	24.86	118.14	907.	0	53.3	18.5	8.3	4.1	2.7	13.	100.	100.	6.
1000–1200	4	1049.	390.	195.	118.	57.73	18.46	259.06	1039.	+ 10.	37.5	18.8	11.4	5.6	1.8	24.9	100.	99.	4.5
1200–1500	1	1300.	572.	120.	150.	64.	62.40	371.60	1300.	0	44.	9.2	8.5	4.9	4.8	28.6	100.	100.	10.
1500+	1	1818.	832.	195.	150.	36.	0	715.	1928.	– 110.	43.2	10.1	7.8	1.9	0	37.	100.	106.1	10.
Total	15	927.80	406.87	157.62	97.55	47.67	24.22	195.27	929.20	– 1.40	43.8	17.	10.5	5.1	2.6	21.	100.	100.2	5.9

GERMANY

Classified Income	Total Families	Average Income ($)	Food ($)	Rent ($)	Clothing ($)	Light and Fuel ($)	Insurance ($)	Sundries ($)	Total Expenditures ($)	Average Surplus or Deficit ($)	Food %	Rent %	Clothing %	Light and Fuel %	Insurance %	Sundries %	Total %	Per Cent of Income Expended	Average Size of Family
$200–$400	0	410.	160.	90.	66.	22.	18.20	53.80	410.	0	39.	22.	16.1	5.4	4.4	13.1	100.	100.	5.
400– 500	1																		
500– 600	0																		
600– 700	1	614.	286.	132.33	62.	36.	26.	88.17	630.	+ 16.67	45.4	21.	9.8	5.7	4.1	14.	100.	102.6	4.
700– 800	3	746.	334.	154.33	61.	33.	61.83	86.17	730.33	+ 15.67	45.7	21.1	8.4	4.5	8.5	11.8	100.	97.9	4.7
800– 900	1	880.	500.	131.50	150.	32.	7.80	58.70	880.	0	56.8	14.9	17.	3.6	9.	6.7	100.	100.	8.
900–1000	1	916.	520.	132.	150.	65.	39.	150.	916.	0	56.8	14.4	17.1	7.1	4.2	16.4	100.	100.	4.
1000–1200	4	1064.75	518.70	199.50	105.25	46.92	47.	117.38	1034.75	+ 30.30	50.1	19.3	10.2	4.5	4.5	11.4	100.	97.2	6.5
1200–1500	5	1343.48	456.60	265.60	113.	54.38	70.36	304.74	1264.68	+ 78.80	36.1	21.	8.9	4.3	5.6	24.1	100.	94.1	6.8
1500+	1	1512.	468.	336.	85.	49.	26.	248.	1212.	+ 300.	38.6	27.7	7.	4.	2.2	20.5	100.	80.2	5.
Total	17	1032.14	429.05	200.62	90.70	44.86	49.54	167.66	982.43	+ 49.71	48.7	20.4	9.2	4.6	5.	17.1	100.	95.2	5.9

TABLE III—Continued

ITALY

Classified Income	Total Families	Average Income	Food	Rent	Clothing	Light and Fuel	Insurance	Sundries	Total Expenditures	Average Surplus or Deficit	Food	Rent	Clothing	Light and Fuel	Insurance	Sundries	Total	Per Cent of Income Expended	Average Size of Family
			(Average Expenditure per Family for)								(Per Cent of Total Expenditure Made for)								
$200–$400	1	$366.50	$200.	$102.	$26.	$29.72	$10.40	$8.60	$376.	–$10.	53.2	27.1	6.9	7.7	2.8	2.3	100.	102.7	3.
400– 500	2	462.50	182.50	134.50	42.	35.52	0	67.78	462.50	0	39.5	29.1	9.1	7.7	0	14.6	100.	100.	5.5
500– 600	1	580	247.	90.	40.	40.	13.	150.	580.	0	42.6	15.5	6.9	6.9	2.2	25.9	100.	100.	5.5
600– 700	2	665	299.	99.	105.	41.20	3.90	136.80	685.	–20.	43.6	14.5	15.3	6.	.5	20.	100.	103.	5.5
700– 800	1	797	271.	216.	30.	38.	31.20	110.80	697.	+100.	38.9	31.	4.3	5.4	4.5	15.9	100.	87.	4.
800– 900	1	867	400.	165.	200.	50.	0	52.	867.	0	46.1	19.	23.1	5.8	0	6.	100.	100.	10.
900–1000	3	935.67	403.07	121.67	103.67	52.78	46.80	213.93	941.92	–6.25	42.8	12.9	11.	5.6	5.	22.7	100.	100.7	8.
1000–1200	2	1086	429.	180.	133.	24.95	46.80	244.75	1058.50	+27.50	40.5	17.	12.6	2.4	4.4	23.1	100.	97.5	6.5
1200–1500	1	1358	512.20	216.	300.	89.	28.60	212.20	1358.	0	37.7	15.9	22.1	6.6	2.1	15.6	100.	100.	12.
1500+	1	1500	624.	270.	170.	48.	0	388.	1500.	0	41.6	18.	11.3	3.2	0	25.9	100.	100.	8.
Total.........	15	846.80	352.29	150.07	109.13	43.74	21.67	164.15	841.05	+5.75	41.9	17.8	13.	5.2	2.6	19.5	100.	99.3	6.6

FRANCE

Classified Income	Total Families	Average Income	Food	Rent	Clothing	Light and Fuel	Insurance	Sundries	Total Expenditures	Average Surplus or Deficit	Food	Rent	Clothing	Light and Fuel	Insurance	Sundries	Total	Per Cent of Income Expended	Average Size of Family
$200–$400	2	351.	153.	115.50	10.25	26.12	10.65	44.48	360.	–9.	42.5	32.1	2.8	7.3	3.	12.3	100.	102.6	2.5
700– 800	1	700.	260.	118.	72.	41.50	0	188.50	680.	+20.	38.2	17.4	10.6	6.1	0	27.1	100.	97.1	5.
800– 900	1	832.	306.80	180.	90.	35.60	30.12	176.48	819.	+13.	37.5	22.	11.	4.3	3.7	21.5	100.	98.4	6.
Total.........	4	558.50	218.20	132.25	45.63	32.34	12.85	113.48	554.75	+3.75	39.3	23.9	8.2	5.8	2.3	20.5	100.	99.3	4.

NORWAY AND SWEDEN

Classified Income	Total Families	Average Income	Food	Rent	Clothing	Light and Fuel	Insurance	Sundries	Total Expenditures	Average Surplus or Deficit	Food	Rent	Clothing	Light and Fuel	Insurance	Sundries	Total	Per Cent of Income Expended	Average Size of Family
$500–$600	1	572.	286.	144.	70.	41.	5.60	25.40	572.	0	50.	25.2	12.2	7.2	1.	4.4	100.	100.	5.
1000–1200	1	1000.	260.	186.	83.	33.	0	268.	830.	+170.	31.3	22.4	10.	4.	0	32.3	100.	83.	2.
1500+	2	1557.50	403.	189.65	76.30	49.50	19.95	269.10	1007.50	+550.	40.	18.8	7.6	4.9	2.	26.7	100.	64.7	3.5
Total.........	4	1171.75	338.	177.32	76.40	43.25	11.38	207.90	854.25	+317.50	39.6	20.8	8.9	5.1	1.3	24.3	100.	72.9	3.5

TABLE III—Continued

SWITZERLAND

Classified Income	Total Families	Average Income	Food	Rent	Clothing	Light and Fuel	Insurance	Sundries	Total Expenditures	Average Surplus or Deficit	Food %	Rent %	Clothing %	Light and Fuel %	Insurance %	Sundries %	Total %	Per Cent of Income Expended	Average Size of Family
			$	$	$	$	$	$	$	$									
$600–$700	1	680.	273.20	151.	36.	37.35	83.20	99.45	680.	+ 0	40.2	22.2	5.3	5.5	12.2	14.6	100.	100.	4.
900–1000	1	904.	434.20	144.	75.	28.	40.80	147.	869.	+ 35.	50.	16.6	8.6	3.2	4.7	16.9	100.	96.1	6.
Total	2	792.	353.60	147.50	55.50	32.67	62.	123.23	774.50	+ 17.50	45.6	19.	7.3	4.2	8.	15.9	100.	97.8	5.
Austria	1	731.	312.	198.	30.	50.	49.20	91.80	731.	0	42.7	27.1	4.1	6.8	6.7	12.6	100.	100.	6.
Scotland	1	832.	364.	120.	76.	68.20	0	203.80	832.	0	43.8	14.4	9.1	8.2		24.5	100.	100.	8.
Cuba	1	450.	208.	132.	40.	20.	23.40	36.60	460.	− 10.	45.2	28.7	8.7	4.3	5.1	8.	100.	102.2	4.

SUMMARY OF INCOME AND EXPENDITURES IN 200 FAMILIES BY THE NATIVITY OF THE HEAD OF THE FAMILY

Nativity	Total Families	Average Income	Food	Rent	Clothing	Light and Fuel	Insurance	Sundries	Total Expenditures	Average Surplus or Deficit	Food %	Rent %	Clothing %	Light and Fuel %	Insurance %	Sundries %	Total %	Per Cent of Income Expended	Average Size of Family
United States	105	816.61	343.34	161.72	87.61	40.09	33.03	138.36	804.15	+ 12.46	42.7	20.1	10.9	5.	4.1	17.2	100.	98.5	5.3
Ireland	35	852.83	403.89	156.04	88.66	46.99	33.68	137.95	867.22	− 14.39	46.6	18.	10.2	5.4	3.9	15.9	100.	101.7	6.4
England	15	927.80	406.87	157.62	97.67	47.55	24.22	195.27	929.20	− 1.40	43.8	17.	10.5	5.1	2.6	21.	100.	100.2	5.9
Germany	17	1032.14	429.05	200.62	90.70	44.86	49.54	167.66	982.43	+ 49.71	43.7	20.4	9.2	4.6	5.1	17.1	100.	95.2	6.6
Italy	15	846.80	352.29	150.07	109.13	43.74	21.67	164.15	841.05	+ 5.75	41.9	17.8	13.	5.2	2.6	19.5	100.	99.3	6.6
France	4	558.50	218.20	132.25	45.63	32.34	11.85	113.48	554.75	+ 3.75	39.3	23.9	8.2	5.8	2.3	20.5	100.	99.3	4.3
Norway & Sweden	2	1171.75	338.60	177.32	76.40	43.25	11.38	207.90	854.25	+ 317.50	39.6	20.8	8.9	5.1	1.3	24.3	100.	72.9	3.5
Switzerland	2	792.	353.60	147.50	55.50	32.67	62.	123.23	774.50	+ 17.50	45.6	19.	7.3	4.2	8.	15.9	100.	97.8	5.
Austria	1	731.	312.	198.	30.	50.	49.20	91.80	731.	0	42.7	27.1	4.1	6.8	6.7	12.6	100.	100.	6.
Scotland	1	832.	364.	120.	76.	68.20	0	203.80	832.	0	43.8	14.4	9.1	8.2		24.5	100.	100.	8.
Cuba	1	450.	208.	132.	40.	20.	23.40	36.60	460.	− 10.00	45.2	28.7	8.7	4.3	5.1	8.	100.	102.2	4.
Total foreign	95	889.81	385.61	162.85	89.39	45.08	31.61	157.20	871.74	+ 18.07	44.2	18.7	10.3	5.2	3.6	18.	100.	98.	6.
Total U. S. and foreign	200	851.38	363.42	162.26	88.45	42.46	32.35	147.31	836.25	+ 15.13	43.4	19.4	10.6	5.1	3.9	17.6	100.	98.2	5.6

surplus of only $15.13, unless the amount paid for insurance be added to this, $32.35—which, as has already been explained, is considered by the people a form of savings.

Table III gives by nativity of head of the family, instead of by size of the family, the classified incomes and expenditures of these families, and shows the per cent of their expenditures for various purposes.

Table III.

In 105, or 52.5 per cent, of all the families in this study, the head of the family (father, or widowed or deserted mother) was native born, and in 95, or 47.5 per cent, of all the families, he was foreign born. Of the 95 foreign born, 35 were born in Ireland, 15 in England, 17 in Germany, 15 in Italy, 4 in France, 4 in Norway and Sweden, 2 in Switzerland, and 1 each in Austria, Scotland, and Cuba. Some interesting racial traits are brought out in this table, in grouping families by nativity and sub-grouping them by amount of income.

Contrasting the two main groups, native and foreign first, it will be seen in the Summary that the average income of the foreign families was $889.81, while in the native families it was only $816.61. This difference is

Foreign and Native Families.

somewhat modified by the fact that the average size of the foreign family was 6 and of the native 5.3. It has already been shown that the income is likely to increase with the size of the family, but, after making this allowance, there remains a considerably larger average income for the foreign families than for the native. This fact presupposes a greater thrift or ability in the foreign families—a condition which must be rather startling to those pessimists who bewail the phenomenal growth of our foreign population in New York City. The difference in surplus is not so marked—$12.46 for the native and $18.07 for the foreign families. The average income and expenditures of the native and foreign families may be compared as follows.

	Average Income.	Expenditure for					
		Food.	Rent.	Clothing.	Light and Fuel.	Insurance.	Sundries.
Native......	$816.61	$343.34	$161.72	$87.61*	$40.09	$33.03*	$138.36
Foreign.....	889.81	385.61	162.85	89.39*	45.08	31.61*	157.20

	Per Cent of Income Expended.	Per Cent Expended for					
		Food.	Rent.	Clothing.	Light and Fuel.	Insurance.	Sundries.
Native......	98.5	42.7	20.1	10.9*	5.	4.1*	17.2
Foreign.....	98.	44.2	18.7	10.3*	5.2	3.6*	18.

It is shown here that the average American family spent a larger percentage for rent, clothing, and insurance than the average foreign family, which in turn expended more for food, fuel, and sundries. Making allowence for the larger foreign family, the percentage spent for food would be about the same. The native families included more grown children, whose expenditure for clothing did not enter into the amount given, so that they really expended a larger proportion for clothing than is here given.

Distribution of Incomes. The distribution of incomes of various amounts in native and foreign families can best be shown by the table on the next page. It will be seen that there were 11, or 11.6 per cent, very poor foreign families in this number, that is, with incomes less than $500., and 16, or 15.2 per cent, native born. In families having the largest incomes, $1000. or over, the foreign families make an even better showing, 33, or 34.7 per cent, coming within this group, contrasted with 24, or 22.7 per cent, of the native born. Further comparisons may be made in other groups of incomes.

Income.	Native Born.		Foreign Born.		Native and Foreign.	
	Number.	Per Cent.	Number.	Per Cent.	Number.	Per Cent.
Income $200– 400....	7	6.7	4	4.2	11	5.5
" 400– 500....	9	8.6	7	7.4	16	8.
" 500– 600....	10	9.5	6	6.32	16	8.
" 600– 700....	18	17.1	11	11.6	29	14.5
" 700– 800....	15	14.3	12	12.63	27	13.5
" 800– 900....	15	14.3	10	10.5	25	12.5
" 900–1000....	7	6.7	12	12.63	19	9.5
" 1000–1200....	11	10.5	17	17.9	28	14.
" 1200–1500....	8	7.6	10	10.5	18	9.
" 1500+ ...	5	4.7	6	6.32	11	5.5
Total.........	105	100.0	95	100.0	200	100.0

Group A further divides the incomes and expenditures of the native families. The largest number of families have in-

Nativity United States.

comes from $500. to $900. The smallest income in an American family was $250., the largest was $2556., which are the two extremes in this investigation. The foreign families seem to have a more equable distribution of income. As was shown in Table II, the tendency is for all expenditures to increase as the income increases, and for the percentage of expenditures for food, rent, light and fuel, and insurance to decrease, for clothing and sundries to increase. The per cent of income expended also decreases as the income increases.

Contrasting these figures with those of foreign nationalities, it is seen that the average Irish incomes extend from $397. to $1500., the English from $400. to $1818.,

Ireland.

the German from $410. to $1512., and so on. In per cent of income expended the Irish lead all other nationalities (with the exception of the one Cuban family, which is not representative), and they have the largest average deficit—$14.39. Every group of this nativity but one shows a deficit, except the poorest family, which came out even. Eighteen of the 35 Irish families had a deficit, 15 came out even, and only 2 had a surplus. The family with an income of $712. for 5 in the family had a surplus of $55. left from $300. "damages" given the widow on the death of her husband during the year by the Elevated Railroad Company, —the other surplus was $5. which a family of 5 with an income of $1100. had managed to save in the Penny Provident Bank.

As might be expected, the German, French, and Italian families were the most provident. The Germans show a surplus in all the average incomes above $700.,

Germany.

except two which came out even. In the family whose income was $614. the deficit of $16. was due to the three months' illness of the head of the family; ordinarily there would have been a surplus in this thrifty family. This is an illustration of one of the dark years which come to every workingmans family, when sickness and unemployment eat up the little savings, and the family is either plunged into debt or forced to become dependent upon charity. The only other deficit in the German families was $28. for the doctor's bill, after the long illness of the mother. (This deficit was eliminated in the average for the group, $700. to $800., and is not shown in this table.)

Only 3 out of the 15 Italian families admitted a surplus at the end of the year, 4 were known to have a deficit, and 8 claimed they just managed to come out even.

Italy.

It is possible that with characteristic Italian secrecy the true amount of the income was withheld, and in a few cases the income may have been larger than was given, and a balance saved. The investigators feel confident that the expenditures were not overestimated. A larger average surplus would be expected in these Italian families, but gifts to relatives, and large families, combined to cut down this surplus.

Although there were only 4 Norwegian or Swedish families and 4 French families in this study, these few examples

Norway and Sweden. present the characteristics of their races. The Norwegians had the largest average income by nationality, $1171.75, the smallest average family, and the least percentage of income expended. All families reported a surplus. One family had a surplus of $650., which was the highest amount saved in any nationality. This family was an interesting and unusual one. The father had been a deck-hand for seventeen years, but had taken a pilot's examinations in Norway and America, and was suddenly made a captain of a tugboat at $125. a month. One month of the year investigated his wages were $9. a week. The wife told the investigator "we got along comfortably on that, and saved a little, too, but now we don't have to count the pennies so carefully". It is not surprising that such a family could show such a large surplus, for the standard of living remained practically the same, except that they moved into better rooms, and were able to give more to their poorer friends and relatives here and in Norway.

The characteristic French thrift cannot be well illustrated here, because of the poverty of two of the families studied.

France. Two out of the four families had incomes of $322. and $380. (for 3 and 2 in the family), yet the latter managed to come out even at the end of the year, and the other was in debt only $18. after a long season of unemployment by the man, who was an ordinary kitchen-helper. Decreased vitality was the result of thrift in this family on this income. The other families had fair incomes, $700. and $832., and reported a surplus.

The two Swiss families were also very thrifty, but in one case the family just managed to come out even, because of illness, though in previous years considerable had been saved.

Switzerland.

The English families were for the most part only able to keep out of debt and saved nothing. Ten out of 15 reported neither surplus nor deficit, 3 families had a total surplus of $140., and 2 families were deeply in debt—one $51. and the other $110. The family which had a deficit of $51. had an income of $626. The deficit was owing on furniture which the woman had been obliged to buy "on time" in order to get a position as janitor. The other instance, the family having a deficit of $110., has already been noted. Three deaths within the year, with funerals and medical attendance costing $448. and no insurance, plunged this family into debt, even though the income was $1818. Hence the English families instead of having a surplus reported an average deficit of $1.40 due to these exceptional circumstances.

English.

The summary of this table shows more clearly than do the different groups this influence of racial characteristics on the incomes and expenditures. The deductions already made from this table are also shown here. In addition to these facts concerning incomes and surplus or deficit, the Summary brings together the various expenditures and compares them by nationality.

Summary of Table III.

First, in regard to the expenditure for food and rent, it is seen that the German families (average size 5.9) spent the largest amount for food and rent, but the Irish families of larger size (6.4) expended more in proportion for food, or 46.6 per cent compared with 43.7 per cent in the German families. The Cuban family spent the largest *percentage* for rent, because of the social

Food and Rent.

condition of the family. The man was a Cuban negro with a German wife, and the children were so dark-skinned that they could only get rooms in a negro tenement and had to pay a high rent, for such quarters, far out of proportion to what their income afforded. Parenthetically, it should be noted, in Groups A to I, that the larger percentage paid for rent seems not so much a matter of nationality as of size of income. Usually the smaller the income the larger the proportion that is spent for food and rent, which are the two absolutely necessary expenses.

The French spent a large per cent on rent because of the small average income of these families. They also show the smallest proportion for food, 39.3 per cent of the total expenditure, which is an obvious racial characteristic.

With the exception of the one Scotch family, the English and Italian families spent the smallest proportion of their total expenditure on rent.

A discussion of the expenditure for clothing must always be limited by the fact that sometimes the amount given does not cover the entire expense for the whole family. This is especially true in the American families, but, on the contrary, the larger proportion (13 per cent) which the Italian families expended did generally clothe all members of the family. The Italian custom is for even the older working children to turn all their earnings into the common purse, and the mother buys clothing for them all. Even the father rarely asks for enough spending-money to clothe himself. It is therefore to be expected that the Italian families should show the highest amount and percentage spent for clothing. It is however probable that the gross amount spent for clothing by the American, Irish, English, and German families is greater than for the Italian families. The Italians love pretty clothes and finery, and the more prosperous dress well, but in these families at least, they dressed more economically, and the women more frequently made the clothes for the family than did the Irish and English women, who usually bought their clothes "ready-made" at greater cost. The Italians also had the largest families, which helps explain this large per cent for clothing compared with other nationalities. The German families were the best and most comfortably dressed of all the families, without the gaudy finery of the Italians and Irish.

The expenditure for light and fuel does not reveal any native characteristics, except the innate French and Swiss economy. The French housewives especially could make a bushel of coal or a bundle of wood last the most surprising length of time.

Light and Fuel.

The general impression that foreign families carry a smaller amount of insurance than do native families seems to be borne out here. The average per foreign family was $31.61, for native families, $33.03. Neither all the foreign nor all the native families carried insurance, only 78 or 82.1 per cent of the foreign, and 96 or 91.4 per cent of the native families reported an expenditure for this purpose. The average amount for those foreign families who carried insurance was $38.50, for the native families who had this expenditure it averaged $36.11. The deduction here is that though a smaller proportion of these foreign families carried insurance, those who did so expended more than the average native family having this expenditure.

Insurance.

The amount spent for "sundries" by nationalities has little significance, unless the various items included in this group are analyzed, which will be done in a later table.[1]

[1] Table VII, p. 103

The foreign families spent more for "sundries" than did the American. The one Scotch family and the average

Sundries. Norwegian family spent the largest amount and percentage for "sundries" of all the families— in the Scotch family this expenditure was principally for drink, in the Norwegian families it was more for the "luxuries of life",—furniture, gifts, recreation, or spending-money.

Comparisons can readily be made between

Comparison of Different Nativities having Same Income. families of like income in the different nativities. For example, a comparison of the average expenditures of 6 Irish and 4 German families, having an income between $1000. and $1200., is as follows:

Nativity.	Average Income.	Size.	Expenditure for							
			Food.	Rent.	Cloth-ing.	Light and Fuel.	In-sur-ance.	Sun-dries.	Total Expen-diture.	Surplus or Deficit.
Irish	$1088.83	7.7	$539.83	164.17	$110.20	$53.20	$34.23	$196.37	$1098.	$− 9.17
German..	1064.75	6.5	518.70	199.50	105.25	46.92	47.00	117.38	1034.75	+30.00

It must be kept in mind in reading this table that the average Irish family was about one larger than the German, but the average income was also larger. The Irish families spent more for food, light and fuel, clothing and "sundries" and had a deficit, and the German families spent more for rent and insurance and saved $30.

The following tables aim to bring together the incomes and expenditures of the 200 families, in order to show the averages

Size of the Family. per family, by *nativity of the head* of the family and by *size of family*. The average size of the native families was 5.3, of the foreign 6. The average for different nationalities was: Ireland, 6.4; England, 5.9;

TABLE IV

INCOME AND EXPENDITURES PER FAMILY BY NATIVITY OF HEAD OF FAMILY AND SIZE OF FAMILY, AND PER CENT OF EXPENDITURES FOR VARIOUS PURPOSES

UNITED STATES

Size of Family	Total Families	Total Income	Food	Rent	Clothing	Light and Fuel	Insurance	Sundries	Total Expended	Average Surplus or Deficit	% Food	% Rent	% Clothing	% Light and Fuel	% Insurance	% Sundries	Total Per Cent	Per Cent of Income Expended
Two in family	5	851.60	270.18	150.60	83.54	32.17	22.25	214.86	773.60	+ 78.	34.9	19.5	10.8	4.1	2.9	27.8	100.	90.8
Three	11	762.27	293.09	148.45	97.59	36.59	26.42	161.91	764.05	+ 1.78	38.4	19.4	12.8	4.8	3.4	21.2	100.	100.2
Four	23	743.52	294.99	165.64	78.71	40.28	26.89	125.67	732.18	+ 11.34	40.3	22.6	10.7	5.5	3.7	17.2	100.	98.5
Five	22	699.61	326.24	152.14	53.26	40.68	34.34	92.25	698.91	+ .70	46.7	21.8	7.6	5.8	4.9	13.2	100.	99.9
Six	18	944.89	361.29	171.33	114.09	42.94	29.14	196.15	914.94	+ 29.95	39.5	18.7	12.5	4.7	3.2	21.4	100.	96.8
Seven	12	832.75	385.92	167.96	68.37	37.08	45.83	108.34	813.50	+ 19.25	47.	20.6	8.4	4.6	5.6	13.3	100.	97.9
Eight	8	1064.75	498.65	175.	119.37	49.36	41.50	183.87	1067.75	— 3.00	46.7	16.4	11.2	4.6	3.9	17.2	100.	100.3
Nine	5	808.80	374.04	151.80	151.30	34.40	46.80	67.26	825.60	— 16.80	45.3	18.4	18.3	4.2	5.6	8.2	100.	102.1
Ten	1	1046.	520.	180.	140.	40.	52.	114.	1046.	0	49.7	17.2	13.4	3.8	5.	10.9	100.	100.
Total	105	816.61	343.34	161.72	87.61	40.09	33.03	138.36	804.15	+ 12.46	42.7	20.1	10.9	5.	4.1	17.2	100.	98.5

Average size of family, 5.3.

IRELAND

Size of Family	Total Families	Total Income	Food	Rent	Clothing	Light and Fuel	Insurance	Sundries	Total Expended	Average Surplus or Deficit	% Food	% Rent	% Clothing	% Light and Fuel	% Insurance	% Sundries	Total Per Cent	Per Cent of Income Expended
Two in family	0																	
Three	6	620.50	280.17	118.83	85.17	37.58	17.58	89.59	628.92	— 8.42	44.6	18.9	13.5	6.	2.8	14.2	100.	101.
Four	8	712.12	326.40	146.62	62.63	41.81	32.44	100.72	710.62	+ 1.50	45.9	20.6	8.8	5.9	4.6	14.2	100.	99.8
Five	7	790.43	361.91	159.86	164.75	54.31	38.66	130.12	798.	— 7.51	45.4	20.	6.7	6.8	4.8	16.3	100.	101.
Six	4	1239.75	559.	174.75	72.98	54.33	43.	291.02	1292.25	— 52.50	43.3	13.5	12.8	4.2	3.3	22.5	100.	104.2
Seven	4	904.25	453.40	131.87	141.67	47.35	31.20	199.20	936.	— 31.75	48.4	14.1	7.8	5.1	3.3	21.3	100.	103.5
Eight	3	1188.33	601.67	249.33		47.60	39.86	108.20	1188.33	0	50.6	21.	11.9	4.	3.4	9.1	100.	100.
Nine	3	918.33	485.34	160.67	114.33	51.73	35.01	96.25	943.33	— 25.	51.5	17.	12.1	5.5	3.7	10.2	100.	102.7
Total	35	852.83	403.89	156.04	88.66	46.99	33.68	137.95	867.22	— 14.39	46.6	18.	10.2	5.4	3.9	15.9	100.	101.7

Average size of family, 6.4.

TABLE IV—*Continued*

ENGLAND

Size of Family	Total Families	Total Income	Food	Rent	Clothing	Light and Fuel	Insurance	Sundries	Total Expended	Average Surplus or Deficit	Food %	Rent %	Clothing %	Light and Fuel %	Insurance %	Sundries %	Total Per Cent	Per Cent of Income Expended
Two	0																	
Three	1	1000.	338.	144.	125.	85.	0	308.	1000.	+ 0	34.	14.	12.5	8.5	0	31.	100.	100.7
Four	4	914.25	344.50	187.70	111.25	46.87	16.90	177.03	884.25	+ 30.	39.	21.2	12.6	5.3	1.9	20.	100.	96.7
Five	2	770.	393.	164.	45.	22.70	27.52	143.28	795.50	− 25.50	49.4	20.7	5.6	2.8	3.5	18.	100.	103.3
Six	3	675.	299.	108.	108.33	41.	37.	81.23	675.	+ 0	44.3	16.	16.1	6.1	5.5	12.	100.	100.
Seven	2	951.	468.	180.	72.50	63.20	21.26	136.04	941.	+ 10.	44.2	19.1	7.7	6.7	2.3	14.5	100.	98.9
Eight	1	675.	364.	142.50	75.	46.	23.40	24.10	675.	0	53.9	21.1	11.1	6.8	3.5	3.6	100.	100.
Nine	0																	
Ten	2	1559.	702.	157.50	130.	50.	31.20	543.30	1614.	− 55.	43.5	9.8	8.	3.1	1.9	33.7	100.	103.5
Total......	15	927.80	406.87	157.62	97.67	47.55	24.22	195.27	929.20	− 1.40	43.8	17.	10.5	5.1	2.6	21.	100.	100.2

Average size of family, 5.9

GERMANY

Size of Family	Total Families	Total Income	Food	Rent	Clothing	Light and Fuel	Insurance	Sundries	Total Expended	Average Surplus or Deficit	Food %	Rent %	Clothing %	Light and Fuel %	Insurance %	Sundries %	Total Per Cent	Per Cent of Income Expended
Two	1	728.	300.	150.	75.	29.	47.20	51.80	653.	+ 75.	45.9	23.	11.5	4.4	7.2	8.	100.	89.7
Three	0																	
Four	3	866.50	416.	188.	73.33	43.89	28.60	121.51	871.33	+ 5.33	47.7	21.6	8.4	5.	3.3	14.	100.	100.6
Five	4	966.50	345.50	216.	71.50	38.92	52.12	165.96	890.	+ 76.50	38.6	24.3	8.	4.4	5.9	18.6	100.	92.1
Six	2	1319.50	413.50	286.50	115.	56.10	66.47	294.43	1232.	+ 87.50	33.6	23.2	9.3	4.6	5.4	23.9	100.	93.4
Seven	3	974.67	535.60	166.	68.67	45.33	77.29	81.78	974.67	0	55.	17.	7.	4.7	7.9	8.4	100.	100.
Eight	3	1113.80	452.67	183.83	108.33	52.34	33.20	210.10	1040.47	+ 73.33	43.5	17.7	10.4	5.	3.2	20.2	100.	93.4
Nine	1	1450.	572.	210.	200.	41.	36.40	305.60	1365.	+ 85.	41.9	15.3	14.7	3.	2.7	22.4	100.	94.1
Ten	0																	
Total......	17	1032.14	429.05	200.62	90.70	44.86	49.54	167.66	982.43	+ 49.71	43.7	20.4	9.2	4.6	5.	17.1	100.	95.2

Average size of family, 5.9.

TABLE IV—*Continued*

ITALY

Size of Family (in family)	Total Families	Total Income	Avg Exp: Food	Rent	Clothing	Light and Fuel	Insurance	Sundries	Total Expended	Average Surplus or Deficit	% Food	% Rent	% Clothing	% Light and Fuel	% Insurance	% Sundries	Total Per Cent	Per Cent of Income Expended
Three	3	$478.33	217.33	$100.	32.67	31.66	$7.80	$92.20	$481.66	− 3.33	45.1	20.8	6.8	6.6	1.6	19.1	100.	100.7
Four	1	797.	271.	216.	30.	38.	31.20	110.80	697.	+100.	38.9	31.	4.3	5.4	4.5	15.9	100.	87.5
Five	1	640.	260.	90.	100.	45.	7.80	137.20	640.	0	40.6	14.1	15.6	7.	1.2	21.5	100.	100.
Six	3	870.	390.	126.33	108.34	35.80	28.60	168.35	857.42	− 12.58	45.4	14.7	12.7	4.2	3.4	19.6	100.	98.6
Seven	1	1162.	416.	216.	166.	24.90	41.60	317.50	1182.	− 20.	35.2	18.3	14.	2.1	3.5	26.9	100.	101.7
Eight	3	953.67	411.33	189.	106.	51.93	20.80	181.77	960.83	− 7.16	42.8	19.7	11.	5.4	2.2	18.9	100.	100.8
Nine	0																	
Ten	2	919.50	384.60	133.50	150.	50.50	22.10	178.80	919.50	0	41.8	14.5	16.3	5.5	2.4	19.5	100.	100.
Twelve	1	1358.	512.20	216.	300.	89.	28.60	212.20	1358.	0	37.7	15.9	22.1	6.6	2.1	15.6	100.	100.
Total	15	846.80	352.29	150.07	109.13	43.74	21.67	164.15	841.05	+ 5.75	41.9	17.8	13.	5.2	2.6	19.5	100.	99.3

Average size of family, 6.6.

FRANCE

Size of Family (in family)	Total Families	Total Income	Avg Exp: Food	Rent	Clothing	Light and Fuel	Insurance	Sundries	Total Expended	Average Surplus or Deficit	% Food	% Rent	% Clothing	% Light and Fuel	% Insurance	% Sundries	Total Per Cent	Per Cent of Income Expended
Two	1	$380.	182.	$120.	10.	26.25	0	$42.20	$380.	0	47.9	31.6	2.6	6.8	0	11.1	100.	100.
Three	1	322.	124.	111.	10.50	26.25	21.30	46.95	340.	− 18.	36.5	32.6	3.1	7.7	6.3	13.8	100.	105.6
Four	0																	
Five	1	700.	260.	118.	72.	41.50	0	188.50	680.	+ 20.	38.2	17.4	10.6	6.1	0	27.7	100.	97.1
Six	1	832.	306.80	180.	90.	35.60	30.12	176.48	819.	+ 13.	37.5	22.	11.	4.3	3.7	21.5	100.	98.4
Total	4	558.50	218.20	132.25	45.63	32.34	12.85	113.48	554.75	+ 3.75	39.3	23.9	8.2	5.8	2.3	20.5	100.	99.3

Average size of family, 4.

TABLE IV—Continued

Norway and Sweden

Size of Family	Total Families	Total Income	Average Expenditure per Family for						Total Expended	Average Surplus or Deficit	Per Cent of Expenditure per Family for						Total Per Cent.	Per Cent of Income Expended.
			Food.	Rent.	Clothing.	Light and Fuel.	Insurance.	Sundries.			Food.	Rent.	Clothing.	Light and Fuel.	Insurance.	Sundries.		
Two in family	1	$1000.	$260.	$186.	$83.	$33.	$0	$268.	$830.	$+170.	31.3	22.4	10.	4.	0	32.3	100.	83.
Three " "	1	1515.	286.	204.	65.60	59.	32.30	218.70	865.	+650.	33.1	23.6	7.5	6.8	3.7	25.3	100.	57.1
Four " "	1	1600.	520.	175.30	87.60	40.	7.60	319.50	1150.	+450.	45.2	15.2	7.6	3.5	0.7	27.8	100.	71.9
Five " "	1	572.	286.	144.	70.	41.	5.60	25.40	572.	0	50.	25.2	12.2	7.2	1.	4.4	100.	100.
Total	4	1171.75	338.	177.32	176.40	43.25	11.38	207.90	854.25	+317.50	39.6	20.8	8.9	5.1	1.3	24.3	100.	72.9

Switzerland

Average size of family, 3.5.

Size of Family		Total Income	Food.	Rent.	Clothing.	Light and Fuel.	Insurance.	Sundries.	Total Expended.	Average Surplus or Deficit.	Food.	Rent.	Clothing.	Light and Fuel.	Insurance.	Sundries.	Total Per Cent.	Per Cent of Income Expended.
Four in family	1	$680.	$273.	$151.	$36.	$37.35	$83.20	$99.45	$680.	$0	40.2	22.2	5.3	5.5	12.2	14.6	100.	100.
Six " "	1	904.	434.20	144.	75.	28.	40.80	147.	869.	+35.	50.	16.6	8.6	3.2	4.7	16.9	100.	96.1
Total	2	792.	353.60	147.50	55.50	32.67	62.	123.23	774.50	+17.50	45.6	19.	7.3	4.2	8.	15.9	100.	97.8

Average size of family, 5.

Nativity of Head of Family.	Size of Family.	Total Income.	Food.	Rent.	Clothing.	Light and Fuel.	Insurance.	Sundries.	Total Expended.	Average Surplus or Deficit.	Food.	Rent.	Clothing.	Light and Fuel.	Insurance.	Sundries.	Total Per Cent.	Per Cent of Income Expended.
* Austria	6	$731.	$312.	$198.	$30.	$50.20	$49.20	$91.80	$731.	$0	42.7	27.1	4.1	6.8	6.7	12.6	100.	100.
* Scotland	8	832.	364.	120.	76.	68.20	0	203.80	832.	0	43.8	14.4	9.1	8.2	0	24.5	100.	100.
* Cuba	4	450.	208.	132.	46.	20.	23.40	36.60	460.	—10.	45.2	28.7	8.7	4.3	5.1	8.	100.	102.2

*One family from each of these nationalities.

TABLE IV—*Continued*

SUMMARY OF INCOME AND EXPENDITURES OF 200 FAMILIES BY SIZE OF FAMILY (U. S. AND FOREIGN)

Size of Family	No. of Families	Total Income	Average Expenditure per Family for						Total Expended	Average Surplus or Deficit	Per Cent of Expenditure per Family for							Per Cent of Income Expended
			Food	Rent	Clothing	Light and Fuel	Insurance	Sundries			Food	Rent	Clothing	Light and Fuel	Insurance	Sundries	Total Per Cent	
Two in family	8	$ 795.75	$ 261.61	$ 151.12	$ 73.21	$ 31.10	$ 19.81	$ 179.52	716.37	$ +79.38	36.5	21.1	10.2	4.3	2.8	25.1	100.	90.
Three " "	17	744.53	272.	140.71	80.71	39.27	21.62	154.78	709.09	+35.44	38.4	19.8	11.4	5.5	3.1	21.8	100.	95.2
Four " "	40	765.15	309.10	162.80	79.50	40.16	25.56	126.67	743.79	+21.36	41.6	21.9	10.7	5.4	3.4	17.	100.	97.2
Five " "	39	728.37	327.24	155.49	58.74	39.95	33.12	106.07	720.61	+7.76	45.5	21.6	8.1	5.5	4.6	14.7	100.	98.9
Six " "	36	896.72	360.66	166.69	97.64	44.70	34.62	172.07	875.98	+20.74	41.2	19.1	11.1	5.1	3.9	19.6	100.	97.7
Seven " "	22	951.82	446.63	172.20	90.75	43.16	48.16	149.96	950.86	+.96	47.	18.1	9.5	4.5	5.1	15.8	100.	99.9
Eight " "	20	992.22	456.14	165.42	102.05	50.56	32.11	183.56	989.85	+2.37	46.1	16.7	10.3	5.1	3.2	18.6	100.	99.8*
Nine " "	9	1006.55	471.91	190.78	153.50	39.50	43.33	107.39	1006.44	+.11	46.9	18.9	15.3	3.9	4.3	10.7	100.	99.99
Ten " "	8	1094.75	518.65	155.50	130.37	49.52	32.96	230.87	1117.87	—23.12	46.4	13.9	11.7	4.4	2.9	20.7	100.	102.1
Twelve " "	1	1358.	512.20	216.	300.	89.	28.60	212.20	1358.	0	37.7	15.9	22.1	6.6	2.1	15.6	100.	100.
Total.......	200	851.38	363.42	162.26	88.45	42.46	32.35	147.31	836.25	+ 15.13	43.4	19.4	10.6	5.1	3.9	17.6	100.	98.2

Average size of family, 5.6.

* Due to older German children being boarders—hence more saved.

Germany, 5.9; Italy, 6.6; France, 4; Norway and Sweden, 3.5; Switzerland, 5, and the others according to the individual family. As has been previously shown, the number of boarders or dependents in these families was not large enough to seriously upset these averages, if the number of children were considered instead of the total family. That is, two in the family generally means no children; three in the family usually one child or occasionally two children and one parent; four in the family means two children, etc. The Italians had families of the largest size—in the 15 families 7 or 46.7 per cent had 7 or more in the family. In 35 Irish families, 14 or 40 per cent had 7 or over. In the 15 English families only 5 or 33.3 per cent had 7 or more, and in the 17 German families, 7 or 41.2 per cent had 7 or over. Among the American families 26 or 24.8 per cent consisted of 7 or over, and 34 or 35.8 per cent of the total foreign had families of this size. Most of the families investigated were of fair size, having five or six in the family.

A comparison can here be made of the income and expenditures of the families of different nativities, according to the size of the family. For example, the 5 native families of 2 in the family had an average income of $851.61. There were 3 foreign families of this size, German, French, and Norwegian. Only the Norwegian family (income $1000.) exceeded the average income of the American families. In the 23 native families having 4 in the family the average income was $743.52. This average was exceeded by the English, German, Italian, and Norwegian families of the same size. The lowest income for 4 in the family was $450. in the Cuban family, the highest was the Norwegian, $1600.

A comparison of the expenditure for *food* in families

Incomes.

having 2 in the family shows the average native expenditure

Food for two in the Family. of $270.18 or 34.9 per cent was exceeded by the German and Swiss families. The German family spent the largest amount, $300. or 45.9 per cent. The French family spent the least, $182., but here the percentage was the highest, 47.9 per cent, the income being only $380.

For 4 in the family the native families spent $294.99 or 40.3 per cent of the total expenditures. The English families

Four in the Family. averaged $344.50, the German $416., and the Norwegian $520. The higher average allowance in these nationalities than in the native families was sometimes due to better food and more of it, sometimes to extravagant management.

The native families of 4 persons averaged $165.64 a year or $13.80 a month for rent, or 22.6 per cent of the total expenditures. This amount for rent is exceeded by all other nationalities having families of the same size, except the Irish and Swiss. The highest rent was paid by the Italian family, $216., or 31 per cent of the expenditure. This was an exceptional family with a high standard of living. The man was a barber during the winter at Tuxedo and Palm Beach, and demanded a good home for the few months he was at home. His wife called him "a sport and dandy".

The incomes and expenditures of all families of the same size but different nativity may be read and compared in the same manner. The averages for each group are the same as in Table III, but here the average size family of each nationality must be borne in mind in comparing the results.

The Summary of this table shows the income and expenditures of 20 families, by size of family, regardless of nativity.

Summary of Table. It is the same as Summary A of Table II. These averages are full of interest. They show the gradual increase in income as size of family increases. The two exceptions to this general rule may be explained. In

In regard to Incomes. the group in which there are 2 in the family, there were two incomes exceptionally large for families of this size. The one was that of a thrifty and hard-working Norwegian longshoreman, who made $1000. in the year; the other instance was a very unusual negro family, in which the man and his wife both contributed to the family income, which was $1134.

The average income drops in the families of 5 members. In this group more than ⅓ had incomes below $600., contrasted with the group of 4 in the family, in which only ¼ had such small incomes. An explanation of this may be that 20 out of the 39 families in this group consisted of father, mother, and three small children, or a widow with four children under 14. In smaller families, the woman was free to add to the family earnings herself, or to take boarders, and the larger families had grown children to add to the family income. In addition this group was burdened with 6 out of the 13 dependents in the entire 200 families. These are sufficient causes for this drop from the normal increase in income as the family increases.

The steady increase in the expenditure for food with the enlargement of the family is also shown here. The other

In regard to Expenditures. expenditures do not increase so regularly, but as has already been noted, in Summary A of Table II, the *tendency* is for all expenses to increase with the size of the family, though not always proportionately. This would be shown for clothing if the total expenditures for this purpose could always be given; and for insurance if the average were not cut down by those families who did not carry it. The *total expenditure* naturally increases with size of family. The two exceptions here were due to rare good management and thrift in a few of the families of each group.

The surplus steadily decreases, and the per cent of income expended increases. In the families of 8, the larger average surplus and smaller percentage expended were due to two German families in which the older children were boarders, and paid their own expenses, so that the mother could save $220. The families of 10 and 12 in the family all had a deficit, or just came out even.

No study of the income and expenditures of a given number of families would be complete without an analysis **The Sources of** of the *sources* of income. The popular im-**Income.** pression, outside the working class, seems to be that the entire income of the workingman's family is from the earnings of the head of the family. This implies that if the head of the family is an unskilled day laborer, the income of his family is of that grade. On the contrary, **From the** some of the largest incomes in this study are **Husband.** of this class. The fact is that there are comparatively few families of wage-earners who are entirely dependent on the earnings of the head of the family. This may be true in families where there are several young children, and the wife's strength is needed at home, but even then it **From the Wife.** is surprising how frequently other sources of income are added, such as gifts from friends, from employers at Christmas, presents of clothing to the children, help from relatives or churches and charitable societies in the poorer families, etc.

As the children grow older and require less of her care at home, the mother takes in sewing or goes out washing, secures a janitor's place, cleans offices, and does whatever she can to increase the weekly income. She feels this to be her duty, and often it is necessary, but frequently it has a disastrous effect on the ambition of the husband. As soon as he sees that the wife can help support the family, his

TABLE V

A Study of the Sources of Income

A. NUMBER OF FAMILIES WITH INCOME FROM VARIOUS SOURCES BY NATIVITY OF HEAD OF FAMILY

B. PER CENT OF FAMILIES HAVING AN INCOME FROM VARIOUS SOURCES BY NATIVITY OF HEAD OF FAMILY

Nativity of Head of Family.	Total Families.	Average Size of Family.	Families with an Income from Occupation of					Per Cent of Families with an Income from Occupation of				
			Husband.	Wife.	Children.	Boarders and Lodgers.	Other Sources.	Husband.	Wife.	Children.	Boarders and Lodgers.	Other Sources.
United States	105	5.3	94	55	34	29	68	89.5	52.4	32.4	27.6	64.8
Ireland	35	6.4	25	15	18	11	22	71.4	42.9	51.4	31.4	62.9
England	15	5.9	13	7	7	6	8	86.7	46.7	46.7	40.	53.3
Germany	17	5.9	14	4	5	12	7	82.4	23.5	29.4	70.6	41.2
Italy	15	6.6	13	5	8	3	7	86.7	33.3	53.3	20.	46.7
France	4	4.	3	3	0	0	3	75.	75.	0	0	75.
Norway and Sweden	4	3.5	4	0	0	1	0	100.	0	0	25.	0
Switzerland	2	5.	2	1	0	0	1	100.	50.	0	0	50.
Austria	1	6.	1	1	0	0	0	100.	100.	0	0	100.
Scotland	1	8.	1	1	1	0	0	100.	100.	100.	0	0
Cuba	1	4.	1	1	1	0	1	100.	100.	100.	0	100.
Total foreign	95	6.	77	38	40	33	49	81.1	40.	42.1	34.7	51.6
Total U. S. and foreign	200	5.6	171	93	74	62	117	85.5	46.5	37.	31.	58.5

TABLE V—Continued

C. AVERAGE AMOUNT OF INCOME FROM VARIOUS SOURCES BY NATIVITY OF HEAD OF FAMILY

D. PER CENT OF INCOME FROM VARIOUS SOURCES BY NATIVITY OF HEAD OF FAMILY

Nativity of Head of Family.	Total Families.	Average Size of Family.	Average Income of all Families from					Total Income of Family.	Per Cent of Income from				
			Occupation of			Boarders and Lodgers.	Other Sources.		Occupation of			Boarders and Lodgers.	Other Sources.
			Husband.	Wife.	Children.				Husband.	Wife.	Children.		
United States........	105	5.3	$564.51	$80.87	$57.68	$51.70	$61.85	$816.61	69.1	9.9	7.1	6.3	7.6
Ireland...............	35	6.4	421.85	87.48	187.69	70.84	84.97	852.83	49.5	10.2	22.	8.3	10.
England..............	15	5.9	541.50	127.85	88.60	135.	34.85	927.80	58.4	13.8	9.5	14.5	3.8
Germany.............	17	5.9	580.	59.65	69.18	303.29	20.02	1032.14	56.2	5.8	6.7	29.4	1.9
Italy.................	15	6.6	487.67	48.87	246.	35.46	28.80	846.80	57.6	5.8	29.	4.2	3.4
France...............	4	4.	436.69	80.75	0	0	40.06	557.50	78.3	14.5	0	0	7.2
Norway and Sweden.....	4	3.5	1145.75	0	0	26.	0	1171.75	97.8	0	0	2.2	0
Switzerland..........	2	5.	754.50	27.50	0	0	10.	792.	95.3	3.5	0	0	1.2
Austria..............	1	6.	624.	107.	0	0	0	731.	85.4	14.6	0	0	0
Scotland.............	1	8.	260.	156.	416.	0	0	832.	31.3	18.7	50.	0	0
Cuba.................	1	4.	72.	75.	275.	0	28.	450.	16.	16.7	61.1	0	6.2
Total foreign........	95	6.	514.29	78.34	141.63	108.38	47.17	889.81	57.8	8.8	15.9	12.2	5.3
Total U. S. and foreign.	200	5.6	540.65	79.67	97.56	78.62	54.88	851.38	63.5	9.4	11.5	9.2	6.4

TABLE V—*Continued*

E. AVERAGE AMOUNT OF INCOME FROM VARIOUS SOURCES BY NATIVITY OF HEAD OF FAMILY

Nativity of Head of Family.	Total Families.	Average Size of Family.	Average Income of Families Having an Income from					Total Average Income.
			Occupation of			Boarders and Lodgers.	Other Sources.	
			Husband.	Wife.	Children.			
United States................	105	5.3	$630.57	$154.39	$178.13	$187.19	$95.51	$816.61
Ireland.....................	35	6.4	590.60	204.11	364.95	225.41	135.18	852.83
England....................	15	5.9	624.81	273.96	189.86	337.50	65.34	927.80
Germany...................	17	5.9	704.29	253.50	235.20	429.67	48.63	1032.14
Italy......................	15	6.6	562.69	146.60	461.25	177.33	61.71	846.80
France.....................	4	4.	582.25	107.67	0	0	54.75	557.50
Norway and Sweden........	4	3.5	1145.75	0	0	104.	0	1171.75
Switzerland................	2	5.	754.50	55.	0	0	20.	792.
Austria....................	1	6.	624.	107.	0	0	0	731.
Scotland	1	8.	260.	156.	416.	0	0	832.
Cuba......................	1	4.	72.	75.	275.	0	28.	450.
Total foreign...............	95	6.	634.51	203.75	336.38	312.02	91.45	889.81
Total U. S. and foreign......	200	5.6	632.34	171.33	263.67	253.63	93.81	851.38

interest and sense of responsibility are likely to lessen, and
he works irregularly or spends more on himself. There
are, of course, many families in which this united income
is needed, when the man's illness or incapacity makes it
imperative for the wife to help. Sometimes it is due to
thrift and an ambition to save money for the future, or for
some definite purpose. Charitable societies generally deplore the prevalence of this custom because of its economic
and moral results on the head of the family.

The average parents in this neighborhood have no higher
ambition for their children's education than that they should
From the "graduate" from the Grammar School at 14.
Children. The time when they can legally go to work is
eagerly anticipated, and frequently parents have declared
the children older than they are in order to get out their
working-papers. Under the new Child Labor Law, however,
documentary evidence of age is demanded.

It is the general custom for all boys and girls between
14 and 18 to bring their pay envelopes to the mother un-
opened, and she has the entire disbursement of their wages,
giving them from $0.25 to $1. a week spending-money, according to the prosperity of the family. After they are 18, the
boys usually pay board of $4.–$8. a week, according to their
wages. They are considered in this study "boarders", and
are no more expense to the family than the usual boarder.
The girls are not usually boarders until they are over 21,
and then they pay from $3. to $6. a week to their mothers.
In some cases they continue to give all their wages to their
mother, who supports them until they are married.

All the larger families having five or more in the
family have from one to five children who are adding to the
family income. As the children become wage-earners the
mother stays at home and does the housekeeping.

In these 200 families there were only 23 in which the earnings of the father were reported as the only source of income; of these, 10 were American, 4 Irish, 2 German, 1 English, 2 Italian, 1 French, and 3 Norwegian. In those families in which the mother was the head, there were no cases in which her earnings made up the total income.

In addition to the earnings of the father, mother, and children, and the income from boarders and lodgers, Table V

From "Other Sources".

(C & E) groups together all the "other sources" of income. These "other sources" are so varied that they could not be classified separately. They include gifts of money or clothing, coal, and groceries (the value of which was estimated) from friends, relatives, employers, churches, or charitable societies; money obtained by pawning various articles, selling furniture, etc.; income from property inherited; savings drawn from the bank; gifts from sons away from home; insurance received on the death of a member of the family, or benefits from benefit societies, unions, or lodges in case of sickness or death; pensions, or "damages" obtained for the injury or death of a member of the family. All these and other sources are a part of the total "household income".

This table is accordingly a study and analysis of these various sources of income, grouped according to the nativity of the head of the family. Tables A and B show the number and per cent of families having an income from various sources, Tables C and D show the average amount of income from these sources for *all* the families, with the percentages computed from these averages, and Table E shows the average amount of income from these various sources for those families *having an income from each specified source*, by nativity of the head of the family.

Tables A and B (of Table V) show that in the 105 families whose heads were native born 94, or 89.5 per cent, of the husbands and 55, or 52.4 per cent, of the wives contributed toward the family income. In 34, or 32.4 per cent, of the families the children also contributed part of the income, 29, or 27.6 per cent, had some revenue from boarders or lodgers, and 68, or 64.8 per cent, of the families had an income from "other sources".

Tables A and B: Number and Per Cent of Families having Income from Stated Sources.

Native.

In the 95 foreign families, 77, or 81.1 per cent, of the husbands and 38, or 40 per cent, of the wives contributed to the family income, and the labor of the children helped in 40, or 42.1 per cent, of the families. Receipts from boarders or lodgers added to the household income in 33, or 34.7 per cent, of the foreign families, while 49, or 51.6 per cent, had some income from "other sources". It is evident that the native families had a larger proportion of families with an income from the husbands, wives, and "other sources" than the foreign families, who, in turn, had a larger percentage of families with an income from boarders or lodgers, and from children.

Foreign.

The Irish families had the smallest proportion of husbands contributing to the family income, while in the Norwegian, Swiss, Austrian, Scotch, and Cuban families, all the husbands contributed something to the family support. The largest proportion of families having an income from wives was 75 per cent of the French families, where in 3 out of 4 families the wives were wage-earners; the Germans had the smallest proportion—only 4, or 23.5 per cent, of the wives contributing to the family income.

Income from Husbands and Wives in Different Foreign Nativities.

The Italians had the largest proportion of families in

which the children were wage-earners, 53.3 per cent of the **From the Children.** families. It should be remembered that the Italians had the largest families, size 6.6 (containing the most children), hence there were more instances of children of working age in that nativity. This fact, together with the inclination to put all the children to work as soon as possible, explains the large percentage. The Irish come next in size of family, 6.4, and also in the proportion of families having an income from the children, 51.4 per cent. The size of the family should therefore be borne in mind in reading these tables. It is indicative of a desire that the children should remain in school longer, that the German families, who come next in size (5.9), have the smallest proportion of families, 29.4 per cent, having an income from the children. This is with the exception of the few French, Norwegian, Swiss, and Austrian families who were smaller in size and had no children working.

The Germans had the largest proportion of families having an income from boarders and lodgers, because the **From Boarders or Lodgers.** older children usually paid board and were classed as boarders. The habit of keeping boarders and lodgers is undoubtedly the strongest with the Italians, though the families in this investigation did not happen to illustrate this characteristic.

The largest proportion of families having income from "other sources" was 75 per cent for those of French nativity, **From " Other Sources ".** with the exception of one Austrian and one Cuban family, each of whom had some income from "other sources". The native families had the next largest proportion, 64.8 per cent, and the Germans had the smallest proportion, only 41.2 per cent of the families having an income from "other sources".

The number and percentage of all families, both native and foreign, show that 171, or 85.5 per cent, had an income from the husband; 93, or 46.5 per cent, had an

Number having Income from Different Sources in both Native or Foreign Families. income from the wife; 74, or 37 per cent, had an income from children; 62, or 31 per cent, had revenue from boarders or lodgers, and 117, or 58.5 per cent, had an income from "other sources". This dist·ibution shows how commonly the total income is from two or more sources.

Tables C and D show the average amount and percentage of income derived from the various sources for *all* the families of each nativity. For example, 105

Tables C and D: Amount and Percentage of Income from Various Sources for All Families. native husbands averaged $564.51, or 69.1 per cent of the total average income of the native families, which was $816.61; 105 wives in the native families averaged $80.87, or 9.9 per cent of the total income; in the 105 native families the average income from children was $57.68, or 7.1 per cent of the total income, and so for all the different sources, as shown in the tables.

The average amount from each source in the Irish families was obtained by dividing the total amount from each source

Comparison by Nativities. by 35, the number of families of that nativity; the total English amounts were divided by 15, the number of English families, etc. By this method the results show that the Norwegian families had the largest average income from the husband, $1145.75, and the largest proportion, 97.8 per cent of the total income. The two Scotch and Cuban families had only $260. and $75. respectively from the husbands, who were both drinking men, but they are not representative of their nationalties. Excepting them, the average Irish husband brought in the smallest amount of income, $421.85, or 49.5 per cent of the total Irish income. The wife in the Scotch family was forced to bring in the largest amount and proportion of income from the wives. She contributed $156., or 18.7 per cent of their total income. The average English wife brought in the next largest amount, $127.85. The German and Italian wives contributed a small proportion of the income, only 5.8 per cent each. In these nativities the children, including older children who were classed as boarders, contributed large amounts to the family income. The Swiss wife only contributed an average of $27.50, or 3.5 per cent of the total, while the Norwegian wives contributed nothing to the support of the family.

The Italians show the largest average amount from the children in *all* the families, $246., or 29 per cent, with the exception of the individual Scotch and Cuban cases, where the children contributed more than half of the income.

With the exception of the German families, where children were classed as boarders, the 15 English families had the largest average amount from the boarders or lodgers, $135., or 14.5 per cent, while the French, Norwegian, Swiss, and Austrian families had no boarders or lodgers. It is not surprising that the Irish families had the largest average amount, $84.97, and percentage, 10 per cent, of the entire income from "other sources", when the character of these sources has been explained. They most frequently consisted of gifts, charity, pawning, former savings, etc.

The total average income of the 200 families, native and foreign, was $851.38; of this $540.65, or 63.5 per cent, came **Averages for All Families from Various Sources.** from the husbands' labor; $79.67, or 9.4 per cent, from that of the wives; $97.56, or 11.5 per cent, from the children; $78.62, or 9.2 per cent, from boarders or lodgers, and $54.88, or 6.4 per cent, from "other sources". On the whole, the husbands bore the greater part of the burden, but the amounts from these other sources are surprising.

If the average income from the different sources is based on the number of families of each nativity who had *any* income *from the specified source,* the results are those shown in Table E. The averages here are for the number of families given in Table A who had an income from that source. Hence constant reference should be made to Table A in reading this table. For example, there were 94 husbands in the 105 native families who contributed to the family income. The average which these 94 husbands brought in was $630.57. There were 55 wives working in the 105 native families, and the average amount which they contributed was $154.39. In 34 of the native families, children were wage-earners; the average amount in these 34 families contributed by the children was $178.13, and so on for the other sources of income in the native families. The average income from various sources in the families of different nativities should be read in the same way. It will be seen that there is considerable difference between the averages thus computed and those in Table C. This table represents more fairly the actual average which the husbands, wives, children, etc., of the different nativities contribute to the total income in those families in which they contribute anything at all. The averages are accordingly higher than in Table C. The Norwegian husbands, the English wives (instead of the Scotch wife), the Irish and Italian children, and the German and English boarders (including the older German children) contributed the largest average amounts to the family income, and the income from other sources was largest in the Irish families, as in Table C. The average amounts from all these sources (except from "other sources")

Table E: Average Income from Different Sources for Families having an Income from the Specified Source.

was higher in the foreign families than in the native families, but the foreign average income was larger, $889.81. Making this allowance, the foreign husbands contributed less in proportion than did the American husbands.

Averages for All Families having Given Source of Income. By this method of averaging the various sources of income the husbands contributed an average of $632.34, the wives $171.33, the children $263.67, boarders and lodgers $253.63, and other sources $93.81, in all families in which there is an income from each of these specified sources.

Table VI is an analysis of the amount and proportion of the distribution of the various expenditures previously classed as "sundries". The 200 families are grouped according to the proportion between their expenditures for "sundries" and the entire expenditure. For instance, there were 21 families, mostly with small incomes, who expended less than 5 per cent of their total expenditures for "sundries". Their average income was $509.; the average for "sundries" was only $14.48. The deduction from this is that families on small incomes must spend practically their entire income for the actual necessities of life, i.e., food, rent, clothing, light and fuel, and that if sickness or death comes they must be helped by some outside source to bear the extra expense; this aid would swell their incomes and put them in a group of families having larger income and larger percentage of expenditure for "sundries". These families spent the largest percentage of the $14.48 devoted to "sundries" for medical attendance, $3.78, or 26.1 per cent, with the exception of the "miscellaneous" expenses, which were too small and too varied to be further classified. These "miscellaneous" expenses cover a great variety of objects, including laundry,

Per Cent of Expenditure for Sundries, less than 5.

Medical Attendance.

TABLE VI

A. Distribution of Amount Devoted to "Sundries" for Families in which Expenditure for "Sundries" is a Given Per Cent of Entire Expenditure

Per Cent of Expenditure for "Sundries".

Distribution.	Less than 5. Expended Amount	Less than 5. Average per Family	5–10. Expended Amount	5–10. Average per Family	10–20. Expended Amount	10–20. Average per Family	20–30. Expended Amount	20–30. Average per Family	30–40. Expended Amount	30–40. Average per Family	40–50. Expended Amount	40–50. Average per Family	Total Amount Expended	Total Average per Family
Recreation	$15.60	$.74	145.15	$3.63	737.70	$9.34	$797.45	$17.72	$180.01	$13.85	$758.50	$379.25	$2634.41	$13.17
Union	3.00	.14	12.	.30	127.70	1.62	99.20	2.20	31.	2.38	0	0	272.90	1.37
Gifts or loans	0	0	33.	.83	267.96	3.39	573.40	12.73	115.88	8.91	245.	122.50	1234.84	6.18
Drink	0	0	418.10	10.45	1485.50	18.80	1604.40	35.65	468.	36.	176.80	88.40	4152.80	20.76
Church	0	0	55.50	1.39	354.82	4.49	275.	6.11	36.20	2.79	22.40	11.20	744.02	3.72
Furniture	29.40	1.40	98.50	2.46	1015.78	12.86	1047.98	23.29	521.85	40.14	43.	21.50	2756.51	13.78
Papers	54.51	2.60	119.82	3.00	448.74	5.68	278.25	6.18	72.02	5.54	13.	6.50	986.34	4.93
Car-fares	20.80	.99	171.60	4.29	645.30	8.17	379.20	8.43	177.48	13.65	0	0	1394.38	6.97
Medical attendance	79.30	3.78	323.77	8.09	1349.48	17.08	1019.58	22.66	517.69	39.82	111.	55.50	3400.82	17.
"Spending-money"	0	0	443.90	11.10	2024.28	25.62	1820.67	40.46	1214.61	93.43	0	0	5503.46	27.52
Education	0	0	64.	1.60	244.56	3.10	353.25	7.85	304.58	23.43	0	0	966.39	4.83
Domestic service	0	0	0	0	47.	.60	445.	9.89	0	0	0	0	492.	2.46
Funerals	0	0	0	0	57.50	.73	1163.	25.85	748.50	57.58	0	0	1969.	9.85
"Miscellaneous"	101.41	4.83	344.09	8.60	1034.39	13.09	957.66	21.28	490.19	37.71	26.	13.	2953.74	14.77
Total "Sundries"	304.02	14.48	2229.53	55.74	9840.71	124.57	10813.64	240.30	4878.01	375.23	1395.70	697.85	29461.61	147.31
Number of families	21		40		79		45		13		2		200	
Average income	$507.		$748.86		$820.43		$1050.70		$1105.46		$1599.50		$851.38	
Av. total expenditures	$510.90		$747.68		$811.56		$998.98		$1103.77		$1599.50		$836.25	

TABLE VI—Continued

B. PER CENT OF DISTRIBUTION OF AMOUNT DEVOTED TO "SUNDRIES" FOR FAMILIES IN WHICH EXPENDITURE FOR "SUNDRIES" IS A GIVEN PER CENT OF ENTIRE EXPENDITURE

Distribution.	Per Cent.						Total.
	Less than 5.	5–10.	10–20.	20–30.	30–40.	40–50.	
Recreation.............	5.1	6.5	7.5	7.4	3.7	54.3	8.9
Union.................	1.	.5	1.3	.9	.6	0	.9
Gifts or loans.........	0	1.5	2.7	5.3	2.4	17.6	4.2
Drink.................	0	18.8	15.1	14.8	9.6	12.7	14.1
Church................	0	2.5	3.6	2.5	.7	1.6	2.5
Furniture.............	9.7	4.4	10.3	9.7	10.7	3.1	9.4
Papers................	17.9	5.4	4.6	2.6	1.5	.9	3.4
Car-fares.............	6.8	7.7	6.6	3.5	3.6	0	4.7
Medical attendance....	26.1	14.5	13.7	9.4	10.6	7.9	11.5
"Spending-money".....	0	19.9	20.5	16.8	24.9	0	18.7
Education.............	0	2.9	2.5	3.3	6.2	0	3.3
Domestic service......	0	0	.5	4.1	0	0	1.7
Funerals..............	0	0	.6	10.8	15.4	0	6.7
"Miscellaneous"......	33.4	15.4	10.5	8.9	10.1	1.9	10.
Total per cent........	100.0	100.0	100.0	100.0	100.0	100.0	100.0

writing-paper, stamps, "late" fines, payment of petty debts,
Miscellaneous   redeeming goods pawned, etc.   None of these
Expenses.   items occur often enough for a separate classification.   In this first group the various petty expenses
averaged $4.83, or 33.4 per cent, of the entire expenditure
for "sundries".   It is interesting that the next highest item
of expense is for "papers".   The "penny-paper
Newspapers.
habit" is common to even the poorest of these
families, who buy it whenever they can, sometimes two or
three times a week, or perhaps only the Sunday edition, which
if bought every Sunday for five cents would amount to $2.60
a year.   This happens to be the average amount spent for
papers in this group.   "Furniture" only aver-
Furniture.
aged $1.40 a year, and was for the ordinary
kitchen and house furnishings, which frequently need re-
plenishing.   No "parlor suites" could be bought by these
families!   Only 4 out of 21 families reported
Recreation.
any expenditure for recreation.   These four
families spent from $1. to $10. in the year, but the average
for the entire group would only be $0.74, a pathetically small
amount to be used for an entire year's recreation.   Nothing
appears for drink in this group, because in six
Drink.
cases the husbands were sick, in nine families
they were dead, had deserted, or were in the penitentiary, and
in three families in which it did not enter, the man was
worthless and added nothing to the family income, only
working occasionally in order to buy drink, which therefore
did not come within the family expenses.

In only one instance was a man in this group
Trade-union.
a member of a trade-union, and that was the
longshoreman's union.   This is an illustration of the fact
that unskilled labor is largely unorganized.

In the next group 40 families had an expenditure for

"sundries" which was between 5 and 10 per cent of their
total expenditures. The incomes were larger

Expenditure for Sundries, 5-10 per cent. (the average was $748.86), so that more could
be expended for "sundries", and the average
expenditure for these expenses per family was .$55.74. The
most significant fact in this group is that "spending-money"

"Spending-money." has entered into the family expenditure, which
was impossible when the incomes were smaller.
Here it averaged $11.10, and is the largest percentage, 19.9
per cent, of the "sundries". Drink has also become a

Drink. regular item of expense in 13 out of the 40
families. In these families it was usually a
pint of beer a day at supper, which costs $0.70 a week, or
$36.40 a year; but the average for the 40 families in the group
was only $10.45 a year. More was paid for papers—$5.68

Papers. a year—than in the previous group, but it
was a smaller percentage of the total expenditure
for "sundries". About five times as much was spent for
recreation, an average of $3.63, or 6.5 per cent, while the

Recreation. average income had increased over $200. This
increasing amount for recreation with larger
incomes is also shown by the fact that 17 of these 40 families, or 32.5 per cent, had an expenditure for recreation,
while only 4, or 11 per cent, of the previous group had any
expenditure for this purpose. Something was also given

Church. to the Church in these families—only an average of $1.39 a year, but the fact is significant.
There was also an expenditure for education; one family
spent $60. for fees and books to send a daughter to
a commercial college, and another family spent $4. for

Education. kindergarten dues. All of the expenditures
have increased over those of the same kind in
the first group, though not always proportionately.

There were 79 families whose expenditures for "sundries"
Expenditure for Sundries, between 10 and 20 per cent. were between 10 and 20 per cent of their total expenditures. Their average income and total expenditures are shown here. The largest item of expenditure among the sundries was "spending-money" for the husbands and older children. It averaged $25.62, or 20.5 per cent. A proportion-
Spending-money. ately larger number could spend money for drink—32, or 40.5 per cent, of the number in this group.
Drink. The average for all these families was $18.80, but 8 of them spent a large amount on drink. Over $52. a year, or a dollar a week, for drink is considered a proportionately large amount for families of this average income.

Medical Attendance. The amount expended for medical attendance increases, but the percentage drops in this group. All of the expenditures have risen above those of the two other groups, and expenditures for domestic service and funerals are added. Two families
Funerals. among this number had to bear the expense of funerals, one costing $47.50 and the other $10. (toward the expense of a father's funeral). Three families paid for
Domestic Service. outside help, which has been called "domestic service", usually in times of the mother's illness. The expenditures for church and for education have increased notably. Six families in this
Church. group reported expenditures either for music lessons or musical instruments, an evening course at Pratt
Education. Institute, and a course in stenography, and kindergarten fees; these have all been considered forms of "education".

The expenditures in the other groups may be read and compared in the same way. The most striking features

about these expenditures are the largely increased expenditure for recreation and drink, the greater
All Other Groups.
ability to make gifts or loans to friends, the
larger contribution to the church, the increased amount
(though smaller percentage) for medical attendance, and
the larger allowance for spending-money, education, domestic
service, and "miscellaneous" expenses. There are a few
exceptional families in these groups. Five
Illustrations of
Exceptional   of the thirteen families who spent from 30
Families.
to 40 per cent of their total expenditure on
"sundries" had seven funerals, which cost $748.50, or an
average of $106.93 for each funeral, and the average expense
to all the families in this group (13) was $57.58. These
funerals raised the expenditure for "sundries" to within
this group. Two families had an expenditure for "sundries"
over 40 per cent of their total expenditure. One was the
family already referred to with the income of $2158., in
which a trip to Germany cost $500., gifts to relatives in
Germany and loans to friends amounted to $245., and table
wines and liquors cost $104., or $2. a week—all of these
expenses coming under "sundries". In the other family
the income was $1041., and the high expenditure for
sundries was due to the fact that the man was a gambler,
"played the races", and had lost over $200. within the
year. This was considered his "recreation" expense. This
family had also spent $97. for medicines and doctor's bills
and $72.80 for drink.

In the analysis of the *total* amounts expended for "sundries" in the 200 families, and the percentages, the largest
average expense was the "spending-money".
Total Families'
"Spending-   An allowance for this was made in 108 out
money."
of the 200 families. In these cases 94 men
received all or part of the amount given, and in 29 families

one or two children had an allowance. The 94 husbands received in all $4641.96, or an average for each one of $49.38. The children in 29 families received $861.50, or an average of $29.71 for each family in which one or more children were given spending-money. The next largest amount and proportion in all the families was for drink, an average of

Drink.
$20.76 a year, or 14.1 per cent of the total expenditures for sundries. The next highest expenditures included under "sundries" were $17. for medical attendance, $14.77 for "miscellaneous" expenses, $13.78 for furniture and necessary household furnishings, and $13.17 a year on recreation. With an average income of $851.38 in the 200 families, and 5.6 persons in the family, none of these expenditures seems disproportionate. In fact the average for recreation seems small, but the father and older children often paid for their recreation out of their "spending-money". The smallest average expenditures were for domestic service and trade-unions. Here the unexpected is that in families of this class there should be as high an expenditure per family as $2.46 for domestic service, and that for trade-unions it should be as low as $1.37 per family. It is encouraging to find that these families averaged even as much as $4.83 a year on "education", in which is included the cost of a piano, violin, or other musical instrument, and the lessons on them, business-college fees, kindergarten dues, etc. This expenditure, though small, shows a laudable ambition in the 20 more prosperous families, in which it averaged $48.32 a year.

In brief, then, Table VI shows that the amount and per cent of expenditure for "sundries" increases with

Summary.
the income; that the largest number of families had an expenditure for "sundries" between 10 and 20 per cent of the total expenditure (the average

expenditure for sundries being 17.6 per cent of the total expenditure), and that the leading items under "sundries" were "spending-money", drink, medical attendance, furniture, and recreation. These expenses reveal interesting aspects of the moral and social life of the people in contrast to the economic life shown in the previous tables.

Table VII continues the analysis of the expenditures for "sundries" by grouping them according to the general nativity of the head of the family. It throws some illuminating side-lights on the standards of living in the foreign and native families.

In general it is seen that more native families had an expenditure for recreation and newspapers, and more foreign **Number of** families for drink, church, and education. **Families.** The number having an expenditure for drink shows the more common foreign custom of having wine or beer with the meals, while the larger number having expenditures for church and education, indicates a devotion to the church and its support, and a desire that the children should have all the advantages and "accomplishments" that can be afforded. The proportion of 11.6 per cent of foreign families having an expenditure for education is not large, but is encouraging when the size of the income is considered, as it indicates the spirit and ambition of these families. The proportion of families having expenditures for trade-unions, gifts, furniture, car-fares, medical attendance, spending-money, domestic service, funerals, and "miscellaneous expenses" did not vary much in the native and foreign families.

The amount of expenditure for these various purposes **Amount of** has been computed in two ways: the first **Expenditures.** column giving the average amount expended by the number of families in each group having the specified

TABLE VII

ANALYSIS OF EXPENDITURES INCLUDED UNDER "SUNDRIES" BY GENERAL NATIVITY OF HEAD OF THE FAMILY

General Nativity of the Head of Family.

Items of Expenditure.	United States						Foreign						United States and Foreign					
	No. of Families.	Per Cent of all Native Families.	Aver. Amount for Families having given Expenditure.	Average Amount for all Native Families.	Per Cent of "Sundries".	Per Cent of Total Expenditures.	No. of Families.	Per Cent of all Foreign Families.	Aver. Amount for Families having given Expenditure.	Average Amount for all Foreign Families.	Per Cent of "Sundries".	Per Cent of Total Expenditures.	No. of Families.	Per Cent of all Families.	Aver. Amount for Families having given Expenditure.	Average Expenditure for all Families.	Per Cent of "Sundries".	Per Cent of Total Expenditure.
Food	105	100.	$343.34	$343.34		42.7	95	100.	$385.61	$385.61		44.2	200	100.	$363.42	$363.42		43.4
Rent	105	100.	161.72	161.72		20.1	95	100.	162.85	162.85		18.7	200	100.	162.26	162.26		19.4
Clothing	105	100.	87.61	87.61		10.9	95	100.	89.39	89.39		10.3	200	100.	88.45	88.45		10.6
Light and fuel	105	100.	40.09	40.09		5.	95	100.	45.08	45.08		5.2	200	100.	42.46	42.46		5.1
*Insurance	96	91.4	37.19	33.03		4.1	78	82.1	38.50	31.61		3.6	174	87.	37.19	32.35		3.9
"Sundries", includ'g:																		
Recreation	58	55.2	31.89	17.61	12.7	2.2	49	51.6	16.02	8.26	5.3	.9	107	53.5	24.62	13.17	8.9	1.6
Union	24	22.9	6.04	1.38	1.	.2	22	23.2	5.82	1.35	.9	.2	46	23.	5.93	1.37	.9	.2
Gifts or loans	22	21.	25.95	5.44	3.9	.7	17	17.9	39.06	6.99	4.4	.8	39	19.5	31.66	6.18	4.2	.7
Drink	32	30.5	48.55	14.80	10.7	1.8	47	49.5	55.30	27.36	17.4	3.1	79	39.5	52.57	20.76	14.1	2.5
Church	34	32.4	7.76	2.51	1.8	.3	43	43.2	11.17	5.05	3.2	.6	77	38.5	9.66	3.72	2.5	.4
Books and papers	85	81.	6.76	5.48	4.	.7	69	72.6	5.96	4.33	2.8	.5	154	77.	6.40	4.93	3.4	.6
Furniture	50	47.6	28.08	13.37	9.7	1.8	44	46.3	30.73	14.23	9.1	1.6	94	47.	29.32	13.78	9.4	1.6
Car-fares	39	37.1	18.00	6.72	4.8	.8	35	36.8	19.69	7.26	4.6	.8	74	37.	18.84	6.97	4.7	.8
Med. attendance	89	84.8	18.75	15.90	11.5	2.6	80	84.2	21.65	18.23	11.6	2.1	169	84.5	20.12	17.00	11.5	2.
"Spending-money"	56	53.3	55.03	29.35	21.2	3.2	52	54.7	46.57	25.49	16.2	2.9	108	54.	50.96	27.52	18.7	3.3
Education	8	7.6	23.95	1.82	1.3	.2	11	11.6	70.44	8.16	5.1	.9	19	9.5	50.86	4.83	3.3	.6
Domestic service	5	4.8	54.60	2.60	1.9	.3	5	5.3	43.80	2.30	1.5	.3	10	5.	49.20	2.46	1.7	.3
Funerals	8	7.6	94.13†	7.17	5.2	.9	9	9.5	135.11†	12.80	8.1	1.5	17	8.5	115.82†	9.85†	6.7	1.2
"Miscellaneous"	85	81.	17.55	14.21	10.3	1.8	79	83.2	18.50	15.39	9.8	1.8	164	82.	18.01	14.77	10.	1.8
				804.15	100.	17.2‡				871.74	100.	18.‡				836.25	100.	17.6‡

* Of the 26 families who did not carry insurance in the total 200, 9 were native born and 17 were foreign born,—5 of whom were Italian, 4 Irish, 4 English, 2 French, 1 Scotch, and 1 Norwegian.

† These figures represent the cost per family for "funerals". In the native-born families the cost per funeral would be the same, as there was only one death in each family; but in the 9 foreign families there were 12 deaths, making the average cost of the funerals in those families $101.33, and in both U. S. and foreign, $98.45 (average for 20 funerals).

‡ For sundries.

expenditure, and the other column giving the average amount for *all* the families in each group. The averages for food, rent, clothing, light, and fuel, which have already been discussed, are inserted here for comparison with the other expenditures. For example, the average expended for insurance in 105 native families was $33.03, but the average for the 96 families having that expenditure was $37.19.

Considering the other expenses in the first column in this way, it is evident that a larger number of native families spent a larger amount for recreation and books and papers, the averages for these purposes being $31.89 and $6.76 against $16.02 and $5.96 in the foreign families. Again, the larger proportion of foreign families had larger average expenditures for drink, church, and education. The higher average for education is especially noteworthy, as it is over three times as much as in the native families. Five more native families, or 3.1 per cent, had an expenditure for gifts, but the average amount which was given was much higher in the foreign families, i.e., $39.06, as compared with $25.95 for the native families. So in the expenditures for furniture, car-fares, and medical attendance, a larger number of native families having those expenditures spent less for these purposes than did the foreign families. On the contrary, a smaller number of native families had a larger average for "spending-money" and "domestic service", while a smaller proportion of native families spent a smaller average for funerals and "miscellaneous expenses". The inference is that the native families considered it necessary or expedient to spend more for recreation, trade-unions, papers, "spending-money" for husband and children, and for domestic service, while the foreign families preferred to spend more for gifts or loans to their relatives or friends, for the church, drink, furniture, and education. The slightly larger expenditure in foreign families for car-fares and miscellaneous expenses does not illustrate any foreign characteristic; and the larger average for medical attendance and funerals depended on sickness and death, which happened to be a greater burden to them during the time of this investigation than to the native families. It is probable that the native families, especially those of Irish parentage, took advantage of the dispensaries more frequently than did the foreign, who generally prefer private physicians of their own race.

In this study the foreign families spent more on "fine funerals" than did the American. This is frequently a characteristic of the Irish and Italians. The most expensive funeral in this study cost $178., in an American family of Irish parentage. The average cost of the 12 funerals in the 9 Italian families was $101.33. This average is brought down by one family, which spent only $10. toward a father's funeral. The father of the head of this family died, leaving no insurance. His funeral cost $140., of which the widow was able to pay $100., and each of his 4 sons gave $10. This is a frequent Italian custom when there is no insurance money. Hence the cost of the funeral to the son whose family was included in this investigation was only $10.

The third section of Table VII gives the average expenditures of the 200 native and foreign families for food, Expenditures for rent, clothing, light and fuel, and insurance, as Sundries for both Native and Foreign well as for all the expenses included under eign Families. "Sundries". The largest number of these families had expenditures (of those expenses included under Sundries) for medical attendance (169), "miscellaneous expenses" (164), papers (154), "spending-money" (108), recreation (107), and so on down in the order of their recurrence. In the column giving the average amounts expended by families having each specified expenditure it is seen that the highest averages were for funerals ($115.82), drink ($52.57), spending-money ($50.96), education ($50.86), domestic service ($49.20), etc. The average expenditure for 107 families on recreation was $24.62, 77 families gave to the church an average of $9.66, 169 families had medical attendance which averaged $20.12, and so on. The average for drink, $52.57, was for 79 families, in which an expenditure for drink was a part of the family expenses. This was in addition to what the man may have spent for drink out of his spending-money, or what he earned and spent on himself, and which did not enter into the household income. Frequently it was a large amount, but it could not be estimated. It was found that ten of these families had paid for some outside service in amounts varying from $10. to $120. a year, but usually it was about a dollar a week, or $52. a year, for a washerwoman. The average for domestic service for these ten families was $49.20. One of the most unexpected and promising discoveries made in this investigation was that 19 families spent an average of $50.86 a year on "education". It was equally surprising to find that in these 200 workingmen's families only 46 families had an expenditure for trade-unions. This number does not include a few instances where the man paid his dues out of his "spending-money". He usually expected his wife to give him extra money for his union dues. In some instances a man had recently joined a union and paid dues for part of the year, in others he had dropped his membership during the year. The dues were from $0.25 to $1. a month, and the average expenditure for these 46 families was $5.93 a year.

The other expenditures under "Sundries" in this column may be read and compared in the same way.

The average expenditures of various kinds for *all* the families in the investigation, which are shown in the next column, are quite different. In the section giving the expenditures for both native and foreign families it will be observed that the results are the same as the totals of Table VI, which have already been contrasted. The averages of the first column are more representative of the individual family having that expenditure. The second column shows the attitude of the entire group of 200 families in each expenditure, and these averages are necessary as a basis for obtaining the proportion of each one of the expenditures under "Sundries" to the total expenditure. "Spending-money" was 3.3 per cent of the total expenditure for the average family, drink was 2.5 per cent, furniture was 1.7 per cent, recreation 1.6 per cent, and funerals 1.2 per cent. The other items were less than 1 per cent of the total expenditure, including the various and scattered items, which brought the "miscellaneous expenses" to 1.8 per cent of the total expenditure.

Table VIII is a summary of the families who reported a surplus or deficit, or neither surplus nor deficit, with the amount of surplus or deficit by nativity of the head of the family. The averages are for the number of families reporting a surplus or deficit, given in the first two columns, and not for the *total* number of families of each nativity. The total amount of surplus or deficit in each nativity is also given, so that the averages for *all* the families in each group may be computed if desired.

The "deficit" does not necessarily mean that those families have exceeded their income to that amount, for in many
Deficit. cases furniture, clothing, or a piano have been bought "on time". The amount remaining unpaid at the end of the year is considered a deficit, for it is

TABLE VIII

FAMILIES REPORTING A SURPLUS OR DEFICIT, OR NEITHER SURPLUS NOR
DEFICIT, WITH THE AMOUNT OF SURPLUS OR DEFICIT BY NATIVITY

Nativity of Head of Family.	No. of Families.	No. of Families Reporting			Amount Reported as		Average Surplus.	Average Deficit.
		A Surplus.	A Deficit.	Neither Surplus nor Deficit.	Surplus.	Deficit.		
United States.....	105	26	30	49	$2300.50	$991.75	$88.48	$33.06
Ireland...........	35	2	15	18	60.	563.50	30.	37.57
England..........	15	3	2	10	140.	161.	46.67	80.50
Germany.........	17	7	2	8	889.	44.	127.	22.
Italy.............	15	3	4	8	177.75	91.50	59.25	22.88
France...........	4	2	1	1	33.	18.	16.50	18.
Nor'y and Sweden.	4	3	0	1	1270.	0	423.33	0
Switzerland.......	2	1	0	1	35.	0	35.	0
Austria...........	1	0	0	1	0	0	0	0
Scotland.........	1	0	0	1	0	0	0	0
Cuba.............	1	0	1	0	0	10.	0	10.
Total foreign....	95	21	25	49	2604.75	888.00	124.04	35.52
Total........	200	47	55	98	4905.25	1879.75	104.37	34.18

an obligation which must be met in the future, even though the family is able to meet the installments when they fall due. There are various kinds of liabilities classed under the general head of "Deficit". In addition to clothing, furniture, or a piano bought on the "installment plan", a doctor's, undertaker's, grocer's, butcher's, or coal-dealer's bill, back rent or insurance, petty debts owing to neighbors— any or all of these obligations may enter into the "deficit".

If money had been drawn from the bank, or charity or gifts from friends and relatives had been received, these Additional Sources amounts were added to the income. Fre-
of Income. quently families with small incomes came out even at the end of the year, or with a small deficit, where the deficit would have been much larger had there not been these

sources of additional income. As these were not actually debts to be paid in the future, they have not been considered a part of the "deficit".

In the 105 native families, 26 reported a surplus, 30 a deficit, and 49 reported neither surplus nor deficit. There were also 49 foreign families who came out even at the end of the year—a larger proportion than in the native families. The foreign families reported 21 instances of surplus and 25 of deficit.

In the different nationalities more contrast is shown in the number reporting a surplus or a deficit, or neither.

Comparison of Deficit and Surplus by Nationalities. The Irish families had the largest number of deficits, in 15, or 42.9 per cent, of all the families. The German families reported the most instances of a surplus, but the Norwegian families had the largest proportion, 3 out of 4 families having a surplus. In the

Italian. Italian families 8 out of 15 reported "neither surplus nor deficit". As has previously been explained, the writer does not believe this is typical of the race. It is probable that some of these 8 families had savings which they would not admit. In those cases the income must have been larger. Yet there were also exceptional circumstances in several of these families which would uphold the accuracy of the statements. Three of the eight families had sent money back to Italy in gifts to relatives, and several had sickness, funeral expenses, and irregular employment to contend against, which used up the former savings and left nothing at the end of the year. Four Italian families reported a deficit, but the amounts were not large, except in one Americanized family, where it was $40., consisting of unpaid bills to the grocer, baker, and wine-dealer. This man was a stonecutter in summer, and his work was irregular in winter, with the result that the family usually contracted

debts in the winter which were paid off in the summer.
The year investigated ended in the spring, and these debts
were the result of the unsteady income of the winter months.
One young family of 3 which had been deserted by the
husband had an income of only $366. and a deficit of $10.
The 2 other families having deficits had had sickness and
death in the family, and the doctors' bills and funeral expenses were not all paid. Two Italian families saved $100.
and $75. each, partly because they had none of these ex-
traordinary expenses. A third family saved $2.75 in the
Penny Provident Bank; in this case the surplus was small,
also due to sickness and death.

The highest average surplus was for the 3 Norwegian
families—$423.33. This leads to the deduction that *thrift*
seems to be most marked in nations in which the preponderance of the income is from the husband, as Table V[1]
showed that 97.8 per cent of the average Norwegian income
was from the husband. The German families had the next
highest average surplus, $127., and the 26 American families
the third highest, $88.48.

The largest deficit was $37.57, in the Irish families, with
the exception of the English deficit of $80.50, which was
increased by the family, so often cited as an exception to
all rules, which had the expenses of three funerals and no
insurance in one year, leaving a deficit of $110. These
unusual circumstances should be taken into consideration
in judging the results in all the families.

In brief, this table shows that among these families there
were more of American birth who reported a surplus, and a
slightly larger proportion, than of foreign
Summary.   birth, but the average surplus for the foreign
families was larger. The average foreign deficit was also

---

[1] Table V, D, p. 85.

larger, due to exceptional circumstances. In the entire
investigation the average surplus for 47 families having
a surplus was $104.37, the average deficit for 55 families
reporting a deficit was $34.18, and in the total 200 families
there was an average surplus of $15.13.

TABLE IX

NUMBER OF FAMILIES OF SKILLED AND UNSKILLED LABORERS, AND OF
CLERKS, ETC., BY CLASSIFIED INCOME

Income.	Unskilled Laborers.		Skilled Laborers.		Clerks and all Others.		Total.	
	Number.	Per Cent.	Number.	Per Cent.	Number.	Per Cent.	Number.	Per Cent.
$200.–$400..	5	5.	3	6.7	3	5.5	11	5.5
400.– 500..	13	13.	1	2.2	2	3.6	16	8.
500.– 600..	12	12.	2	4.45	2	3.6	16	8.
600.– 700..	19	19.	4	8.9	6	10.9	29	14.5
700.– 800..	12	12.	6	13.3	9	16.4	27	13.5
800.– 900..	13	13.	8	17.8	4	7.3	25	12.5
900.–1000..	9	9.	4	8.9	6	10.9	19	9.5
1000.–1200..	11	11.	10	22.2	7	12.7	28	14.
1200.–1500..	5	5.	5	11.1	8	14.55	18	9.
1500.+	1	1.	2	4.45	8	14.55	11	5.5
Total......	100	100.	45	100.	55	100.	200.	100.

The incomes of families of unskilled and skilled laborers,
and of clerks and men of various other occupations, are
Division of   here classified to show the number of families in
Classes.   each group by classified incomes.   Under Table
I the nature of the occupations included in each of these
classes was defined. For example, unskilled laborers include
truckmen, longshoremen, stablemen, etc.; skilled laborers
are all those who have a "trade"—carpenters, plumbers,
machinists, stone-masons, etc.; and "clerks and others"
include clerks, janitors, bookkeepers, letter-carriers, and
all others which cannot be included in the two other classes.
By this classification 100 families were those of unskilled

laborers, 45 those of skilled laborers, and 55 belonged to the class of "clerks and others".

Of the 100 unskilled laborers' families, the largest number, 19, or 19 per cent, are shown in this table to have had incomes between $600. and $700. In the skilled laborers' families the largest number, 10, or 22.2 per cent, had incomes between $1000. and $1200. In the other class, 9, or 16.4 per cent, had incomes between $700. and $800. There were 30, or 30 per cent, unskilled laborers' families having incomes under $600., while only 6, or 13.35 per cent, of the skilled laborers' incomes were under that amount, and in the clerical group 7, or 12.3 per cent, had incomes less than $600. This "clerical" class had the largest number and proportion of incomes above $1200.,—16 families, or 29.1 per cent. In this number are some of the petty shopkeepers, who were quite prosperous, and others having the largest incomes in the investigation.

Unskilled Laborers and Others Compared by Income.

The difficulty in classifying the incomes in this way is that the "family income", or more correctly the "household income", is seldom entirely from the head of the family, but frequently from various sources, so that while the head of the family may be an unskilled "laborer" some of his children may be skilled, or even if they are not, the total income of his family from other sources may be quite large and not at all representative of his particular grade of labor. For this reason it has not been considered desirable or valuable to compute the total average income for each class—skilled or unskilled labor.

Difference in Skill in Members of Same Family.

On the other hand, the skilled laborers occasionally had the smallest incomes, due to illness, drink, or irregular employment. For example, a carpenter's family had an income of only $360., a cigar-maker $450., seamstress $260., while a longshoreman's income was $1288., a stableman's $1054., a waiter's $1134. In the latter instances the income was increased by the combined earnings of several members of the family, receipts from boarders, etc. Often, too, the unskilled laborer, by industry and frugality, brings in a larger income himself than does the skilled laborer. For instance, a longshoreman in this investigation earned $1000. in the year.

Of all the incomes derived from whatever degree of skill, the largest number came within $600. and $900.; 81, or 40.5 per cent, coming within these limits. The average income for all families was $851.38, and a further study of Table IX will show how the different classes of skilled and unskilled labor went above or below this average.

Supplementary to this classification of skilled and unskilled laborers' families, according to their incomes, is the following table (Table IX A), which shows the relative skill of the American and foreign-born heads of families.

It is seen from this comparison that 51, or 48.6 per cent, of the native-born and 49, or 51.6 per cent, of the foreign-born heads of families were unskilled; 26, or 24.7 per cent, of the native and 19, or 20 per cent, of the foreign were skilled; and 28, or 26.7 per cent, of the native and 27, or 28.4 per cent, of the foreign heads of families belonged to the class of "clerks and others". The Americans had therefore a slightly larger per cent (4.7) of skilled laborers and a slightly smaller proportion of miscellaneous workers, which the foreigners have a tendency to become. It is surprising to find that foreign families had only 3 per cent more unskilled workers than the Americans, and it has been frequently observed that the children of the foreign-born parents show a remarkable tendency to become skilled workers and far exceed their fathers in ability.

TABLE IX A

SKILLED AND UNSKILLED LABORERS, AND CLERKS AND OTHERS, BY
NATIVITY OF HEAD OF FAMILY

Nativity.	Number.				Per Cent.			
	Un-skilled	Skilled	Clerks and Others	Total.	Un-skilled.	Skilled.	Clerks and Others.	Total.
United States....	51	26	28	105	48.6	24.7	26.7	100.
Ireland..........	23	3	9	35	65.7	8.6	25.7	100.
England.........	6	3	6	15	40.	20.	40.	100.
Germany........	7	2	8	17	41.2	11.8	47.	100.
Italy............	8	5	2	15	53.4	33.3	13.1	100.
France..........	3	1	..	4	75.	25.	100.	100.
Sweden and Nor'y.	1	1	2	4	25.	25.	50.	100.
Switzerland......	...	2	..	2	.....	100.	.....	100.
Austria..........	...	1	..	1	.....	100.	.....	100.
Scotland........	1	..	..	1	100.	.....	.....	100.
Cuba............	...	1	..	1	.....	100.	.....	100.
Total foreign...	49	19	27	95	51.6	20.	28.4	100.
U. S. and foreign	100	45	55	200	50.	22.5	27.5	100.

The nationalities which had only one or two representatives in this study, i.e., Swiss, Austrian, Scotch, and Cuban,
cannot be considered typical of their races in regard to skill,
but of the other nationalities, the Irish have by far the
largest proportion of unskilled laborers, the Italians the
largest proportion of skilled workers, and the Germans of
the clerical class. Of the 4 French families, 3 happened
to be unskilled workers, but this is not representative of
the race, nor the fact that only 1, or 25 per cent, of the Norwegian families was skilled, for the Norwegians are frequently
skilled artisans. The other nationalities have enough
families represented to show some interesting and characteristic results.

TABLE X A

INCOMES AND EXPENDITURES OF "DEPENDENT" FAMILIES

Schedule Number	Income $	Size of Family	Nativity	Amount of Aid $	Food $	Rent $	Clothing $	Light and Fuel $	Insurance $	Sundries $	Total Expended $	Surplus or Deficit $	Source of Aid.*	Cause of Dependence.
15	250.	3	American	26.	150.	84.	10.	14.80	10.40	8.80	278.	−28.	Settlement, Church, Diet Kitchen.	Drink
8	260.	4	Irish-Amer.	40.	130.	92.75	18.	13.	0	6.25	260.	0	St. Vincent de Paul and C. O. S.	Drink and desertion by husband
109	322.	3	French	30.	124.	111.	10.50	26.25	21.30	46.95	340.	−18.	A. I. C. P. and Settlement	Illness and unemployment
24	360.	6	Scotch-Am.	37.	200.	109.	45.	31.	15.80	35.20	436.	−76.	C. O. S. and A. I. C. P. and Church	Illness of husband
81	380.	4	American	32.	143.	144.	35.	25.	26.60	14.40	388.	−8.	Church	Old age
101	390.	6	American	94.	182.	98.	32.60	30.30	20.80	26.30	390.	0	C. O. S.	Insanity of husband, due to drink
103	397.	5	Irish	16.	182.	120.	20.	32.	39.	4.00	397.	0	C. O. S.	Sickness
106	400.	6	English	24.	195.	84.	30.	20.	52.52	18.48	400.	0	C. O. S.	Drink
26	410.	5	German	10.	160.	90.	66.	22.	18.20	53.80	410.	0	Church	Death of husband
16	420.	5	Irish-Amer.	41.†	190.	120.	50.	38.	20.80	27.20	446.	−26.	C. O. S. and Widows' Aid Soc.	Death of husband
137	436.	8	Italian	20.	160.	161.	52.	45.45	0	17.55	436.	0	Trade School	Inefficiency of father and large family
150	450.50	5	Irish-Amer.	10.	182.	144.	36.	20.	46.80	26.20	455.	−4.50	Settlement	Unemployment

* Abbreviations under 'Source of Aid" are for the two organized charitable societies—Charity Organization Society and Association for Improving the Condition of the Poor. Four of these families received additional aid.

† + $60. from friends.

WAGE-EARNERS' BUDGETS

TABLE X A—*Continued.*

Schedule Number.	Income.	Size of Family.	Nativity.	Amount of Aid.	Food.	Rent.	Clothing.	Light and Fuel.	Insurance.	Sundries.	Total Expended.	Surplus or Deficit.	Source of Aid.	Cause of Dependence.
	$			$	$	$	$	$	$	$	$	$		
90	496.	9	Irish-Amer.	100.	234.	128.	60.	20.	20.80	47.20	510.	−14.	Diet Kitchen, Settlement and C. O. S.	Drink
120	509.	5	Irish	4.	286.	108.	80.	32.50	0	2.50	509.	0	C. O. S.	Death of husband
123	514.	9	Scotch-Am.	136.	312.	108.	36.	10.	15.60	32.40	514.	0	C. O. S., Church, everywhere	Drink and inefficiency
31	530.	5	Irish-Amer.	16.*	260.	120.	62.	30.	25.	53.	550.	−20.	Settlement	Drink and desertion by husband
53	557.	6	American	15.†	260.	106.	51.	55.	15.60	89.40	577.	−20.	Settlement	Drink and unemployment
125	560.	8	Irish	48.	312.	158.50	35.	42.	18.20	24.30	590.	−30.	C. O. S.	Death of husband
172	574.	5	American	25.	312.	156.	46.	16.92	0	108.08	639.	−65.	Church	Drink
95	575.	5	Irish	55.	299.	132.	22.	32.	26.	85.	596.	−21.	Settlement and Diet Kitchen	Sickness
121	626.	5	English	20.	286.	160.	40.	36.40	26.	128.60	677.	−51.	C. O. S.	Sickness
167	640.	6	American	100.	390.	102.	25.	26.40	7.20	89.40	640.	0	Church	Drink
37	675.	8	English	30.	364.	142.50	75.	46.00	23.40	24.10	675.	0	A. I. C. P. and Settlement	Death of husband
78	693.	6	American	16.	234.	180.	50.	42.	25.20	161.80	693.	0	Church	Sickness
14	810.	10	Irish	36.‡	416.	138.	175.	48.	0	108.	885.	−75.	Church, Settlement, everywhere	Unemployment
133	868.	8	Eng.-Amer.	5.	409.	108.	100.	43.	26.	162.	848.	+20.	Church	Unemployment
5	880.	8	German	20.	500.	131.50	150.	32.	7.80	58.70	880.	0	Church	Death of husband

*+$20. from sister for rent.   †+$35. from man's father for rent and clothing.   ‡+$55. from wife's father and mother.

The question of the relation of the incomes and expenditures of the families in this investigation who have received outside aid, the so-called "dependent" families, to the average incomes and expenditures of all the families has often been touched upon in this study.

Table X A.

A table has therefore been made, showing the incomes, size of family, nativity of head of family, amount of aid received, and the expenditures for various purposes by each one of the "dependent" families in this investigation. A second table compares the average incomes and expenditures of these "dependent" families with those of like incomes who were not dependent, and also with the averages for all the families.

It has been difficult to decide what families were dependent. Almost every family of small income received some help or other from friends or relatives in the form of clothing for the children, money for the rent, or occasional gifts to carry the family over a tight place. In the entire number investigated there were over 60 instances discovered of this fraternal helpfulness. To each of these families personal friends or relatives had given from $5. to $150. in money or in clothing. Frequently, were it not for their friends, these families would have been obliged to go to some organized charity for aid, but as they did not, they cannot properly be classed as dependents, according to our definition of dependency. In addition to gifts from more prosperous parents, relatives, sons away from home, and friends, this assistance often came in the form of small legacies, gifts from former employers, Christmas gifts from landlords and present employers, allowances from sick-benefit societies, gifts to the children from their godparents, and so on. Assistance of this nature cannot be considered as making

Distinction between "Dependent" and Independent Families.

the recipients dependent. The line of distinction cannot be sharply drawn between dependent families and those that are not, but after carefully eliminating all the families who received gifts from the sources just described, we have left 27 families out of the 200 in this investigation who received some aid through the usual channels of charity. Some of these families did not ask for aid, but it was given voluntarily by a church, settlement, or district worker who knew the needs of the family. This table shows in addition to the incomes and expenditures of these dependent families and the amount of aid received, the "source of aid" and the "cause of dependence" in each case. Among Sources of Aid. the "sources" were 15 instances of help from organized charities—including the Charity Organization Society, the Association for Improving the Condition of the Poor, St. Vincent de Paul Society, French Benevolent Society, Diet Kitchens and Widows' Aid Society; 7 received aid only from the churches, 3 from Settlements only, and 2 from various sources. The kinds of charity given were usually clothing, shoes, groceries, coal, milk from the Diet Kitchens, medicines, or payments toward rent—the value of all these gifts has been estimated in money in order to give uniformity. Of the 43 families having incomes below $600. in this study, 20 or 46.5 per cent had received "charity" from some church or society, 11 received money or clothing from friends, which kept them from being dependent, and 12 families claimed they had received no help at all.

Turning to the table, it will be seen that these 27 families were only partly dependent, and that relief given them in the form of rent, clothing, groceries, or coal was usually but a small proportion of their income. The 3 families with the larger incomes who received aid were very large, 8 and 10

in the family. The family with the income of $868. had
a period of unemployment, and during that time the church
gave the children a hat, shoes, and a few other little things that
have been valued at $5. In the last case, income $880. for
8, the church, which had helped the woman when she was
left a widow with three small children, still continued to
give her a good deal of clothing, although her income was
increased by a boarder and the wages of a son. The amount
of clothing given by the church during the year of investigation was valued at $20. According to the definition given
for dependency in this study, these two families were added
to this table, but because they are exceptional instances
and not representative of the dependent class, they have
been omitted in making further classification, leaving only
25 families considered actually dependent. This leaves
only one family with an income over $800. among the
dependent families. This family of 10 is the most completely
pauperized one in the study. Owing to a most irregular
income and a large family under 14 years of age, with only
two wage-earners, the father and one son (one or the other of
whom was usually out of work), this family received charity
from whatever source it could be obtained. As its character
was well known to charitable societies, they gave relief only
in small amounts, which we have estimated at $36. for the year.
In addition to this, the woman's parents sent them $55., and
even with this outside aid the debts to the butcher, grocer,
etc., amounted to $75. This is a striking example of a truly
dependent family in spite of a fair-sized income. The
causes of dependency were a large family under working
age, lack of ambition and perseverance on the part of the
father, which resulted in irregular and infrequent employment and unsteady income. The wife was a good manager,
but was handicapped by such an irregular income.

The "causes of dependency" in the 27 families are given in the last column of this table,—drink and unemployment **Causes of Dependency.** (generally due to intemperance), illness, and death of the husband, the principal wage-earner, are the chief reasons for charity in these families. In addition to these causes, the size of the family and the fact that few of the children were of wage-earning age are explanations for dependency in families with incomes of medium size. Among the 36 children in the 7 families in this table having incomes over $600. only 5 were old enough to contribute to the family income. There were also two dependent adults in these families.

Nativity of Dependent Families. The nativity of the dependent families shows that 15 heads of families were native-born, of whom 5 were of Irish parentage; 5 were born in Ireland, 3 in England, 2 in Germany, and one each in Italy and France.

In regard to incomes it is not surprising that the preponderance of families had very small incomes,—in fact 20 **Incomes.** out of the 27 families had incomes less than $600.,—and their average size was 5.6; 4 had incomes between $600. and $700. with an average size of 6.2; and the 3 families who had incomes between $800. and $900. had an average family of 8.7. The increased income is here offset by the increased size of families.

Omitting the two exceptional families already described, the 25 dependent families are classified according to their incomes and expenditures in Table X B, which may be compared with the results for all the families of like incomes given in the summary of Table II.

Such a comparison shows that "dependent" families on about the same income have larger families to support, and also that the average income (including the aid given)

TABLE X B

COMPARISONS OF INCOMES AND EXPENDITURES OF DEPENDENT FAMILIES, WITH AVERAGES FOR ALL FAMILIES BY CLASSIFIED INCOMES

25 DEPENDENT FAMILIES—INCOME UNDER $900

Income.	Number of Families.	Size of Families.	Average Income.	Average Aid Given.	Average Expenditure for						Total Expenditure.	Surplus or Deficit.
					Food.	Rent.	Clothing.	Light and Fuel.	Insurance.	Sundries.		
$200.-$400	7	4.4	$337.	$39.29	$158.72	$108.39	$24.44	$24.62	$19.13	$20.27	$355.57	-$18.57
400.- 500	6	6.3	435.41	34.17	186.83	121.17	49.	27.57	26.52	31.74	442.83	- 7.42
500.- 600	7	6.1	545.57	42.72	291.57	126.93	47.43	31.20	14.34	56.38	567.86	- 22.29
600.- 700	4	6.2	658.50	41.50	318.50	146.12	47.50	37.70	20.45	100.98	671.25	- 12.75
800.- 900	1	10.	810.	36.00	416.	138.	175.	48.	0	108.	885.	- 75.00
Total below $600	20	5.6	439.52	38.95	213.65	118.72	39.85	27.81	19.67*	36.35	456.05	- 16.53
Total below $900	25	5.9	489.38	39.24	238.52	123.87	46.48	30.20	19.01*	49.56	507.64	- 18.26

124 FAMILIES—INCOME UNDER $900. (From Table II.)

Income.	Number of Families.	Average Size.	Average Income.	Average Expenditure for						Total Expenditure.	Surplus or Deficit.
				Food.	Rent.	Clothing.	Light and Fuel.	Insurance.	Sundries.		
$200.-$400	11	4.2	$344.09	$158.14	$109.07	$26.10	$23.45	$17.14	$23.83	$357.73	-$13.64
400.- 500	16	4.7	454.97	205.28	119.94	43.13	28.75	20.72	45.10	462.92	- 7.95
500.- 600	16	5.2	549.88	280.79	125.16	47.44	33.77	17.74	55.10	560.	- 10.12
600.- 700	29	5.1	651.14	299.06	142.55	59.16	37.36	30.04	88.78	656.95	+ 5.81
800.- 900	25	5.9	836.80	380.36	154.89	85.55	44.59	26.10	139.87	831.28	+ 5.52
Total below $600	43	4.8	461.92	221.32	119.10	40.37	29.27	18.69*	43.38	472.13	- 10.21
Total below $900	124	5.2	643.78	294.49	140.01	59.95	38.21	26.68*	86.62	645.96	- 2.18

* Not all families carried insurance.

TABLE X C

INCOMES UNDER $600

	Number of Families.	Average Size.	Average Income.	Food.	Rent.	Clothing.	Light and Fuel.	Insurance.	Sundries.	Total Expenditure.	Surplus or Deficit.
Dependent families..........	20	5.6	$439.52	$213.65	$118.72	$39.85	$27.81	$19.67*	$36.35	$456.05	−$16.53
† Independent families.........	23	4.1	481.39	227.99	119.52	40.82	30.53	17.76*	49.49	486.11	− 4.72
Total for all families.........	43	4.8	461.92	221.32	119.10	40.37	29.27	18.69*	43.38	472.13	− 10.21

Average Expenditure for

INCOMES UNDER $900

	Number of Families.	Average Size.	Average Income.	Food.	Rent.	Clothing.	Light and Fuel.	Insurance.	Sundries.	Total Expenditure.	Surplus or Deficit.
Dependent families...........	25	5.9	$489.38	$238.52	$123.87	$46.48	$30.20	$19.01*	$49.56	$507.64	−$18.26
† Independent families...........	99	5.	682.77	308.63	144.09	63.35	40.23	28.62*	95.97	680.89	− 1.88
Total for all families.........	124	5.2	643.78	294.49	140.01	59.95	38.21	26.68*	86.62	645.96	− 2.18

* Not all families carried insurance.

† Those families who have received no assistance from an organized charity.

is less in each group of incomes than the average income of all families in the investigation. From these facts two further causes for charity in these families are evident—larger families and smaller incomes than the average for all the families in the investigation whose incomes are less than $900.

Table X C compares totals in another way. First, the incomes, expenditures, and size of family of dependent, independent, and all families having incomes under $600. are compared; and then the same comparison for families of these different classes having incomes under $900. is made. In these groups it is also shown that the families are larger and the incomes smaller in dependent families. This is more marked in comparing the dependent with the independent families (those who have received no assistance from organized sources) than in a comparison with the total averages for each group. It is also noteworthy that the expenditures for the various purposes named are smaller in the dependent families than in the independent ones, and yet the deficit is larger. This shows a careful expenditure and justifies the receipt of charity. Insurance in families having incomes below $600. is the only item which was larger in the dependent families, and that is not a marked difference.

The averages of the expenditures of the so-called independent poor families—that is, with incomes below $600.—
Incomes Below $600. seems a fair average minimum expenditure for existence in New York City, without receiving outside aid. Eleven of these families have already been shown to have received aid from friends and relatives, which makes their income slightly higher. The writer does not consider these expenditures "requisite to maintain physical efficiency" with the present cost of living in this city, for each one of these families suffered moral and

physical deterioration, and some of them are in a state of disintegration which must prove fatal to the family group unless conditions change and a larger and steadier income is possible in the immediate future. The average size of these families was 4.1. Families of 2 or 3 with wonderful management might live on this income without going to pieces, but it does not seem possible for families of 4 or over. How much worse is the condition of the dependent families in this group! Even with the help received, they tried to support an average family of 5.6 on an average income of $439.52. Their expenditures for the necessaries of life fell below the normal standard of other poor families, and even then they were burdened with a deficit of $16.53.

The statistics of the incomes and expenditures of "dependent" famil es and of all those having incomes less than $600. a year, which are given in the three sections of Table X, show how inadequate such incomes are to support families of average size without assistance or without indebtedness

CHAPTER V

THE STANDARD OF LIVING. GENERAL

THE "Standard of Living" is a relative phrase depending
not only upon the amount of income and expenditures of a
The Standard   family, but also on its attitude toward life.
of Living.   The plane of living which is sometimes forced
upon a family by stress of economic circumstances is not
necessarily its standard. The amount of comfort attainable
on a given income varies greatly in different families, according to the size of the family, its thrift or extravagance,
intemperance or other waste, as well as upon the ideals and
ambitions of each family. A family with a small income
frequently has a higher standard and lives more comfortably
than another family with a much larger income.

The tabulations in the preceding chapters dealt with
the actual figures of income and expenditure in 200 workingmen's families, but in addition to these facts the schedules
from which the statistics are drawn also contain an abundance
of information on the individual standards and characteristics of each family.

The following sample of the schedule used in the investigation shows the nature of the questions that were asked.

125

GREENWICH HOUSE COMMITTEE ON SOCIAL INVESTIGATIONS

STANDARD OF LIVING

1. Name. . . . .
2. Address. . . . .
3. Members of the family. . . . .

	Native-born.	Native-born of Foreign Parentage.	Foreign-born.	Age at Marriage.	Years in United States.	Years in N. Y. City.
Man.						
Woman.						

Children:

AT HOME.					NOT AT HOME.				
Sex.	Present Age.	In School.	Not in School.	Age at Marriage.	Sex.	Present Age.	In Institutions.		Age at Marriage.
							Ref.	Dep.	

Others in family. . . . .
. . . .
. . . .
. . . .

4. Number of rooms occupied....... 5. Sanitary conditions.........
6. Appearance of rooms. ....
....
....
7. Income and occupations:

Contributors.	Occupations or Source of Earnings.	Actual Income per Week.	Possible Income per Week.
Father.............			
Mother.............			
Children...........			
1..................			
2..................			
3..................			
4..................			
5..................			
Lodgers.			
Relatives.			
Neighbors.			
Church............			
Benefit Societies. ...			
Charitable Societies..			
	Home work: Day Night		

8. Allowance to be made for lost time by head of family per year, owing
   to—(a) Unemployment.....................................
   (b) Illness................. (c) Irregular habits..............
9. Estimated total income per year. ....
10. Amount paid for rent (per month). ....
11. Expenditure for food (per week). ....
12. Description of food consumed. ....
....
....
....
13. How are meals served?...................................
14. Is food wholesome and adequate in quantity?...................
15. Expenditure for drink (per week). ....
16. Habits in reference to drink. ....
....
....
17. Expenditures for clothing (per year).........................
18. Are second-hand clothes bought?.........................

19. What is the standard of dress?...................................
    (a) For father?...
    (b) For mother?...
    (c) For children?...
20. Expenditures for light and fuel (per year)........................
21. Observations on light and fuel used..............................
    ....
    ....
22. Expenditures for recreation—(a) For father......................
    (b) For mother...............(c) For children..................
23. Expenditures for insurance—(a) On father........................
    (b) On mother...............(c) On children...................
24. Expenditures for union..
25. Expenditures for books, magazines, or papers.....................
26. Expenditures for car-fares......................................
27. Expenditures for medical attendance—(a) Private physician........
    (b) Dispensary................(c) Medicines.....................
28. Expenditures for furniture......................................
    ....
    ....
29. Gifts or loans to relatives or neighbors.........................
    ....
30. Other expenditures..
    (a)...
    (b)...
    (c)...
31. Estimated total expenditure per year............................
32. Amount saved, and where deposited or invested...................
    ....
    ....
33. Church connection...
34. Membership in clubs...
35. Relation to political organizations.............................
    ....
36. Standard in reference to funeral expenses.......................
    ....
    ....
37. What articles are bought on installments?.......................
38. Is pawnshop resorted to?..
39. Has family been dependent, and under what circumstances?........
    ....
    ....
    ....

40. Frequency of removals.......................................
... .
... .
41. Other observations or remarks bearing on the standard of living, ...
... .
Name. ....
Address. ....
    Period of investigation:
        From.....................to........................
        Investigator. ....

This schedule served as an excellent working basis for obtaining the kind of information desired. When answered in full the 41 questions give a picture of the economic and social condition, and the moral and ethical standards of each family. Such questions as those bearing on the manner in which meals are served, the kind of food consumed and its quality and quantity, the standard of dress, the installment system, the pawnshops, the attitude toward funeral expenses, the appearance of the homes, etc., have a direct bearing on the life of each family. The schedules of 200 families described so minutely give a composite picture of the daily life of various classes of workingmen's families, and from them the following observations have been made on subjects which have not been fully covered in the preceding chapters.

In regard to the number of children living at home, it was found that only 8 families had children who were married or permanently living away from home. In two instances boys were in the Juvenile Asylum, and one boy was in the Truant School for five months. Three families had children in the Catholic Protectory, and three had children with relatives. Five boys and one daughter were working outside the city, and one boy was being sent to college by a friend of the family.

Children at Home or Away from Home.

When the children were away from home all the year and were no expense to the family, they were not considered as economic members of the family. The "others in the family" were boarders or dependents, i.e., fathers or mothers-in-law, nephews or nieces, or occasionally old women taken in out of charity. These were considered members of the family.

As to the number of rooms in the apartments:

2 apartments consisted of 1 room.

17   "   "   " 2 rooms.

70   "   "   " 3   "

Number of Rooms Occupied. 83   "   "   " 4   "

21   "   "   " 5   "

6   "   "   " 6   "

1 apartment   "   " 7   "

It will be seen that over three-fourths of the apartments consisted of 3 or 4 rooms. The average number of rooms for an apartment was 3.6. The average rent paid for these rooms was $13.50 a month, or $3.75 per room. The average number of persons in each apartment was 5.75.

The evils of overcrowding are not so noticeable on the lower West Side in New York as on the East Side. Writers **Number of Persons in a Room.** on social questions generally agree that overcrowding exists when the average number of persons per room is more than two. According to this definition, only 37 families, or 18.5 per cent of the whole, were overcrowded. In that number were several instances of 8 persons living in 3 rooms, 10 persons in 4 rooms, one family of 6 lived in 2 rooms, but the two worst examples of overcrowding were 10 persons in 3 rooms. In all, 137 families had less than 2 in a room, 26 families had 2 for each room, and 37 families had more than 2 in each room.

The average number per room was 1.6. Therefore it cannot be said that these families as a whole were overcrowded in their homes.

The extremes of housing conditions in this neighborhood are shown both in the sanitary condition and in the general

Sanitary Conditions.
appearance of the rooms. There are four types of apartments here represented. The most wretched sanitary conditions are usually in very old rear houses. Some of these houses have no water-supply except from a hydrant in the yard, which is likely to be frozen all winter, and water has to be carried from the front house. The halls of these houses are dark, stairs rickety, floors almost worn through, and the whole house so filthy and foul-smelling that it would be impossible to make it clean. In one of these dilapidated houses (not a rear house) a notice was posted in the hall saying: "This building will sustain 20 lbs. per sq. foot. All tenants are urged to place heavy furniture parallel to side walls." In houses such as this, 2 rooms rent for $7. or $7.50 a month and are the cheapest to be found in the district. Many families live in basements of old houses or old tenements. Some of these apartments are damp, dark, and unhealthy, others are quite light and dry. They rent from $8.50 to $10. for 3 rooms (at the time of this investigation, 1903–1905).

The second class of apartments are in the "old-law" tenement-houses. The rooms on the first floor of these houses are generally dark and damp. Only the front rooms have outside windows. The kitchen is the middle room and has a very small window, about 2 ft. square, opening on a narrow air-shaft or into the public hallway. The one or two bedrooms have only a small window into the public hall. The kitchen is lighted by glass partitions between it and the front room, but an artificial light is usually necessary all day. These old tenement-houses are from four to six stories high and have four apartments on each floor, two on each side of the hall, front and back. Three or four rooms like those described bring $10. to $15. a month.

Next in degree of comfort are the *better* class of old tenements, which have two apartments on each floor,, one on each side of the hall. These consist of four or five rooms extending from the front to the rear of the house—the "parlor" in front, two or three bedrooms in between, and the kitchen in the rear. The inner bedrooms have windows into the hall or none, but the front room and kitchen are light and airy and the circulation of air through the bedrooms is good. These apartments rent for from $15. to $25. a month.

The best and most expensive apartments are in the "new-law" tenement-houses, in which all the rooms have outside windows and are light and airy. Apartments in such houses contain five or six rooms and often a bath and private hall. They rent for $18. to $32. a month. The highest rent paid by any family in this study was $32. a month, by an Irish family for six rooms and bath. There were nine in the family, including two boarders, who each had a room, paying $5. a week for board and room.

The appearance of the rooms shows the standard of each family more surely than anything else. The ideals and
Appearance of ambitions of a family are usually first reflected
Rooms. in the home surroundings, which may be neat and clean, no matter how poor the family is.

The typical home of the wage-earners in this district is quite well furnished and fairly neat and clean. The
"parlor" is usually gaudy with plush furniture
A Typical Home. (sometimes covered with washable covers),
carpet on the floor, cheap lace-curtains at the windows,

crayon portraits of the family on the walls, and usually religious pictures of saints, the Virgin Mary, or "The Sacred Heart," sometimes a couch, and the ubiquitous folding-bed. The bedroom is only large enough for a white iron bed, generally covered by a white spread, and is quite clean. The kitchen, which is also the dining-room, is just large enough for a stove, a cupboard, a few chairs, and the table covered with white oilcloth. The rooms are likely to be crowded with too much furniture and bric-a-brac and littered with piles of clean clothing. On the whole, however, it is quite a comfortable home.

The poorest homes are in striking contrast. They are often dark, dirty, and bare of furniture. One of these homes **Example of a** consisted of two rooms. The house was only two **Very Poor Home.** rooms deep, so that both rooms were light, but the plaster was falling down from the ceiling, and the floor was almost worn through. The rooms were kept scrupulously neat and clean. The only furniture was a white iron bed in one room, and in the other a stove, a cheap oak rocking-chair, a table covered with a dark-colored oilcloth, a dilapidated old couch, an oak bureau, two kitchen chairs, no curtains, no carpet or oilcloth on the floor, no bric-a-brac, and no pictures on the walls.

At the other extreme are to be found homes of real comfort and taste. Here the furniture is good and not gaudy; **Homes of the** in the parlor is a leather couch, a bookcase **Most Prosperous** and desk with a few good books, frequently **Families.** a piano, a pier-glass (bought second hand), a carpet or Wilton rug (usually with brilliant coloring and glaring patterns), the usual family portraits and bric-a-brac, red-plush albums, "tidies" on the chairs; a separate dining-room with dining-table and sometimes a sideboard; and occasionally a sewing-machine, and plants at the windows. These homes are well cared for and the owners take much pride in them.

A few quotations from the investigators' notebooks will illustrate these different types:

"Untidy and careless; things always look at sixes and sevens, and a general air of discomfort pervades the place. One feels reluctant to 'sit a spell' even if one can find an unoccupied chair."

"House in good condition. It gives you the atmosphere of a well-to-do family in a small town. Furnishings ugly, but at the same time home-like."

"Looks like a place where people work and live; not a parlor. Everything clean at bottom, but littered about."

Turning from the homes of the people, the next question on the schedule relates to the various occupations and many sources of income in each family. The total amount of these incomes has already been tabulated. "Home work" consisted of making artificial flowers, collars or stocks, washing, or sewing given out by the churches. Comparatively little "sweat-shop clothing" is made in the tenements in this neighborhood.

Incomes and Occupations.

Some of the wages paid for different occupations were as follows:

Hod-carriers, $2.50 a day.

Truckmen, $9.–$15. a week.

Grocers' clerks, $8.–$10 a week.

Longshoremen earn from a few dollars to $25. or more a week. The wages paid are $0.25 an hour on non-union and $0.35 an hour on union docks, and $0.60 an hour for night work and Sundays.

Icemen, $15. a week.

Factory boys and girls, $3.–$9. a week.

Tailors, $10. a week.

Map-engravers, $24. a week.

Cloth-examiners, $24. a week.

Stone-cutters, $4.–$5. a day (work irregular).

Silversmiths, average, $18., possible $24. a week.

Steam-fitters, $3.50 and more a day.

Steam-fitters' helpers, $2.65 a day.

Waiters, usually $5. a week, and tips; at one place, 5 per cent on bills and all tips.

Porters, $8.–$12. a week.

Stablemen, $12. and $13. a week.

Elevatormen, $10. a week.

Automobile engineers, $30. a week.

Machinists, $13.–$18. a week.

Cabinet-makers, $16.–$17.50 a week.

Painters and paper-hangers, $12. a week.

Expressmen, $50. and $75. a month.

Many more examples could be given, but these will illustrate the scale of wages. Employment was so irregular during these two years that these wages could scarcely ever be relied upon for the entire year. Often a man only worked two or three days a week, during the months of the slack season, and then for some weeks during the rush season made a great deal working overtime. In estimating the total income, allowance has been made for all these exceptions. It was interesting to find that many men had two occupations, summer and winter; for example, oysterman and tent-maker, oysterman and watchman, carpenter and longshoreman, etc. Wages in some occupations rarely rise above a certain point. One man has been a truckman for one firm for thirty-two years, and his wages are now only $14. a week. Another man was with an ice company for twenty years and still receives $15. a week. This is true in practically all unskilled occupations. One of the most pathetic con-

ditions is found in cases where men have been in business
for themselves and failed, and are now working for $10.
to $15. a week. For example, one man was an independent
ice-dealer, another started a produce commission business,
one owned his own truck and horses, and one man owned
a saloon and failed, his wife said, "because it was impossible
to make money out of a legitimate saloon, and he would
have no other kind"!

The various amounts of expenditures for different purposes can best be understood by a knowledge of the char-
Expenditures   acter of the women who are the managers of
Dependent on   the family income. The standards of a well-
Character of the
Women.   ordered household in this neighborhood recognize the wife as the financier of the family group. It
is not an unattained ideal condition, but the regular standard
of respectability that a good husband should turn over to
his wife all his wages, receiving one or two dollars a week for
his personal use. One man boasted that he always gave
his wife every cent he earned, whether it was five cents or
$25. It was a matter of pride with him. The earnings of
the younger children all go to the mother, and also the board
of the older ones.

Provided the income is of average size and fairly steady,
the comfort of the whole family depends upon whether the
Many Admirable   mother is a good manager or not. Hence the
Managers.   character and ideals of the women are of the
highest importance in determining the standard of living
of each family. Many of them are admirable managers
and show intelligence and foresight in their household
economy. Probably their wits have been sharpened by
necessity. One little Frenchwoman remarked: "I ought
to know how to manage, for I always had to earn my living
by the sweatness of my forehead".

One finds women who would be exceptional in any position, who are refined in manner with a sweet and sunny **Intelligent and** disposition, in spite of a hard life. An inves- **Refined.** tigator's comment on one woman is typical of many: "Mrs. B—— is a neat, ambitious little woman with a tongue that wags at both ends, but wags in a kindly fashion". In some families the woman was a servant before her marriage, and the care these women take of their children's diet and health presents a striking illustration of the superiority of domestic service over factory training for developing intelligent home-makers.

It is a sad thing to find an attractive, ambitious wife who is a good manager, but completely discouraged because **Hard-working.** of small and irregular income due to drink, unemployment, illness, or lack of enterprise on the part of her husband. One woman who has a worthless husband does scrubbing at the Battery and walks down there at 5 A.M., back at 10, down at 5 P.M., and back at 7 P.M. every day, except when very stormy, for $20. a month. This was at least five miles a day in addition to the work. It is therefore not surprising that "Mrs. Smith is rather complaining, but she has cause, with a husband who is abusive, lazy, drunken, and sick, a daughter who has fits, and a truant son".

The women must plan for the future, and if they are improvident and shiftless, the standard of the family is **Plans for the** equally so. But women of the better class **Future.** have definite methods of management. They set aside certain amounts, from $20. to $100. during the busy season to be drawn out when work is slack and income irregular, and so they "just manage to keep out of debt". Many plan to keep the rent equal to the weekly income, or about one-fourth of the total income. This is an unformulated economic ideal with them. They move to better rooms as the income increases.

The lives of the women are very narrow, and they have few interests outside their homes. A high grade of intel-

Relations with Husbands. ligence on national issues or industrial questions is occasionally found among the men, but the women have no time to read the papers, except the fashion or society notes, or some famous scandal or murder case. There is seldom any mental companionship between husband and wife. He rarely ill-treats her, but "restricted education and a narrow circle of activities hinder comradeship". Occasionally one finds a very attractive, affectionate home life, but a common ideal of domestic felicity was expressed by one woman who told the writer, "We've been married fourteen years and he never said to me 'You're a liar,' nor I to him".

Illustrations of a laudable ambition on the part of the mothers to make the home attractive and give the boys and girls every possible advantage are frequent.

Ambitions: (1) in their Homes. One woman spent $20. "on little things for the house, such as plants for window-boxes". Another saved a few cents each week in order to buy some cheap lace curtains as an Easter surprise for the children. An Italian family fitted up at Christmas in their home an elaborate crèche, of no artistic value beyond mechanical ingenuity in the arrangement of the lights and architectural effects. One American family of 7 was content to live under wretched conditions, poorly nourished and with a generally low standard, for the sake of some day having a home on Long Island. Out of an income of $700. they saved $100. during the year of investigation. The little piece of land is already paid for, and they are building a home as rapidly as they can get the money. As soon as many of the better-class families can afford it, they are moving out of the city to Orange, Hoboken, or Jersey City, where they can have more air and sunshine for their money.

The expenses for education show that some families are making great efforts to send a child to a business college. One boy who was forced to go to work at 14 **(2) In the Education of the Children.** went to night school for three years. His ambition was to get into the mechanical engineering course at Cooper Union, but his education was so elementary that he was unable to enter until given private evening lessons by a settlement worker. A common Irish ambition is to get on the police force. One Jewish family, having an income of $797., saved $123. in the year toward sending their two boys (now aged 9 and 13) to Columbia University.

The most common ambition of the mothers is to have a piano in order that the children may "take lessons", whether they possess any musical ability or not. As one woman expressed it, "It would be so grand to have Adelphine sit down to an old rattle-box and knock out a tune". Many of the children take lessons, paying $0.50 a lesson, sometimes practising on a neighbor's piano. One family pays a dollar a week for lessons for two children, and $10. a month toward the piano. The pianos are always bought "on time".

The amounts of those expenditures which depend largely upon the personality of the wife have already been given in the tabulations. A fuller description of the expenditures for food and clothing will be given in connection with the budgets—showing the character of the diets and the prices paid for food and clothing. (Chapter VII.) There are some kinds of expenditure for which the women are not responsible. Such divergent expenses as drink and trade-union dues are of this character.

Unfortunately there are many families in this neighborhood in which the woman also drinks, but in those cases the Expenditure for woman was not reliable enough to give the Drink. information desired for these schedules and was dropped from the investigation. One of the saddest aspects of the drink question is frequently the despondency of the wife over the situation. In several instances among these families the wife had become despondent and was beginning to drink herself, where formerly she had been a good manager, attractive and ambitious. The influence of drink is one of the questions which statistics can only touch upon. In this investigation only 79 families reported an expenditure for drink which amounted to from $0.30 to $3. a week, but was usually $0.70 a week for a pint of beer daily for supper. The average expenditure for all the families in the study was only $20.76 a year; or $52.57 a year for those families who had that expenditure. These facts show only part of the real situation. In addition, there were 42 families in which intemperance had affected the family standard, and in some of them the family was going to pieces because of it. As has already been explained, the men who were the hardest drinkers did not bring home all their wages, or only worked for enough to buy liquor, so that this part of their earnings did not appear in the "household income" and could not be estimated. The reason that more suffering is not shown as the result of intemperance in this study is because there frequently happened to be other members of the family whose earnings brought up the family income, and the man's earnings were not relied upon. Yet there were some cases of extreme suffering due to intemperate husbands. The two poorest families having incomes of $250. and $260. a year were the result of this. Table X shows how often dependency was due to this cause. It has been estimated that the average sum spent a week for drink by families of the working classes of England is 6s. 10d., or about $1.70.* Undoubtedly, it was not nearly as high among these workingmen's families, but it must be remembered that an average of $20.76 a year or $.40 a week does not represent the actual amount spent, but only that which came out of the "family or household income".

It has already been noted that the expenditure for trade-unions is surprisingly low—only 46 families reported an average expenditure of $5.93 a year. In a few instances the man paid his dues out of his spending-money, but whenever the wife knew the amount it was deducted from the allowance for spending-money. There is a noticeable lack of enthusiasm for labor organizations in these families. There are several apparent reasons for this attitude: an inability to see the ultimate general good when the immediate personal need is so great, the dread of strikes, sometimes failure to gain admission into certain unions, or success in obtaining employment without belonging to a union and thus avoiding an expense which is considered an unnecessary burden. The books of some unions are only open for membership twice a year, when a limited number are admitted. This excludes many. Others are unwilling to join because the incidental expenses of a union are frequently considerable. The disadvantages connected with labor organizations seem therefore more real to this group of wage-earners than do their merits.

Trade-unions.

The expenditure for "books, magazines, and papers" was usually confined to one daily penny paper, which, with the Sunday edition, costs $.11 a week or $5.72 a year. The more sensational newspapers which claim to "champion the cause of the

"Books, Magazines, and Papers".

* B. Seebohm Rowntree, *Poverty*, p. 142.

workingmen" most aggressively, and bring out the most illustrated editions, are the ones universally read. Occasionally both morning and evening papers are bought. The foreigners usually read their own papers also. The few magazines bought include the *Ladies' World, Collier's Weekly, Munsey's*, and *Everybody's*. One exceptional family spent $25. on papers and magazines. The man was a printer and bought a great many papers, *The Sun, World*, and *Journal* every Sunday, the *Saturday Evening Mail and Express*, a daily morning paper, and two evening papers. He also bought *Munsey's*, the *Argosy*, and *Everybody's* every month. This family could discuss current news intelligently. There seems to be no general love of reading, however, in this neighborhood, as there is on the East Side.

The forms of recreation have already been mentioned. The amount spent varies from nothing to $500. for a trip to

Recreation. Germany, and averaged only $13.17 a year. The usual attitude toward any expenditure for pleasure is that it is a luxury which cannot be afforded. Only 107 families had any expenditure for recreation besides what came out of the spending-money. These families spent an average of $24.62. The more intelligent mothers, who can afford nothing else, take their children to Central Park or to the small parks, and occasionally on street-car rides. The Fresh Air parties in summer are eagerly anticipated by the children. The usual outings, which are any expense to the family, are a couple of trips to Coney Island and perhaps to Fort George, and to the theatre a few times in the winter, costing in all about $10. a year. Yet the amount which some of the more prosperous families spend on the theatre is surprising. Some of the women go regularly every week all winter to Proctor's, Weber and Field's, or the Fourteenth Street Theatre, but rarely to an uptown theatre.

They buy fifty-cent seats. One family rented a furnished tent at Ulmer Park for six weeks, and estimated that the rent of the tent ($48.) was the only additional expense, as the expenses for food, etc., were the same as at home. Another family, mother and 3 children, went to the country for two weeks, and paid $13. a week for the four. Such summer trips are, however, very unusual among these families. An exceptional instance of extravagance in recreation was where the father and son went fishing almost every Sunday, summer and winter, costing at least $2. a trip. Allowing for stormy and cold Sundays, when they could not go, they estimated that this cost $80. a year. In addition, the whole family of eight went twice to Midland Beach and twice to New Dorp in the summer, and " $5. for the day is nothing for a family of eight," said the mother— so that family's annual recreation cost about $100.

Going to funerals of friends is considered an obligation, but is at the same time a kind of outing. The usual price is $5.50 for a coach, and some families have gone several times in the year, and this is frequently mentioned as the only recreation the family had.

And, finally, all the lodges and societies and political clubs have social nights, and are centres of recreation for those who can afford to belong to them. The most popular lodges are the "Forresters", "Royal Arcanum", "The Shepherds of Bethlehem", and "The Daughters of America". Many also belong to Church Societies, such as the "Holy Name Society" in the Catholic Church.

The death-rate of this ward is unusually high, due to either the bad sanitary conditions of the old houses, the nationality of the people, or to some other cause. Tuberculosis is the scourge of the district. In many of these families the high expenditure for

Health and Medical Attendance.

medicine was largely for special food for tuberculous members of the family. For example, one family with an income of $810. spent $124.80 for medicine,—this included two bottles of cod-liver oil ($1.46), special milk, ten cents a day, or $.70 a week; and pills, $.24 a week; or, in all, $2.40 a week for the man, who seemed likely to recover from tuberculosis on this treatment. A priest claimed that the Italians have so much sickness because they are improperly nourished; they bring a "macaroni diet" to this country, where the climate is so different, and the work so much harder, that they often break down under the strain.

Some families have the "medicine habit"—one family spent $25. a year on patent medicines. The Dispensaries are universally used by the poor families, though the more prosperous scorn them as a charity and have sometimes a very poor opinion of the medicines given there! The prejudice against hospitals is lessening, though there is still a common belief that people die if they go there, and the women can seldom be persuaded to go for a confinement. The very poor women frequently have a free physician and nurse from a hospital, but the majority have a private physician or midwife, who is willing to be paid for services in installments. It is unusual for a woman to save enough for her sickness beforehand. The usual expenditure for medicine, when there is no long illness in the family, is about $5. for household remedies, such as salts, magnesia, and cough medicines; the larger average amount, $17., was due to the exceptional cases.

The standards of the working-class in regard to funerals have often been criticized. The expenditures for this purpose were discussed under Table VII. The insurance is almost invariably entirely spent on the funeral, sometimes the family runs into debt in addition, and in

Funerals.

the cases in which there was no insurance the family was years in paying for the cost of the funeral. The undertakers are often unscrupulous, and sometimes obtain possession of the insurance policy, and make the cost of the funeral equal to the whole amount. Funerals of children cost from $10. to $90., and for adults from $100. to $200. The larger amounts include the cost of a grave or opening a grave, shroud, flowers, hearse, and several carriages. The ostentatious display in the flowers and number of carriages is much to be regretted. One family, which was dependent most of the time, insisted on having two carriages for the funeral of their son, with no one to ride in the second one, but, as the mother said: "Sure, it's all I can do for him". They were burdening themselves with a debt which it would take years to pay. In one case the funeral of a child four years old cost $84., and there was no insurance. The mother has been five years trying to pay for it, but has not been successful, for "the money is so much needed for other things".

Buying on the installment system is almost universal among the working-class. This system has some merit, **Installment** but many evils. Many times it is the only **System.** way in which very necessary furniture can be bought, but, on the other hand, occasionally a family fails to make payments, loses all they have already paid, and forfeits the goods. The universal feeling is that it is a necessity at times, but is hated. "I'm glad I'm out of that" is the frequent testimony. Furniture is most frequently bought "on time", especially pianos and sewing-machines, so that a discussion of the prices paid for furniture properly belongs here. Sewing-machines cost from $25. to $60., and are paid for at the rate of $1. a week. Pianos cost about $300., and at $10. a month it takes two years and a half to pay for them. Occasionally young people have saved enough to buy all their furniture for cash when they set up house-keeping, but most frequently it is bought "on time". One young couple paid $200. for furniture in this way when they were first married, another $68., and another $50. The most extravagant tendency is to buy elaborate parlor furniture "on time", which is far out of keeping with the family's income. Yet even this indicates ambition and a higher standard. One family bought a parlor set for $97.; they paid $45. the first year, $40. the second, and were still owing $12. when the furniture looked about worn out. Another family paid $112.90 for a parlor set and carpet, and it took eighteen months to pay for them. A few women feel they would rather do without than buy "on time". One woman who was particularly disgusted with the system said that she paid $5. for a rug in this way, and later saw one exactly like it in a department store for $1.98.

Some of the prices paid are as follows:

Stoves	$11.00–$15.00
Couch	5.00
Lace curtains	4.00– 6.50
Family portraits	6.00
Religious pictures	4.50– 6.00
Refrigerator	10.50
Mattress	5.00– 14.00
Linoleum for kitchen	5.00– 6.25
Pianos	275.00–300.00
Sewing-machines	25.00– 60.00
Parlor furniture	75.00–125.00

Clothing bought "on time" is not so common as furniture, but the habit is even more deplorable, for it is invariably of the cheapest quality and is often worn out before it is paid for. The women know they pay much more than the value of a coat or skirt, but the excuse always is "we had not the cash, and this way can pay $.50 a week". Clothing is usually bought from Jews who go from house to house to sell, and come regularly Monday mornings to collect. From 20 to 100 per cent more than the value of the clothing is paid under the installment system, and the temptation is to buy far more than can be afforded. There are few families among this number who are not generally paying from $.50 to $1.50 a week for something. Probably only the more shiftless women buy clothing on time, but even thrifty managers will buy furniture. The purchase of a sewing-machine in this way seems justifiable, for a woman can often manage better and more economically if she can make her children's clothes, even if she is paying $1. a week for a machine, than if she bought them ready-made.

Closely linked to the installment system, with none of its merits, is the pawning habit. It is perhaps more common than the women would admit. They are all
Pawnshop. ashamed of it, even when trying to justify themselves by saying "what else can poor people do?"

The women agree that if the habit is once fixed upon them it is difficult to overcome. It is an easy way to get ready money. Articles of clothing are often "put in" from Monday morning to Saturday evening, but in the meantime 3 cents on every dollar is forfeited. One woman who had a particularly hard winter claimed that she lost from $.25 to $.50 a week by pawning articles and then redeeming them as soon as she had a little money ahead. This is an unusual example of improvidence. Some startling evidences of shiftlessness were discovered in this custom. One family which had been given $100. in clothing, money, and rent by the church paid $25. for a watch "on time" when a child of fourteen "graduated", and had barely paid for it when it was pawned for $5. This family would beg things to pawn. Other instances were found where clothing, watches, jewelry, and furniture had been bought "on time" and then pawned before they were paid for. Jewelry and unnecessary things are the first to be pawned when hard times come. One man pawned his wife's wedding-ring for drink, and she bought a ten-cent brass one "to keep the respect of the children", she said.

Many families in this investigation did not have the pawning habit, and always paid cash for everything—"German style", as one woman expressed it. There is not the Monday morning pilgrimage to the pawnshop that there is in some neighborhoods, but both pawning and "buying on time" are typical of every workingman's neighborhood.

In regard to child labor, there seems to be a general feeling among parents that they would like to keep the children in school longer *if* they could afford it, but that they cannot, and the result to be gained did not **Child Labor.** seem worth the sacrifice. This feeling was expressed by one woman when she said: "I know Josie (13) ought not to stay out of school, but what could I do? I needed the money and he had the chance". She promised to send him back to school in a few weeks, but, unless the truant officer appears, these promises are soon forgotten! With an intimate knowledge of the family struggle for existence, it is easy to understand this eagerness to put a child to work as soon as possible. The immediate gain is all that can be realized and not the ultimate harm to the child. Yet there is a universal desire that the children should become skilled workers and "learn a trade". Many bright and capable men and women in this neighborhood would undoubtedly have been able to occupy high positions in the industrial world if they had not been forced into unskilled work when young.

The church connection of each family was asked and the

amount of contribution to the church, in the hope that these
Religion. questions would throw some light on the influence of the churches. There were about as many
Catholic as Protestant families—80 Catholic and 85 Protestant, while 33 had no church connection, and 2 were Jewish.
Frequently the children of non-church people or of Catholics
attended Protestant Sunday-schools. The majority of parents
did not attend church regularly nor make any contribution to
the support of the church. The mother was unable to go and
the father indifferent. In many families church-going is
confined to the children and young people. There is frequently a desire that the children should have some religious
training. One woman said that she did not consider the
parochial school as good as the public, but she wished her
children to have a good religious training in the beginning.
"It is necessary for young girls to have some religious standard
when they are between fourteen and twenty", she said. She
also summed up an ethical standard very shrewdly: "In
Ireland you are taught that if you find something you must
find the owner. Here, you must not let the owner find
you".

When there was any church contribution at all, it usually
amounted to from $.05 to $.25 a Sunday, or from $2.60 to
$13. a year. The average for 77 families who had such
expenditure was $9.66 a year, for all families it was only
$3.72. Table VII shows that foreign families gave twice
as much to the church as did the native-born. The Catholics
consider it more of an obligation than do the Protestants.
Good Catholics contribute regularly $.10 a Sunday for all
who have been confirmed. The contributions of the Protestant
families were generally confined to the pennies which the
children took to Sunday-school. Yet the two largest con-
tributors were Protestants. In these cases the head of the

family gave $50. a year to the church. One was a German grocer with an income of $1304., who was the leading member of a struggling little Lutheran church. His family only spent $5. on recreation. The other was a Methodist, who had an income of $1140. These were exceptional cases. As a race the Italians are devout, with their simple peasant beliefs and religious rites. The Italian-Americans of the second generation have not the same devotion to the church. On the whole, the direct influence of the Christian churches on these families seems to the writer to be regrettably unimportant.

The question of present dependency in these families has been analyzed in Table X. Many families, however, who did **Dependency.** not come in the dependent class in this year are shown by the answers to Question 39 on the schedule to have been dependent at some time in the past, usually during periods of illness or on the death of the principal wage-earner. This fact supports the statement frequently made in this monograph, that the average wage-earner's family in a city like New York is continually on the verge of dependence.

There have been numerous definitions by sociologists of the "poverty line". The amount of income necessary to keep a family under ordinary circumstances above the "poverty line" has been variously approximated. If it is assumed to be "that rate of earnings which puts the family intermittently in the dependent class", then all the families in this study who have been unable to save for the future are near that line.

Fully half of these families are shown by this question to have been dependent at some time. The ultimate causes of their poverty, such as low rate of wages, periods of industrial depression, etc., have not been considered, but the *immediate circumstances* of their dependence were given. They were about the same as for the dependent families in Table X, namely, inefficiency or death of chief wage-earner, unemployment, illness, intemperance, or large family with small or irregular income. There is, however, an admirable spirit of independence in this neighborhood. When questioned by the investigators as to any previous dependent condition, those who have always been independent usually reply that they hope they will never come to that, or that they have never asked for five cents from anybody. This is a matter of great pride with them. It is only when forced to it by pressure of circumstances that the self-respecting family will become dependent. They will frequently struggle along on the edge of dependence for years before coming to this.

These, then, are some of the characteristics of wage-earners' standards of living, which have been brought out by a study of the information collected in connection with these 200 schedules. Some of the great problems of existence have been merely touched upon, but it is hoped that some light has been thrown upon the workingman's attitude, and that of his family, toward these problems.

CHAPTER VI

THE STANDARD OF LIVING: TYPICAL FAMILIES

In order to illustrate characteristics of the standards of living of families whose economic and industrial conditions are different, an attempt has been made to select some typical families for description. Twelve families have been carefully chosen to illustrate some of the most vital and salient features of the standards of this neighborhood.

The incomes vary from $260. to $1512. a year, and are representative of all grades of prosperity in the district.

INCOMES BELOW $600.

Of the 200 families studied 43 are in this class. The following three examples will give a fair idea of their standard of living:

SCHEDULE No. 8

SEAMSTRESS   INCOME $260.

This is a family whose standard of living is much above the amount of income. Both father and mother have seen more prosperous days. They were married in Boston, where the man owned a small stationery store. He began to drink and they soon lost everything. Mr. M. was a good salesman. He came to New York and had a fine position with a book

152

firm, until he began drinking again and lost his position. His wife had him arrested for non-support and drunkenness, and he was sent to the Island. After serving that term, he was arrested for forgery and sent to the penitentiary for a year. This was the year during which this study was made. Mr. M. contributed nothing to the support of the family, and so was not considered a member of the family, which consisted then of Mrs. M. and three children, a girl aged 13, boy 12, and a little boy of 3. Mr. M. was born in Ireland, his wife in Boston of Scotch-Irish parents.

Their home consists of two rooms in an old tenement on a poor street. The sanitary conditions are fair, front room light with two windows on the street, the bedroom dark with one small window on an air-shaft. The rooms are clean but bare, almost all the furniture having been sold or pawned, until only a bed, stove, table, bureau, and a few chairs and the woman's sewing-machine are left. The rent is $7.50 a month. They lived eight months in this house, before that in two other places where the rent was $8. and $8.50. Mrs. M. moves often so that her husband cannot find her when he comes out of the penitentiary. The family was entirely dependent upon the mother's earnings and charity. The little girl, 13, worked for six weeks in the summer in an artificial-flower factory and earned $14. The total income from all sources during the year was as follows:

Mrs. M., sewing, 14 weeks, averaged $5.00 a week. .	$70.00
" " " 38 " " 3.00 " ..	114.00
Girl, 13, earned in summer	14.00
Mother, extra work.	20.50
St. Vincent de Paul Society, grocery tickets	26.00
" " " " " shoes.	4.00
Charity Organization Society, for rent.	11.50
Total.	$260.00

This is estimating the income as high as possible. The woman had very little work, and worked for starvation prices until the Settlement discovered her and gave her work at better prices. She is very proud and unwilling to ask for aid until forced to. She is very delicate and seems half-starved. The children, too, show poor nourishment. Her usual weekly expenses for food are: bread, $.70; milk (3 cans condensed), $.30; 1½ lbs. of butter, $.38; ½ lb. tea, $.20; 2 qts. potatoes, $.20; meat, $.30; oatmeal, $.10; 1 lb. sugar, $.06; child's dinners at the Day Nursery, $.25; total, $2.49. The usual diet is bread and milk and tea. It is evident that this food is entirely insufficient to properly nourish three growing children. The expenditure for clothing is very low. Fortunately the woman is able to make over clothes they had in better times, and the children always look clean and neat. She insists that she bought no more clothing than the following during the year:

Woman—1 pair stockings	$ .10
Girl (13), 2 pairs shoes	3.00
Stockings for two children, 40 cts. a month	4.80
Skirt for girl	1.25
Material for three waists	.70
Boy (12), shoes	1.50
Boy (12), pants	.25
Boy (12), waists	.65
Boy (12), shirts	.25
Baby, 2 pairs of shoes	.85
Baby, 4 pairs of stockings	.40
Baby, shirts, etc	.25
Value of shoes given	4.00
Total	$18.00

The expenditure for light and fuel is equally low. Gas was burned very sparingly by the "quarter meter", and cost $.50 a month for ten months in one house, and $.25 a week for nine weeks in another, total, $7.25. Wood was gathered by the boy on the streets, and was largely used for fuel. No coal was bought from April to November 1. For five weeks in mid-winter coal averaged $.40 a week (4 pails at 10 cents a pail), and for the other fifteen weeks about $.25 a week—total for coal, $5.75. No oil was burned. The total for light and fuel is therefore $13. There were no expenditures for recreation, no insurance, furniture, books or papers, car-fares, etc. One dollar was spent for medicine and $3. for moving expenses. Itemized the expenditures for the year were:

Food.	$130.00
Rent.	92.75
Clothing.	18.00
Fuel.	13.00
Medicine.	1.00
Moving expenses.	3.00
Sundries.	2.25
	$260.00

Nothing was saved, but they managed to keep out of debt. This seems to show what a family of four can exist on in New York, with a minimum allowance for food, fuel, and rent. But such an existence was not without physical deterioration for each member of the family. They were sent to Sea Breeze for two weeks in the summer, and the boy was sent with a Fresh Air party to Valhalla. The girl comes to clubs at the Settlement, which is the only recreation she has. Nothing has been bought on installment for several years, but the pawnshop was resorted to until, during the year of the investigation, there was nothing left to pawn. Mrs. M. is a good manager, but is utterly disheartened and discouraged. This family will rise to a more prosperous level when the boy and girl are old enough to work.

SCHEDULE No. 26
WASHERWOMAN (WIDOW)   INCOME $410.

This family had a larger income than the previous one, and consists of a widow and four children, aged 12, 11, 8, and 4 years. The father was a grocer's clerk at $10. a week, and the family had been comfortable on that with the most careful management. Mr. S. died early in the year of investigation. Nothing had been saved and the insurance of $125. just paid for the funeral expenses. Both Mr. and Mrs. S. were born in Germany. The man added $80. to the income before he died. He was sick only a few days. Mrs. S. went out working even before he died, and worked four or five days a week. She estimates that she earned on an average $5. a week for fifty weeks. This family has "not received five cents from anybody", but the church visitor and the ladies for whom Mrs. S. worked gave her some clothing which was valued at $10. The total income from all sources was:

Man earned in 8 weeks........................	$ 80.00
Woman averaged $5.00 a week.................	250.00
Girl (12) addressing envelopes in summer.........	20.00
Boy (11) errands after school, $1.00 a week.......	50.00
Value of clothing given......................	10.00
Total..................................	$410.00

The two rooms in which they live are very untidy and crowded, though clean. The sanitary conditions of the house are very bad. It is in one of the worst "courts" of the neighborhood, where the old frame, three-story tenements are almost falling down, halls are dark, stairs rickety, floors almost worn through, and it is altogether a wretched home for such a respectable family. The rent is $7.50 a month, or $90. a year. Mrs. S. is a very neat, quiet, nice-appearing woman, and the children are pretty and well-behaved. They seem out of place in their surroundings. Greenwich House had a station of the Library and Penny Provident Bank in their rooms one night a week for the children of the "court." The boy (11) put every cent he earned into the "bank" until his mother needed it for some purpose. He saved $5. in about a month, which he gave his mother for rent. The children also saved in their stamp-books for clothing. Mrs. S. kept a careful and accurate budget for six weeks. During that time the expenditure for food averaged only $2.25 a week (during February and March). She said it was a trifle higher in summer, and also more when her husband was living (8 weeks), so that the expenditure for food for the entire year is estimated at $160., or about $3. a week. A complete statement of the income and expenditure for the six weeks (February 2 to March 14) is as follows:

Income

Mrs. S., sewing, washing, and "day's work"	$27.13
Boy (12) earned $1.00 a week	6.00
Children earned by errands	2.00
	$35.13

Expenditures

Food	$13.55
Rent for 2 months	15.00
Coal and oil	1.13
Clothing, including mending shoes	2.88
Insurance, at 35 cents a week	2.10
Medicine	.45
Total	$35.11
Balance	$ .02

The expenditure for coal and oil is low, for Mrs. S. belongs to a co-operative coal club at a settlement, where she bought a half-ton of coal for $2.88. This lasted her two months, and she paid what she could for it each week. During this time she was only able to pay $1., because of two payments of rent. The children gathered enough wood from a building which was being torn down to last all summer and winter, with the addition of two half-tons of coal and three pails a week ($.30) for about thirty weeks. The total expenditure for fuel was about $16. Mrs. S. burned more than Mrs. M. in the previous schedule, because she took in washing. The oil was bought by the gallon for 13 cents, and was estimated to cost $6. a year. With a total income of $410. for the year, the expenses were approximately as follows:

Food.	$160.00
Rent.	90.00
Clothing.	66.00
Light and fuel	22.00
Insurance.	18.20
Newspapers.	5.72
Car-fares.	5.00
Medicine and doctor.	11.00
Miscellaneous (soap, washing powder, etc.).	32.08
Total.	$410.00

This woman would not buy second-hand clothes or articles on installment nor go to the pawnshop. With the clothing which is given them, and which Mrs. S. makes over, the children always appear well dressed. The mother is always neatly dressed in black on the street, and wears wrappers at home. The clothing account for the year is:

Mrs. S., skirt, $5.00; 2 pairs shoes, $3.00; extras, 40 cents; total.	$ 8.40
Girls, 12 and 8 years, 2 dresses, $6.00; hats, $2.00..	8.00
Stockings for all (6 pairs apiece for 4) at 15 cents a pair.	3.60
Shoes: Boy (11), 4 pairs at $1.50, $6.00; mending, $1.60; 2 girls, 6 pairs each at $1.00 a pair, $12.00, mending, $4.80; boy (4), 6 pairs at 75 cents, $4.50; total for shoes.	28.90
Two suits for boys.	6.00
Underwear, etc.	1.10
Value of clothing given.	10.00
Total for clothing.	$66.00

The diet of this family of four as shown in the budget consists mostly of bread and milk and vegetables, with little meat. It is described as "wholesome, but not adequate in quantity" by the investigator. The meals are served irregularly and are mostly prepared by the 12-year-old girl. As $3. a week has been estimated as a fair average expenditure for the whole year, the week during which the food cost nearest that amount has been selected to illustrate the character and amount of the purchases.

Expenditures for food—week of March 7–14: Milk .05, bread .05, butter (1 lb.), .25, macaroni .05, tomatoes .05, cornstarch .08, green peas .04, rice .07, bread .05, milk .05, coffee .09, milk, .10, bread .10, ham .05, onions .10, 3½ lbs. sugar .16, coffee .18 (1 lb.), soup-greens .03, 1 lb. tea .40, bread .05, 1 quart potatoes .12, milk .05, pork-chops .16, bread .05, milk .05, corned beef .35, cabbage .07, cake .10, prunes .08, bread .05—total $3.08.

It will be noticed that this family had meat only twice in the week, and then pork and corned beef. As is customary, everything is bought in small amounts, because of lack of storage facilities and of more than enough money for each day's needs.

This family lives better than the previous one, and will also reach a higher standard of comfort when the two older children, who are both industrious and ambitious, are able to go to work.

SCHEDULE No. 151

FACTORY WORKER   INCOME $489.

Another illustration of an independent family on a small income is this young couple with one child, a baby of 16 months. The man was born in Italy, and has been three years in this country; the woman was born in Ireland, and

has been here 9 years.   They are 26 and 23 years old and have
been married over two years.   The circumstances of their
marriage are unusually romantic.   The woman is the cousin
of a successful Milwaukee doctor, with whom she lived when
she first came to this country.   She came from there to New
York to accept a clerical position in the Booklovers' Library.
Here she met Mr. G., who told her he was an Italian noble,
and urged her to marry him and go to live at his country
place on Lake Como.   She believed him, and when they were
married he took her to a good hotel, and told her he had
deceived her, and that he had not a cent in the world.   She
said that the revelation almost killed her and the worst of it
seemed to be that he was an Italian.   She hated him at first,
but has gradually become very fond of him, and has forgiven
him the deception.   She idolizes her baby and their home life
is very simple and attractive.   She worked at first but could
not after the baby came.   She is a plucky girl, determined to
make the best of circumstances.   The man is much inferior
to her in every way, and is an unskilled worker in a metal
novelty factory, but is gradually earning better wages.   He
earned from $8. to $9. a week during the year of investigation
(1904), with a total income of $489.   The previous year it
was only $336.   Mrs. G. earned $5. for a short sketch in the
Ladies' Home Journal on how a Western girl can succeed!
She has kept an itemized account ever since her marriage of
income and expenditures, which she turned over to the investigator.   She said that there may have been a few pennies
which she sometimes forgot to enter, but they would not
amount to a dollar in all.   The following statement is, then,
as exact an account as it is possible to get.

Income, January 1, 1904, to January 1, 1905, $489.

Expenditures

Food (about $4.00 a week).....................	$205.00
Rent, $9.00 a month..........................	108.00
Gas and coal................................	26.00
Clothing....................................	24.00
Clothing for baby...........................	8.00
Furniture...................................	45.00
Books and papers............................	7.80
Charity.....................................	3.00
Recreation in summer........................	7.00
Gifts.......................................	6.00
Loan.......................................	27.00
Kitchen needs...............................	8.00
Miscellaneous (stamps, paper, thread, pins, etc.)...	14.20
	$489.00

They really saved the $27. which they were able to lend, but the account shows that they came out even. At the end of this year they had a lodger at $7. a month, and Mr. G. was earning $9. a week, so that they were planning to save $10. a month regularly. Mrs. G. is the real "head of the family", her husband realizes her ability and superiority and turns over every cent of his wages to her. The standard of this little family is therefore influenced by her ambitions and ideals. These can best be shown by giving extracts from a letter written by her to the investigator.

"Enclosed is a list of our expenditures. Should you use same as a model for somebody to live by, I would say regarding amounts spent for food, rent, gas, or coal (we use mostly gas) that a family such as we could keep healthy and strong on amounts mentioned, by buying plain nourishing food, and can also find sunny healthy rooms, and have to be very economical with gas or coal. I think gas is best to use if possible, as in these small rooms coal makes so much dust and dirt. The other expenses depend on what a person wishes to spend. I will say, though, that I would think life not worth living if I could not have amounts expended by us. We have gotten along on $50. worth of furniture, but couldn't on less. Clothing we needed very little, and then I make and fix over my own clothes, hats, etc. Baby was not much expense to us. Mr. G.'s family sent him 1000 lire, equal to $200., just after he was born. Of course that is the baby's, though I think he would loan it to us should we need it very badly. Kitchen needs, such as soap, etc., it is impossible to do without. I think by investing in papers, a book, etc., you earn more than they cost. I should like to be able to spend more in reading matter. Church expenses differ. If you are Catholic and meet the requirements of the church, you are obliged to attend church each Sunday and pay at least ten cents. We are indifferent to church rules. Charity, I wish I had lots of money at my disposal for same. I think summer trips, outings, etc., save doctor's bills. . . . When we were married, neither had money and we started on nothing. We have got along all right, but it has been impossible to save anything until now we are beginning to save at least $10. every month, for Mr. G. earns more and works overtime occasionally."

Here is the experience of one woman at first hand, which illustrates the possibility of a family of three, with a small child, living comfortably and independently on an income, which would ordinarily be quite inadequate. It would be entirely so with a large family, or if there were the slightest waste or extravagance.

This family lives in three small rooms in an old house, where all the rooms have outside windows, and the sanitary conditions are good. The appearance of the rooms is bright and home-like, but plain. No furniture was bought until it could be paid for in cash. The pawnshop was only resorted to in the first few months after their marriage, and is hated.

The life of this family illustrates thrift and providence on a small income, but it is an exceptional case, for few women situated as was this woman have the intelligence and ability to manage as she did.

INCOME $600.–$900.

Families in this group represent more nearly the average families in this investigation. Their incomes are more typical of the working-class as a whole and the conditions under which they live more normal than in the preceding group. Four families have been selected for description out of the 81 families which belong to this class.

SCHEDULE No. 51
STABLEMAN   INCOME $600.

This household consists of father and mother, both born in Ireland, and two boys, 8 and 9 years of age. The man is a steady, temperate, unskilled laborer. Neither Mr. nor Mrs. R. have known any higher plane of living than their present surroundings; both are uneducated, but the woman especially possesses considerable native thrift and intelligence. This family is representative of the average family of this size on a fairly steady income of $12. a week, with no drink, sickness, or unusual conditions to make it abnormal. The man was out of work for six weeks in the year, but that is not unusual. The woman is neat, honest, and reliable, and trys hard "to get ahead". Mr. R. was greatly interested in the investigation, which he said would "prove it is impossible to get ahead on wages of $12. a week". For three months he had night work as stableman at $13. a week. The family has never been dependent, but while the man was out of work a sister gave them $25. as a present, and they were obliged to draw $10. from the little which they had saved in the Bank. The total income for the year was:

Mr. R.: 33 weeks at $12.00 ⎱ 13 " " 13.00 ⎰	$565.00
Drew from Bank.............................	10.00
Gift from sister..............................	25.00
Total...................................	$600.00

The estimated expenditures were as follows:

Rent: 2 mos. at $10.00, 7 mos. at $12.00, 3 mos. at $11.00.................................	$137.00
Food, from $4.00 to $7.00 a week................	277.00
Drink (pint of beer at supper daily)...............	36.40
Clothing.....................................	40.00
Light and fuel................................	52.00
Insurance from 50 to 75 cents a week............	29.25
Papers, 11 cents a week.......................	5.72
Church, 35 cents a week (for 50 weeks)..........	17.50
Man's spending-money.........................	25.00
Sundries.....................................	2.63
Total...................................	$622.50
Deficit...................................	$22.50

This deficit consisted of bills owing to the butcher and grocer amounting to $10., back insurance payments equal to $2.50, and clothing bought "on time" on which $10. was still unpaid. The rent varied because the family had moved twice in the year, looking for cheaper rent. They were never dispossessed, and always paid their rent in full before leaving. They have always lived in this neighborhood. The last rooms, for which they paid $10. a month rent, were three dark, small rooms. The light of the "parlor" at the back of the tenement was almost shut off by a large factory built close to it. The windows in the kitchen and bedroom opened on an air-shaft. The rooms, however, were very neat, lace-curtains at the windows, plush furniture, pictures of the family, carpet on the floor, and all the bric-à-brac usual in homes of this class. There was a white iron bed in the bedroom, with the customary folding-bed for the children.

The expenditure for food varied greatly. A budget kept for a week showed $7. spent for food, but Mrs. R. said they could only spend that much when the man was working steadily or when there was no rent to pay. The weeks in which semi-monthly payments of rent were made, the food allowance was cut down to about $4. a week. Whenever there was any unusual expense the food suffered. During the six weeks the man was not working they did not spend more than $4.50 a week for food. This is an illustration of a very common condition among wage-earners and is due to the fact that on the prevailing rate of unskilled wages, it is difficult if not impossible for a family to prepare for such emergencies. Mrs. R. estimated that $277. had been spent for food in the year, making these allowances, and that the average per week would be about $5.33. On the whole, the food was adequate and wholesome, and the entire family appeared to be in good condition. They had no illness during the year. Mrs. R. could not remember that she had spent a cent for medicine, not even the usual expenditure in these families for magnesia, salts, and cough mixtures.

The standard of dress is classed as "medium". They had few clothes, but took good care of them. The father had plain working-clothes, the mother always wore wrappers at home, and only had one street dress, as she never went anywhere except to church. The boys were neat and clean. Mrs. R. bought clothing "on time"—she was ashamed of it, but said the boys could not have new suits for Easter unless she did. She itemized the expenditures for clothing for the year as follows:

Man, 1 pair shoes.................................	$ 2.00
Woman, 1 pair shoes..............................	1.25
Two boys: 2 suits.................................	7.00
2 overcoats............................	11.00
4 pairs shoes at 75 cts., 4 pairs at 69 cts..	5.76
Mending shoes........................	2.80
2 pairs pants, $1.00; 4 sets underwear $1.60.............................	2.60
4 shirt-waists; 2 at 50 cts. and 2 at 30 cts.	1.60
4 caps..................................	.70
Miscellaneous.................................	5.29
Total......................................	$40.00

Mrs. R. cannot sew, and buys all their clothes ready-made of a cheap quality, but the little boys are not hard on their clothes. Her sister knits stockings for the entire family.

The expenditure for coal and gas and oil was rather high, owing to the dark rooms. Coal was bought by the bushel, and the man brought home wood free for kindling. Gas was burned in two places where they lived, and the gas-bills for nine months amounted to $11.20. In all, coal cost $37.75 (at $.25 a bushel), and oil for three months about $3.05—total $52.

This family did not spend one cent for recreation, except what the father had out of his "spending-money". This was very little, for while he was earning $12. a week his wife gave him not more than $.40 a week and often only $.25 ($.15 for tobacco and $.10 for a shave), but when he earned $13. a week (for 3 months) he kept out a dollar a week for "spending-money". His allowance for the entire year would not exceed $25. He gave all the rest to Mrs. R., who said he was a "model husband". They are very religious and go to the Catholic Church every Sunday, only missing two Sundays in the year. They pay 10 cents each for a seat, put 10 cents in the collection, and give the boys each 2 or 3 pennies for the collection, making a total of $.35 a Sunday.

They were all insured for $.50 a week, $.15 for the man, $.15 for the woman, and $.10 each for the boys, until the man's wages were raised to $13., when his wife raised his insurance policy and paid $.40 a week for him. This extra amount was more than they could afford to pay, for in those 13 weeks they dropped behind $2.50 on the insurance payments.

The only reading is the penny papers. The boys are sent to the parochial school, and the parents are very ambitious for them. Unless sickness or unemployment comes, this family will be able to make up the deficit of $22.50 on the man's wages of $13. a week, but it is very evident from a study of these expenditures that it will be impossible to save any considerable sum for the future. They have not the intelligence of Mrs. G. in Schedule No. 151, but as far as they know how are thrifty and provident.

SCHEDULE No. 20

DRAFTSMAN   INCOME $850.

This is a typical young American family of the working class, and as the income is near the average income for the entire investigation ($851.38), it has been selected for description. Mr. and Mrs. B. have been married five years and have two children, aged 4 years and 1 year. The man was born in New York, his wife in Ireland, but she was brought to this country when quite a little girl. The only source of income is from Mr. B., who is a draftsman in an architect's office and earns $15. a week. He has been with the same firm for seven years and has the confidence of his employers, for whom he also collects rents. He also has the opportunity to make a few dollars extra in drawing up plans and specifications.

This amounted to about $70. for the year, making the total income $850. The young man is a bright, capable fellow, who is likely to succeed. He never goes out evenings except with his wife, and usually brings home work from the office to do at night. Their home consists of three rooms in an "old law tenement", for which they pay $13. a month. The sanitary conditions are very bad, the bedroom is perfectly dark, with only a small window about two feet square opening into the hall. The kitchen is small, and has a small window opening on an air-shaft. The parlor has two large windows, but they are close to a factory in the rear. The rooms are very well furnished. The furniture cost over $200., bought "on time" when they were married. It was paid for in two years. The rooms are never in order, piles of clean clothes are everywhere, usually unwashed dishes are on the table, and everything is very untidy, but not dirty. Mrs. B. is pretty, bright, and ambitious, but entirely untrained and without system in her work. She is a devoted wife and mother. Their expenditure for recreation was $50. and was most carefully estimated. They went regularly once a week to the theatre all winter. This cost about $16. They also went to six or seven balls ($.50 each), as Mrs. B. is very fond of dancing. In the summer they take the children several times a week on trolley-rides in the evening, besides trips to Coney Island and Fort George. Last summer they spent two weeks at Far Rockaway, where they paid $9. for two furnished rooms and boarded themselves. In all they have a good deal of pleasure and recreation. The man belongs to no club or lodge, but intends joining the Y. M. C. A. on Twenty-third Street for gymnasium privileges, and will get his lunch there. Mr. B. gives his wife his entire earnings every week, including what he makes overtime, and she gives him $1. for lunches and $1. for spending-money. He spent this all in ways his wife knew of, and so it has been divided into different expenditures: drink, books, papers, etc.

The total expenditures for the year, with an income of $850., were as follows:

Food, including lunch-money, $7.00 a week.......	$364.00
Rent, $13.00 a month..........................	156.00
Clothing......................................	65.00
Light and fuel................................	52.60
Insurance.....................................	62.40
Recreation....................................	50.00
Books and papers.............................	18.00
Drink, 30 cents a week, not more than..........	20.00
Medical attendance, including dentist, $30.00.	45.00
Sundries (tobacco, shaving, etc.)................	10.00
Total......................................	$843.00
Surplus....................................	7.00
	$850.00

Mrs. B. had saved $37., but $30. had to be drawn out of the Bank for the dentist's bill, so that only $7. was saved at the end of the year. They are anxious to save, but at the same time have a high standard and wish to live well, and so have only $47. in the savings-bank. They live very comfortably and have many pleasures in life. Mrs. B. kept a budget of her household expenses for four weeks.

The total expenses for each week were as follows (income being $15. a week):

First week....................................	$11.98
Second week..................................	9.70
Third week...................................	10.30
Fourth week..................................	9.40
Total......................................	$41.38
Average per week...........................	10.35

This includes rent, food, light and fuel, sundries, and nothing else, not even Mr. B.'s allowance for lunches and spending-money. The food expense averaged $6. a week, with lunch-money it was $7., and they lived extremely well for a family of four. The expenditure for meat was very high, almost one third of the total amount. They had plenty of vegetables, and more fruit and pastry than most families of their class. A sample week's expenditure for food is as follows:

Saturday evening, Jan. 23d: 1 lb. butter .29, 1 lb. coffee .25, 3½ lbs. sugar .18, ½ lb. tea .25, 1 qt. potatoes, .10, 1 loaf bread .05, vegetables .12, meat .75, cake .20, fruit .10, 1 qt. milk .05, oatmeal 10; total $2.44

Sunday, Jan. 24th: Bread .05, milk .05, biscuits .10. . .20

Monday, Jan 25th: Milk .05, rolls .05, jam .10, bread .05. 25

Tuesday, Jan. 26th: Milk .05, bread .05, meat .25, vegetables .15, pie .10. 60

Wednesday, Jan. 27: Bread .05, milk .05, meat .25, vegetables .18, rolls .05, 1 lb. butter .29. 87

Thursday, Jan. 28th: Milk .05, bread .05, meat .25, vegetables .18, rolls .05. 58

Friday, Jan. 29th: Milk .05, bread .10, fish .22, 4 eggs .14, vegetables .15. 66

Saturday morning, Jan. 30th: Milk .05, bread .05, rolls .05, meat .30. 45

Mr. B., lunch-money for week. 1.00

Total for food. $7.05

The expenditures for light and fuel are higher than the average. Gas was burned extravagantly, and the bills averaged $2.20 a month for six months in winter, and $1. a month in summer, when it was used for cooking. It cost approximately $19.10 a year, coal $29., wood for kindling at .02 a bundle about $4.50. Coal was bought by the 100-lb. bag at .40 a bag.

There were no expenditures for union, church, gifts or loans, furniture, or car-fares. The father and mother were well-dressed, but the children were too small to need much. Mrs. B. is unable to sew and spends more than is necessary,

but she buys clothes of good quality and in good taste. Mr.
B. is fond of reading the daily papers and the cheaper magazines, and spends .30 to .35 a week for them. The insurance
is high because they are also paying the insurance for the
man's mother—.50 a week. Mr. B's. insurance is .30 a week,
Mrs. B's., .20, and .20 for the children—total $1.20 a week
or $62.40 a year.

The standard of living of this family may be called high,
and it is typical of that of many young couples of this class—
extravagant in some ways and provident in others, with a
fair degree of comfort and prosperity, but very little provision
made for the future.

SCHEDULE No. 84

HARNESS-CLEANER   INCOME $870.

An example of good management with a large family on a
moderate income is presented by this case. The B. family in
the preceding schedule were prosperous and extravagant on a
smaller income, because there were only four in the family.
This family of ten on a larger income had a hard struggle to
make ends meet and keep out of debt, but they succeeded.
Mr. and Mrs. H. were both born in Ireland, but have been in
this country eighteen and sixteen years respectively. They
were married about fourteen years ago and have 8 children,
whose ages range from 13 years to 6 months. They live
in four rooms, the whole top floor (third floor) of a rear house.
This house is in unusually good condition, the halls and stairs
are clean and are covered with oilcloth. Even the yard is
clean. The rooms are neat, rather bare, but light and airy,
and all have outside windows. There is a kitchen, parlor
(with a folding-bed and an old velvet carpet on the floor, which
was evidently given to them), and two bedrooms. There are
a few good pieces of furniture, probably bought second-hand,
and no senseless pieces of bric-à-brac. The family have lived

here for five years, and before that lived on the street in which
Greenwich House is now located, until, as Mrs. H. said, "we
could stand it no longer". It was evidently too noisy and
crowded for them. The rent of these four rooms is $13. a
month. The man is a harness-cleaner and has worked in one
stable for six years, and did not lose a day's work during the
year of the investigation. He earned $14. a week, and for
fifty weeks earned a dollar a week extra by acting as watchman on Sunday nights. The boy (13) delivered laundry after
school and earned $2. a week. Mr. H. is steady, sober, and
intelligent, and was much interested in the purpose of the
investigation. Mrs. H. is a most attractive Irishwoman,
bright, capable, neat, and a splendid manager with so large a
family. The children are all pretty, clean, and well-behaved.
She seems to be a devoted wife and mother.

The income and expenditures for the year were as follows:

Income

Man, 52 weeks at $14.00.	$728.00
Man, extra work.	50.00
Boy (13), $2.00 a week for 46 weeks.	92.00
Total.	$870.00

Expenditures

Rent.	$156.00
Food at $8.50 a week.	442.00
Clothing.	69.80
Light and fuel.	57.20
Recreation.	5.00
Insurance.	58.24
Papers.	5.72
Car-fares.	2.00
Doctor and medicine.	11.50
Man, spending-money.	18.20
Stove $14.00, and house furnishings $10.00.	24.00
Church.	8.00
Sundries (soap and washing materials, eye-glasses, etc.).	12.34
Total.	$870.00

Mrs. H. kept a household budget for three weeks, during which time their diet seemed to consist mostly of bread, milk, potatoes, and oatmeal. The food was carefully chosen for its wholesomeness, but it is doubtful whether it was adequate in quantity for a family of that size. Mrs. H. estimated that their expenditure for food averaged about $8.50 a week. Mr. H. came home for his lunch, so there was no additional lunch-money. The meals were served regularly, but it was impossible for all the family to sit at the kitchen-table at once. The usual weekly expenditure for food was as follows:

Milk, 2 bottles a day..........................	$1.12
Eggs, .50 worth a week........................	.50
Three cans of condensed milk for tea ("and to spread on bread when the children can have no butter").	.27
One quart of potatoes a day at .10 a quart........	.70
Vegetables, .10 a day..........................	.70
Bread, 5 loaves at .05=.25 a day................	1.75
(.08 loaves are bought when they are a day old for .05)	
One and one-half pounds of butter at .30 a pound....	.45
Jam, .05 a day, except on Sunday................	.30
One-half pound of tea, no coffee	.20
One can of Baker's cocoa.......................	.18
7 lbs. of sugar at .20 for 3½ lbs...................	.40
Meat, .25 a day................................	1.75
Sundries......................................	.18
Total.	$8.50

This is certainly a model distribution of food for so large a family on such a small income. Mrs. H. was one of the few women in the neighborhood who felt it desirable to buy bottled milk at 8 cents a quart, rather than in bulk at 5 cents a quart.

The expenditure for clothing was itemized. It came to $69.80, including shoes for them all. This was only $4.80 higher than the B. family's expenditures for 4 persons. Mrs. H. made all the children's clothes and the materials cost very little—they were cheap but warm. She and her husband had practically nothing new. The clothing was selected with the same care and intelligence as the food, and a small expenditure was made to go very far. The man was very neat, in a white shirt and black clothes which showed careful brushing, the woman wore a shirt-waist dress in the house, instead of the inevitable wrapper. All the children were very plainly dressed, but neat and clean. A little clothing had been given them by the kindergarten teacher, but its value was too small to be estimated.

The expenditure for light and fuel was $57.20. Mrs. H. did not like to have the children gather wood on the street. Coal was bought by the bushel, and a gallon of oil a week was burned all year. The cost of coal and wood was carefully estimated at $50. and oil $7.20.

They had no recreations that cost anything, except that the two boys (13 and 12 years) were given $.25 a week for car-fares all summer to play ball every Sunday afternoon. The mother is very anxious to give them this pleasure, as she says they ought to have some, and that this only costs about $5. a year. In the summer the kindergarten teacher sent Mrs. H. and some of the children to the country for two weeks, and Mr. H. took his vacation then and kept house for the rest of the family. He urges her to go again this year. There seems to be a very attractive home life and a kindly spirit in the family. They are good Catholics, but "could only give $8. to the church", which was far out of proportion to their means in comparison with what is given by most families.

The father, mother, and 7 of the children were insured, making a total of $1.12 a week or $58.24 a year. The man gives all his earnings to his wife and she gives him $.35 a week for spending-money—$.20 for 2 shaves and $.15 for 3 packages of tobacco. He does not drink, and they never have beer in the house. The children were all well during the year, but about $10. was spent for household medicines, such as salts, magnesia, cough medicines, and Castoria for the baby. They had a private physician once which cost $1.50. When the woman was confined the last time, she went to Sloane Maternity Hospital, and her sickness was no expense to the family.

Here, then, is an illustration of a large family living on an average workingman's earnings, where, with the most careful management, they are just able to make ends meet and keep out of debt, but have not been able to save a cent. If the man should be taken ill or lose his employment, they would be forced to become dependent upon charity, which they have so far been able to prevent.

SCHEDULE No. 12

FIREMAN (STOKER)   INCOME $895.

In striking contrast to the careful management in the preceding family is the improvidence and shiftlessness of this family. Mr. and Mrs. G. were also born in Ireland and married in New York. There were 6 children from 2 to 12 years old. This family's income was influenced by exceptional circumstances, i.e., the death of the oldest boy and the addition of an insurance policy of $240. to the income; but the expenses of the funeral also swelled the family expenditures. The man is a steady worker, but lost eight weeks because of illness. He earns $12. a week. The total income of this family from various sources was:

From man's wages, $12.00 for 44 weeks	$528.00
From legacy of sister in Ireland	100.00
From insurance on boy who died	240.00
From bank (from former savings)	20.00
Boy (12) earned in summer	7.00
Total	$895.00

This family of eight lived in 3 rooms in a typical old tenement. The bedroom was dark, and there was no window in the kitchen except the glass partition between it and the "parlor", which was at the rear of the house. This one room was bright and sunny. The appearance of the rooms was most forlorn, very little furniture, no carpet nor curtains, bare floors always greasy and unswept, with crumbs on the floor, dirty dishes and food always on the kitchen-table, dirty clothes everywhere, and everything untidy and dirty. The investigator went in to see Mrs. G. many times, but she never found her cleaning the house. She was always playing with the children or chatting with a neighbor. She is a pleasant, good-natured Irishwoman, with a winning manner and smile, but is very slovenly and untidy herself, and her children are as ragged and dirty as any in the neighborhood. Mrs. G. is utterly lacking in method or system, but everybody likes her, and she is a most kindly, helpful neighbor. She usually has some children with her, whom she is "keeping for a neighbor". The man is steady and sober and has worked in the same office building for 10 years. He has stomach trouble and is sick quite frequently. The standard and plane of living in this family are both low and have probably never been any higher. Mrs. G. is always glad to help any one, and was very willing to keep a budget for the investigator for six weeks. This was kept very carefully and exactly, no expenditure was too small to be remembered. She evidently preferred doing this to cleaning her house! A typical week's expenses are taken from this note-book and given verbatim (with Mrs. G.'s spelling).

SUNDAY

Meat.	$1.05
Bread.	.20
Horseredish.	.05
Rice.	.08
Oranges.	.25
Vegetables.	.06
Milk.	.15
Butter.	.25
Potatoes.	.10
Vinegar.	.02
Paper.	.05
Tobacco.	.05
Carfair.	.25
Church money.	.25
	$2.81

MONDAY

Carfair.	$ .25
Coffee.	.25
Tea.	.16
Sugar.	.18
Bread.	.15
Milk.	.15
Eggs.	.12
Tobacco.	.05
Paper.	.01
Onnions.	.05
Potatoes.	.10
Coal.	.25
Rent.	4.00
Insurance.	.85
	$6.57

TUESDAY

Bread.	$ .15
Milk.	.15
Carfair.	.25
Potatoes.	.10
Tomatoes.	.08
Oatenmeal.	.14
Paper.	.01
Tobacco.	.05
Meat.	.20
Shoes (mending).	.30
Total.	$1.43

WEDNESDAY

Carfair.	$ .25
Bread.	.15
Milk.	.15
Potatoes.	.10
Paper.	.01
Gas.	.25
Coal.	.25
Eggs.	.14
Meat.	.29
Tobacco.	.05
Total.	$1.64

THURSDAY

Carfair.	$ .05
Oranges.	.05
Potatoes.	.10
Milk.	.15
Meat.	.25
Paper.	.01
Bread.	.15
Tomatoes.	.08
Tobacco.	.05
Eggs.	.08
Butter.	.13
Slate.	.05
Total.	$1.35

FRIDAY

Fish.	$ .15
Bread.	.15
Milk.	.15
Tobacco.	.05
Eggs.	.08
Paper.	.01
Potatoes.	.10
Rice.	.08
Carfair.	.25
Total.	$1.02

SATURDAY.

Meat.	$ .29
Potatoes.	.13
Bread.	.15
Tobacco.	.05
Paper.	.01
Milk.	.15
Eggs.	.08
Onnions.	.05
Shoes (mending).	.30
Carfair.	.25
Total.	$1.46

TOTAL FOR WEEK

Food.	$8.47
Coal and gas.	.75
Carfair.	.85
Tobacco.	.35
Church.	.25
Papers.	.11
Rent.	$4.00
Insurance.	.85
Mending shoes.	.60
Slate.	.05
Total.	$16.28

It will be seen that they had meat almost every day, and an unusual amount of eggs. There seems to be enough food bought, but a great deal of waste in cooking. The meals are served very irregularly, usually "piecemeal".

The expenditure for car-fare, $.25 a day, included the man's lunch-money, $.15 a day, which has been added to the food expense. The average expenditure for these six weeks was $15.60 a week, and the average cost of food $8.50. The man's income was only $12. a week. Mrs. G. spent at least $15. a week all winter, because she had the balance left from her insurance ($153.40) and the $100. from her sister to draw from, but when this was used up she continued to spend at this rate, and was already $46. in debt, with no prospect of any larger income than $12. a week. When asked what she was going to do when she couldn't borrow any more, she merely smiled and said she didn't know! The thought of the future didn't seem to trouble her in the least.

The total estimated expenditures for the year were as follows:

Food, $9.40 a week (including lunch-money)......	$481.60
Rent, $9.00 a month...........................	108.00
Clothing....................................	61.90
Light and fuel..............................	33.00
Insurance...................................	44.20
Recreation..................................	1.00
Union.......................................	6.00
Drink.......................................	31.50
Church......................................	13.00
Papers......................................	5.40
Car-fares...................................	24.00
Medical attendance..........................	26.80
Man, spending-money.........................	18.00
Funeral of boy..............................	86.60
Total...................................	$941.00
Deficit..................................	46.00

The standard for clothing was very low, though almost as much was spent for this family of eight as for the family of ten in the preceding schedule. It affords a striking illustration of the difference which the mother's ability to make the clothes of the family makes in their appearance. Mrs. G. bought everything ready-made, of a cheap quality, and no care was taken of their clothes when they had them. The man was fairly well dressed, but the mother and children were always ragged and dirty and half-clothed. Mrs. G.'s itemized account of the clothing bought within the year follows:

Expense of Clothing for Year

Mr. G. : Suit $11.50, 2 flannel working shirts $5.00, 2 outing shirts $1.00, summer shirts .50, 2 ties .50, hat $1.25, 4 pairs shoes $5.00, 2 pairs shoes $3.00, wool for socks $1.00. . . . . $28.75

Mrs. G.: Cape $3.00, hat $1.50, 1 pair shoes $1.25, 2 pairs stockings .20, 2 shirt-waists .50. . . . .   6.45

Boy (12) (lived 8½ months in year): Suit $2.50, suit $2.00, 3 pairs shoes $3.00, underwear .50, caps .20, 4 pairs stockings .40, 2 ties .30. . . . .   8.90

Boy (10): Suit $1.50, 2 pairs pants .20, 2 pairs shoes $2.00, 2 caps .20, underwear .75, 2 waists .50, wool for 2 pairs stockings .70. . . . .   5.85

Girl (8): Dress $1.00, 2 aprons .50, 3 pairs stockings .30, underwear .60, hat .49, 2 pairs shoes $2.35. . .   5.24

Girl (6): Dress $1.00, 2 pairs stockings .20, hat .25, coat $1.50. . . . .   3.93

Girls (4 and 2): Dress $1.00, 2 dresses at .25 = .50, apron .10, 2 pairs shoes .98, 2 pairs stockings .20.   2.78

Total. $61.90

It will be seen that, with the exception of Mr. G. and the oldest boy, they all had a minimum of clothing. It was all of the cheapest quality and none was given them. A few of the articles were bought at a clothing sale at Greenwich

House, and were of a better quality. Mrs. G. knits stockings for part of the family.

The man had a pint of beer for supper every day, but denied himself this during Lent, so that the expense for beer does not appear in the budget which was kept during Lent. The family have absolutely no recreation which is any expense, except that Mr. G. goes annually to the Firemen's Ball (costing $1.), but his wife does not go with him. She had only been to church a few times and to the settlement occasionally during the entire year. The younger children were sent to the country in a Fresh Air party during the summer. Mr. G. and the older children go regularly to church and pay .25 a week for seats and the collection. His only spending-money is .05 a day for tobacco. The insurance costs .85 a week for the entire family. When the boy (12) died, they received $240. insurance. They had quite an elaborate funeral, with a hearse and two carriages and some beautiful flowers, which cost in all $86.60, and was paid for at once. Mrs. G. does not buy clothing " on time ", but has so bought furniture in the past. She said that she had not gone to the pawnshop during this year. If so, it was because they had nothing worth pawning. Five years ago, when the man was out of work, she pawned her wedding-ring and has not been able to redeem it since!

This family is on the edge of dependence all the time, though they have never yet been dependent on organized charity, but, unless they can struggle along by borrowing right and left or are aided by gifts from relatives until the children are old enough to work, they will surely become dependent. Their standard of living is very low and is typical of a shiftless and improvident class,—the standard of the average workingman's family with such an income being much higher.

INCOME $900. TO $1200.

There were 47 families studied whose incomes were between $900. and $1200. Two have been chosen for description, one illustrating a high standard of living and the other, although with a larger income, a standard kept down by the intemperance of the father.

SCHEDULE No. 22

TRUCKMAN INCOME $970.

The acquaintance of the investigator with this family covered several years. The household consisted of the man, his wife and four children, and a nephew aged 9, who had been adopted. The children's ages were from 3 to 15 years during the period of investigation. Both Mr. and Mrs. H. were native-born Americans, whose families had been in this country for several generations. They occupied a floor consisting of 5 rooms in an old house. The rent was $15. a month, but was later raised to $16. The house was in very good condition. The parlor and kitchen were large bright rooms with two windows each. The bedrooms were small. Mrs. H. rented one of them for six weeks at $1.50 a week. The rooms were very neat and furnished tastefully. The furniture was good and substantial, nothing gaudy or showy. Mrs. H. was accustomed to a much higher standard of living than she has had since her marriage. Her mother is very prosperous, and owns several greenhouses in New Jersey, and a married sister is in very comfortable circumstances. They help the family a great deal. In fact, it would be impossible for this family to maintain its high plane of living were it not for much help from relatives. It affords an excellent illustration of a family which is not dependent on outside sources, because of assistance given by relatives. Mrs. H.'s mother and sister buy all of her clothes and dress the little girl, and Mr. H.'s brother gives him his clothes. The value of this clothing was carefully estimated by Mrs. H. at $50. a year. Mrs. H.'s mother also gives her $5. a month toward the rent, and the money for the insurance, doctor and medicine, recreation for herself and children, etc. These gifts and special gifts at Christmas amounted to $188. in the year. With all this outside assistance, Mr. H. quite naturally did not feel full responsibility for supporting his family. He was a truckman and earned $12. a week, out of which he regularly kept $2. which was spent for drink. The family were not pauperized, unless it was the man, for Mrs. H. would have starved rather than receive aid from any one outside her family.

The total income was as follows:

Man, $12.00 a week for 44 weeks................	$528.00
Boy (15), $3.00 a week........................	156.00
Lodger, 6 weeks at $1.50......................	9.00
Board for nephew, $3.00 a week for 13 weeks......	39.00
(The boy was with them all year, but his father only gave $39.00 toward his support.)	
Gifts from mother and sister in money..........	188.00
Gifts from relatives in clothing.................	50.00
Total....................................	$970.00

Mrs. H. kept a budget of her household expenses for four weeks. The food averaged $7. a week, including lunch-money for the man. The food was very wholesome and adequate for the family of seven on that amount, because Mrs. H. was an exceptionally good manager and cook. Her mother sent them fresh eggs, and a brother who was a baker sent bread every day. They had meat once a day, and always soup and cocoa for the children. The meals were served regularly at a dining-room table in the kitchen, with a white table-cloth on it. Mrs. H. watched grocery sales closely and bought very carefully. She always bought all her dry groceries for the week on Saturday night, from \$4. to \$5. worth. She bought broken crackers at a cracker factory— 4 lbs. for \$.25. This is a sample of her thrift.

The estimated expenditures for the year were:

Food, \$7.00 a week	\$364.00
Rent, \$15.00 a month	180.00
Light and fuel	33.44
Clothing	125.00
Insurance, .65 a week	33.80
Union dues	6.00
Papers, .16 a week	8.32
Recreation	14.00
Drink for man, \$2.00 a week while working	88.00
Gifts at Christmas	10.00
Furniture	13.50
Car-fares	10.00
Medical attendance	22.00
"Spending-money", man \$13.00, boy \$13.00	26.00
Sundries	5.94
Total	\$940.00
Surplus	30.00
	\$970.00

For ten months the woman was just able to make ends meet, but when she received board for the nephew, she was able to save and had put \$30. in the Bank in the other two months. The expenditure for light and fuel was very moderate, for the man brought home on his truck all the wood they needed, and they used it almost entirely in summer. Coal was bought by the ton as being more economical, one ton lasted from March 1st to September 15th, all spring and summer, with the wood. For three months she could not afford to buy it by the ton, and bought about 3 bushels a week at 25 cents a bushel, then she bought one ton which lasted from December 15th to March 1st. Total cost of coal \$20. There was no gas in the house, they burned oil for light, about a gallon a week.   All summer she burned about 3 gallons a week in an oil-range—total for oil, $13.44.

The expenditure for clothing, $125., included the value of clothes given them.   Mrs. H. estimated that if they had bought these clothes, or an inferior quality to take their place, they would have cost at least $50., which was therefore their value to her.   She watches sales at department stores and buys very carefully and wisely.   She makes almost all the children's clothes out of remnants of goods.   The children are very neatly and attractively dressed.   She buys the boys each two suits a year.   She belongs to a Friendly Society connected with a church where she can buy good second-hand clothing very cheaply.   She once paid $.50 and $1. for suits of clothes for the little boys, and bought her husband an overcoat for $.50.   She never buys furniture or clothing "on time" nor goes to the pawnshop.   The cost of the clothing for her three boys for the year was as follows:

6 new suits for 3 boys..........................	$18.00
Shoes at $1.25 and $1.50 a pair, with mending....	38.90
Clothes at Christmas (pants and flannel waists). . .	10.00
2 shirt-waists apiece at .20 each (material)........	3.60
Underwear, 2 sets each at .75 a set..............	4.50
Total.	$75.00
Clothing given man, woman, and little girl.	50.00
Total.	$125.00

The little nephew's father clothed him, making him no expense to the family for clothing.

Their recreation consisted of trips to the cemetery—the mother went regularly every week all summer and took several children with her, costing her $1. a trip.   The oldest boy (15) saved his allowance for spending-money (25 cents a week) for a trip in the summer.   He is a fine manly little fellow.   All the children are bright and interesting.   The man was a kind father, but spent too much on drink. In addition to the $2. which he spent each week for drink, his wife had to give him car-fare, shaving-money, union dues, and lunch-money. His "spending-money" (25 cents a week) was for shaving.

The standard of this family was dominated by the mother's influence, and their home and home-life was very comfortable and pleasant on this income, because of her management. A year after this study was made the family were much more prosperous. The man's wages had been raised to $15. a week and he had steady work, and the boy (16) was earning $5. a week. Their prospects seemed much brighter than ever before, when the father was suddenly killed by a street-car, and the family had to fall back again on their relatives for assistance.

SCHEDULE No. 9

GLASSWORKER   INCOME $1040.

One of the most interesting families in the investigation, because of the personality of the wife, is this Irish family. There are eight in the family, including 6 children under 16 years. Mr. K. is a glassworker. He has been with the same firm for eighteen years and "has never lost a day through drink", a fact of which his wife is very proud. Nevertheless it is drink that keeps them down. The man is very ugly and exacting, and his wife is his slave. He earns $14. a week (perhaps more which his wife does not know about) and keeps $2. out of the wages every week for "spending-money", "which means drink and shaving", his wife says. Mrs. K. also buys him two pints of beer every night for his supper (.20) and occasionally some whiskey, making an expenditure for drink of at least $3. a week for him. His wife goes to the saloon to buy his beer and whiskey for him, for she says he drinks less than if he

went to the saloon himself. She does not drink herself
nor allow the children to touch it. The whole family are
afraid of the father, and he is very brutal when he has been
drinking. Mrs. K. is the janitor of the tenement in which
they live, and they have three rooms on the ground floor,
which they are given rent-free for her services. She works
like a slave, and is wiry and nervous. She appears to be
the hardest-working woman in the neighborhood. Their
rooms are small, and only the front room is light, the bedroom is absolutely dark, and the kitchen always has a lamp
burning. There is very little furniture, but the rooms are
as neat as possible with so many children. The kitchen
is clean. Mrs. K. is always scrubbing and cleaning. She
is a good cook and gives the children nourishing food,
and her husband demands the best of everything. The
children are fat with red cheeks, and look like country
children. The mother is so high-strung, nervous, and over-
worked that she has no control over her children. Her only
method of punishing them is to beat them, or else, as she
expressed it, "give them the full content of me tongue",
which she can do with true Irish skill. She is devoted to
them and very ambitious for them. She "lived with the
best families" before she was married, and is very anxious
that the children should have every advantage she can
give them. She tried hard to keep her boys in school, but
they would not go. Peter was in the Truant School for six
weeks, and Mrs. K. gave two boys ten cents one day to take
Jimmie to school, which they proceeded to do, in spite of
his kicks and screams, much to the amusement of the entire
neighborhood. Mrs. K. realizes her lack of control over the
children and says, "Mr. K. and the children are too much
for me". She is anxious to have the little girls take music-
lessons, and one of them is now doing so, practicing on a

neighbor's piano, with no immediate prospect of their being able to buy a piano of their own even "on time". Mrs. K. is a most interesting and attractive personality. She is full of keen Irish witticisms and has much native intelligence. The total income and expenditures of this family were as follows:

Income

Man, 51½ weeks at $14.00 (3 holidays deducted)..	$721.00
Woman, for janitor's services, rent-free.........	132.00
Boy (15), 22 weeks at $3.50, 25 weeks at $4.00...	177.00
	$1030.00
Gift from landlord at Christmas................	10.00
Total...............................	$1040.00

Expenditures

Food, $10.00 a week, including lunch-money.....	$520.00
Rent.....................................	132.00
Clothing..................................	85.00
Light and fuel.............................	48.50
Insurance, .60 a week........................	31.20
Papers, .11 a week..........................	5.72
Union dues.................................	6.00
Drink for man, $3.00 a week..................	156.00
Medical attendance..........................	27.00
Church.....................................	13.00
Recreation for father and oldest boy...........	10.00
Sundries...................................	5.58
Total...............................	$1040.00

Mrs. K. had $9. in a Penny Provident bank-book, but she owed neighbors that amount, so that her accounts just balanced. She tries hard to get ahead, and she is a good manager, but she says that sickness and drink keep her back. She is constantly getting into debt, and then paying back little by little. She is very honest and methodical and never forgets a debt.

Their food is abundant and nourishing. They have plenty

of good meat, soup for the children with macaroni and rice, home-made bread, potatoes and some vegetable every day. Mrs. K. buys ends of meat at a wholesale butcher's and gets it much cheaper that way. They are all very hearty eaters. Mr. K. takes 35 to 40 cents a day for lunch-money, which is very unusual, but "he likes a good dinner" (the customary amount is 15 cents), and the boy has 10 to 15 cents a day for his, making 50 cents a day which must come out of the food allowance. The mother and children must sometimes have a very cheap lunch. One day they had soup which cost just 6 cents, 4 cents for macaroni, 1 cent for an onion, and 1 cent for a piece of salt pork. It smelled and tasted very good and appetizing. A couple of pages from the budget will give a fair idea of the usual daily expenses in this family, not including rent, clothing, nor insurance.

FEBRUARY 15		FEBRUARY 16		FEBRUARY 18	
Bread	.10	Milk	.10	Meat	.45
Milk	.10	Bread	.30	Coal	.10
Steak	.10	Lunch-money	.40	Bread	.10
Lunch-money	.35	Steak	.10	Candy	.05
Coal	.10	Milk	.05	Beans	.10
Bread	.20	Matches	.01	Milk	.20
Steak	.25			Fish	.25
Tea	.30			Bread	.20
Coffee	.25			Lunch-money	.45
Meat	1.00			Coal	.10
Sugar (7 lbs.)	.45			Milk	.10
Coal	.15			Beer	.25
Beer	.25			Potatoes	.20
				Cake	.20

Mrs. K. was not baking bread at this time. She usually bakes fine bread, which is quite unusual in this neighborhood.

The expenditures for light and fuel were the usual amount. Gas was burned by the quarter-metre, coal by the ton if possible, if not, then by the bushel, and wood was free from the street.

The standard of dress is fair; the father has very good clothes, and also the oldest boy, the mother has nothing but wrappers, and the children have very little, but are usually clean. Mrs. K. will lend her's or the children's clothes to neighbors at any time. She is almost the only woman in this investigation who admitted buying second-hand clothes from Jews. She says the material is better than could be bought new for the same money. The item-ized account for clothing shows that Mr. K.'s clothes cost $15. (at the end of the previous year he had bought a suit and overcoat for $20.), including 1 pair of shoes $3., blue flannel shirt $2., and underwear $4. Mrs. K.'s cost $7., including 2 wrappers $2., 2 pairs shoes $2., and 2 waists $1. The clothing for the six children cost $63. Everything was bought ready-made, as Mrs. K. had no time for sewing.

They have had considerable sickness, the usual children's diseases, and always have a private physician. During the year one child had pneumonia and the doctor's bill was $15., medicines for the entire year amounted to about $12. None of the family have any recreation except the father and oldest boy. Mrs. K. usually gives the latter 15 to 40 cents on Sunday for a ball-game, etc. She went on a day's outing with a Fresh Air party and said it was the first time she had been anywhere for seven years! Mrs. K. never goes to church, but sends the older children with 25 cents every Sunday. Five years ago, when the man's work was slack, they ran into debt about $60., but were not depend-ent on charity, and this has all been paid back. She was very emphatic that she never went to the pawnshop, as she hated the system.

It is greatly to be hoped that this family will respond to

the mother's ambition for them—at present they are a happy, high-spirited lot, content to live on a much lower level in every respect than the mother desires for them.

INCOME $1200. AND OVER

These families are the prosperous families of the neighborhood. Twenty-nine had incomes ranging from $1200. to $2556. In most instances their standard of life is higher than that of families of smaller income, but this is not always so. They are as typical of a class in the neighborhood as are the poorest families. Only two had incomes over $2000. Two large families with incomes of $1500., one Italian and the other Irish, have been selected as illustrations of this class; and also one of smaller size.

SCHEDULE No. 2

OYSTER-SELECTOR   INCOME $1500.

This is an interesting family, because of its size and its extravagance. Mr. B. is an Irish-American who is much older than his wife. The latter is a fine-looking woman, who says she will look well and dress well even if she has seven children, and she does. She is the second wife and was only 15 when she was married. They have seven children, 5 boys and 2 girls —the oldest daughter is 20 years old, the youngest child is a boy 3 years old. They have 4 rooms on the top floor of an old tenement-house. The rooms extend from the front to the back of the house. The two middle rooms are bedrooms without windows, but the circulation of air through them is good. They pay only $14. a month rent and have lived there three years. They have lived twenty years in the neighborhood. The rooms are neat and clean and well furnished. The parlor is gaudy, but comfortable. Mrs. B. is very anxious that her daughters shall have an attractive home to bring their friends to. The man's occupation is "selecting" or "sorting" oysters. He has been at it for thirty years. In his best days his wife claims he could make as high as $200. a week, before there were so many oyster-markets. The work is very irregular. He only works steadily for five months—September to February. The rest of the year he does odd jobs, such as watchman, etc., and part of that time he can work from two to five days a week as an oyster "counter" at $3. a day. During the busy season his earnings are surprising, as high as $75. a week for a few weeks. He does not turn over all his wages to his wife, but most of them. He is a hard drinker, but this does not seem to interfere with his ability to earn money. The amount he spent for drink could not be estimated, because it is not included in the income which Mrs. B. receives. She says he sometimes spends from $2. to $3. a day when he is "drinking hard". A careful estimate of the "household income" is as follows:

Man: September 1st to February 1st (busy season)	$780.00
" 7 months averages 3 days a week at $3.00 a day.	270.00
Daughter (20), $5.00 a week for 50 weeks.	250.00
Boy (15), $4.00 a week for 50 weeks.	200.00
Total.	$1500.00

This is the "household income" which passes through the mother's hands. The man may earn more which he does not bring home. Mrs. B. is a good manager in that, while her husband is earning "big money", she buys all the clothing they need for the year; but she also buys extravagantly, because she has so much money on hand at once, and spends every cent she has. Some of the expenditures for the year are startling in comparison with what the average family spends.

Expenditures

Food, $10.00 a week.	$520.00
Rent, $14.00 a month.	168.00
Clothing.	560.00
Light and fuel.	55.00
Insurance, $2.05 a week.	106.60
Recreation.	10.00
Christmas gifts.	15.00
Papers, .11 a week.	5.72
Furniture.	33.00
Car-fares.	25.00
Medical attendance.	18.00
Sundries.	3.68
Total.	$1520.00

Mrs. B. was in debt $20. (or more, she could not remember just how much!), because the year of investigation ended the first of August and in a month her husband's busy season would commence and she would be able to pay it back. She does not have any idea of saving, her only desire is not to get more in debt than can be paid when her husband is working steadily again.

Mrs. B. says she *ought* to have $2. a day for food for her family of nine (and this was the testimony of all women with large families), and she did spend this much during the short busy season, but in the summer had to spend considerably less, so that she thought $10. a week for the entire year was a fair average. She kept a budget of her expenditure for food for one week in May and it amounted to $10.55. She used 4 lbs. butter $1., 3 lbs. coffee .93, 1 lb. tea .40, 14 lbs. sugar .68, a week; and 4 loaves of bread .32, 2 quarts of potatoes .24, 2 quarts of milk .10, and meat .35, a day. The meat for Sunday is usually $1.50. In addition to this they generally have one vegetable for dinner, but there is little variety in their diet. The food seems wholesome and sufficient, but monotonous. The meals are served regularly at the kitchen-table, which is covered with a white oilcloth, but there is not room for all the family to sit at the table at once.

They are the most extravagant family in the neighborhood in the amount spent for clothes. A family that spends $560. for clothing and useless finery, and is content to live in rooms for which they pay only $14. a month, presents an unusual and interesting standard of living. Neither Mrs. B. nor her daughter can sew; everything is bought ready-made or is made by a dressmaker. Mrs. B. likes housework, but not sewing. Every article in the total amount of $560. was itemized by Mrs. B., who has an accurate memory. It is too long a list to give in detail, but the prices of the articles will give an idea of the standard in buying. Mrs. B. bought a coat for herself for which she paid $18.50, a black skirt for $10.50, a velvet skirt for $14., a waist for $5., a summer silk which cost $7.25 (including making), three hats costing $4. to $5. each, 3 pairs of shoes at $3.50 a pair, etc. Her expenditures for herself amounted to over $104. She always appears exceedingly well dressed on the street: no one would imagine that her home was on —— Street. The man's clothing was much cheaper in quality and price. He had one suit which cost $9., flannel underwear $7., 2 flannel working shirts $5., 2 white shirts $1., 4 pairs shoes (at $2.50) $10.,—his clothing in all (which his wife bought) did not amount to $35. The oldest daughter (20) dressed in about the same style as her mother; some of the expenditures for her were: winter suit $15, coat $9.98, dress skirt $4.50, summer suit $14., silk waist $4., summer-silk dress $6.35, 3 hats $7., 4 pairs shoes $10., etc.—almost $100. in all. The clothing for the five boys, big and little, was not exceptional; they were well dressed on Sundays, but were very hard on their clothes. The most startling expenditure was for shoes. Mrs. B. counted up that for her family of nine she spent $144.25 for shoes in the year. She says they almost support the cobbler, too, in having them mended, as they always have some shoes there being mended. In July the cobbler's bill was $3., and that was not a hard month on shoes. In all, she calculated that she had spent $43. a year in having shoes mended. She often buys $18. worth of shoes at a time, to go around the family. She buys a good quality of shoes, too, never less than $1.25 a pair for the boys, and $2.50 and $3.50 a pair for herself, husband, and oldest daughter. They are all hard on shoes and take no care of them: $187.25 seems a large proportion out of $560. to go for shoes. The stockings for the family cost $51.24 for the year; most of the children had a new pair (at .10) each week; Mrs. B. would not do any darning, and they were thrown away when worn out. This estimated expenditure for clothing is as accurate as possible without keeping an account for a year. Such an account would probably show a larger expenditure rather than less.

The expenditure for light and fuel is not unusual. Five lamps are burned, so that the expenditure for oil is higher than usual ($20.75). Coal is bought both by the ton and by the bushel ($34.25). No gas is burned, and the boys bring the kindling wood from the streets. The total expenditure was about $55.

The insurance costs $2.05 a week, which is unusually high. The 7 children are each insured at 10 cents a week, Mrs. B. at 25 cents, and Mr. B. at $1.10 a week. Mrs. B. has increased her husband's insurance 50 cents a week, which he knows nothing about. She remarked: "Sure, I'm going to get more from him than enough to bury him, which is all he would leave me "!

The outlay for furniture amounted to $33. and consisted of 2 mattresses $8., sheets and comforters $5.90, portières $7.50, mantel-cover $3.50, bisque ornaments $4., etc.

The recreation for the entire family, except the father, did not amount to more than $10. a year. The father often goes to the theatre on cheap seats, and pays for it out of his own money; Mrs. B. goes to the theatre only when she is invited, and the oldest boy goes occasionally on 25-cent seats. The ten dollars a year includes car-fares to go to see a sister uptown.

They are Catholics, but are indifferent and attend church irregularly. Mrs. B. is very ambitious for her children, and wants them to "learn a trade"—the two older children are in factories, much to her regret. She is very proud of her children. She wanted the girl (14) to enter the trade school, but she preferred to work in a factory. The mother had her take piano lessons and took her twice a week to her sister's in Harlem to practice, but the child did not show any ability.

This seems a good example of a workingman's family on a large income, which has always been received, and yet out of which not one cent has been saved. They even pawn rings and jewelry during the slack season, when the income is *only* about $18. a week!

A year after this study was made the family moved to a better house, where they have 5 rooms and a bath, for $17. a month rent. The family seem much more prosperous. The visitor counted 50 pieces of bric-à-brac in the parlor! They have bought a second-hand piano and the girl is still taking lessons. To have her "play the piano" is one of her mother's fondest ambitions. Mrs. B. bought the piano and moved to better rooms "so that the children can have a home they can be proud of".

The standard of living of this family is high, even if extravagant, and fairly representative of their class.

Schedule No. 174

BARTENDER	INCOME $1500.

This is an example of a prosperous Italian family whose income is increased by the earnings of several children. The children are so thoroughly Americanized that their manner of living cannot be said to be Italian. Mr. and Mrs. P. have been in this country twenty-eight and twenty-five years respectively. They had six children at home (including a daughter who died during the year), and a son working in Albany. The father is a bartender and earns $13. a week, less than half the total income. The total income and expenditures for the year were as follows:

Income

Man, $13.00 for 52 weeks........................	$676.00
Woman, averages $3.00 a week making collars at home..	156.00
First daughter, $7.00 a week (boarder).........	364.00
Second daughter, $3.50 for 34 weeks...........	119.00
(Girl lived for 34 weeks of the year.)	
Third daughter, $2.50 for 52 weeks.............	130.00
Son sent home...............................	55.00
Total...................................	$1500.00

Expenditures

Rent, $22.50 a month.........................	$270.00
Food, $12.00 a week (for 8)....................	624.00
Clothing for 7...............................	170.00
Light and fuel...............................	48.00
Union, .25 a month...........................	3.00
Papers, .11 a week...........................	5.72
Machine $26.00 and house-furnishings $10.00....	36.00
Church......................................	11.60
Medical attendance...........................	26.00
Sundries....................................	33.68
Spending-money (man $52.00, girl $34.00, girl (16) $26.00)..............................	112.00
Funeral.....................................	160.00
Total...................................	$1500.00

This is an example of a family with an absolutely steady income all year, and the wages all turned over to the mother, except those of the oldest daughter, who is considered a boarder at $7. a week. This daughter (22) is a fitter at Forsyth's and earns $9. a week. She keeps $2. a week and clothes herself. The other daughter (18) also worked there for eight months and earned $3.50 a week. She was sick only two days and died of spinal meningitis. The funeral cost $160., and was all paid by the end of the year. There is no expenditure for insurance for any of the family. The third daughter (16) is learning the millinery trade and earns $2.50 a week. The oldest girl is a pretty, refined girl who goes with girls of a better class. She tries to improve her home and make it pleasant for the younger ones. They are all exceptionally devoted to one another and interested in the school work of the younger children. The mother is very thrifty and can make very attractive clothes. Everything she does is done well. The father has a very bad temper and makes things very uncomfortable at home at times. Until the girls were able to work they were very poor and unable to save much. What they had saved this year had to be spent on the funeral. Mrs. P. insists that she has not saved a cent over that amount. The large amount for "sundries" may be partly savings which she has in the house, but they have no bank account. Their expense for living has increased proportionately with the income, so nothing has been saved. The man brings all his wages home to his wife, and she gives him $1. a week "spending-money". He does not drink much, though he could have plenty given him at the café where he works. They do not drink at home, because the daughters say "it is not refined". The daughters resent being called Italians, as they want to be considered Americans. Their home is very attractive. They have four rooms, and the sanitary conditions are good. The rooms are exceedingly neat and well kept. The floor of the parlor is carpeted, there is plush furniture, crayon portraits on the walls, and lace curtains. They have white iron beds with brass trimmings. Things look rather ornamental. Mrs. P. kept a budget for two weeks in the summer. A week's expenditure for food is as follows.

SATURDAY, MAY 20
1 lb. butter....	$0.25
1 lb. coffee....	.25
1 can tomatoes.	.10
1 coffee-cake...	.10
Milk..........	.05
Bread.........	.15
1 qt. potatoes. .	.10
1 cabbage.....	.06
Cake..........	.10
1 lb. chops.	.18
Salad.........	.05
1½ lbs. spaghetti	.12
½ lb. cheese....	.12
6 eggs........	.12
2 qts. peas.	.06
1 qt. str'g beans	.06
Cucumbers....	.06
2 lbs. steak....	.36
2½ lbs. veal....	.38
Ice...........	.10
Oranges.......	.12
Lunch-money. .	.30
	$3.19

SUNDAY, MAY 21
1 qt. milk.....	$0.05
Steak.........	.15
	$0.20

MONDAY, MAY 22
Buns..........	$0.10
1 qt. milk.....	.05
Ice...........	.05
1½ lbs. soup-meat	.18
3 loaves bread. .	.15
1½ lbs. steak....	.29
1 lb. pork-chops	.12
Lunch-money. .	.30
	$1.24

TUESDAY, MAY 23
1 qt. milk.....	$0.05
Buns..........	.10
3 loaves bread.	.15
3½ lbs. corned beef........	.44
Ham..........	.15
Lunch........	.30
1 qt. potatoes. .	.10
1 cabbage......	.06
Salad.........	.05
Olive-oil.......	.50
Ice...........	.05
Bananas.......	.16
	$2.11

WEDNESDAY, MAY 24
1 qt. milk......	$0.05
Buns..........	.10
Ice...........	.05
Lunch-money. .	.30
2½ lbs. steak....	.48
Salad.........	.05
Radishes......	.05
Fish..........	.11
	$1.19

THURSDAY, MAY 25
1 qt. milk......	$0.50
Buns.........	.15
3 loaves bread .	.15
Ice...........	.05
1 lb. butter....	.25
Eggs..........	.25
2 pails potatoes.	.20
1 qt. str'g beans	.06
Berries........	.08
¼ lb. cheese....	.10
Lunch........	.30
	$1.64

FRIDAY, MAY 26
1 qt. milk......	$0.05
Buns..........	.10
3 loaves bread. .	.15
Radishes......	.05
1¼ lbs. chops ...	.16
Bananas.......	.06
Ice...........	.05
Lunch-money. .	.30
	$0.92

The total expense for food for the week was $10.49. This account was kept after the daughter's death, when there were seven in the family, and food was cheaper than it had been in the winter. Taking these circumstances into consideration, it does not seem that Mrs. P's. estimate of $12. a week average for all the year is too high. It will be seen that the diet was attractive and abundant and much more varied than that of the family in the preceding schedule. This family's standard is to spend more on food and less on clothing. They are as well dressed as the B. family and in better taste, and only spent $170. a year for seven, not including the oldest daughter, who dressed herself. This daughter had pieces of goods and waists given her at the store, and the mother makes them over. She makes all their clothes and then remodels them several times for the younger children. This is a remarkable example of what care of clothes, good management, and ability to sew, can do in making a good appearance. Assuming that the oldest daughter spent $50. on her clothing (which is a liberal estimate), this family of eight spent no more than $230. for clothing, and are as well dressed as the B. family of nine in the preceding schedule, who spent $560. Both of these families desire an attractive home and are ambitious, but this family appears to live on a higher plane than the other. There is no expenditure for insurance to keep them back, and none for recreation, except what comes out of the spending-money of the father and daughters. Furniture or clothing is never bought "on time". A sewing-machine was bought for $26. cash during the year. The pawnshop is never resorted to. They always have some money ahead in the house for any unexpected expenses, and so keep out of debt. In short, the manner of living and standards of this family are comfortable for any neighborhood.

SCHEDULE No. 200
POLICEMAN　　　　INCOME $1512.

One other illustration of a family on an income of about $1500. will show how a small family, with thrift and management, can save $300. in a year. This family consists of a policeman, his wife (both born in Germany), and two children, a girl of eight and a boy 2 years old. The man's salary is $1200. a year, and they have a boarder, another policeman, who pays $6. a week board, making the total income $1512. Their home is very pleasant; they have six rooms and bath in a very good apartment house, and pay $28. a month rent. The rooms are very attractively furnished, with carpets, pretty pictures, and good furniture. It is a very pretty little home. They have been married about ten years and have lived that long in the city. Before that they both lived in the country, and the woman still keeps her country ways of living. Her home is as neat as wax and she is always neatly dressed at home, in shirt-waist dresses, with a collar. She makes all the children's clothes for them and they are prettily dressed. Mrs. W. says her husband is an "honest policeman" and he always comes home as soon as his work is done. He is a very religious man, a Methodist, and they go to church regularly and contribute 25 cents each Sunday, or $13. a year.

Their expenditures for the year were as follows:

Rent, $28.00 a month.	$336.00
Food for 5, $9.00 a week.	468.00
Clothing for 4.	85.00
Drink.	52.00
Light and fuel.	49.00
Recreation.	25.00
Insurance.	26.00
Papers and magazines.	7.72
Doctor and medicine.	10.00
Church.	13.00
Spending-money (man).	83.20
Washerwoman, $1.00 a week.	52.00
Sundries.	5.08
Total.	$1212.00
Saved.	300.00
	$1512.00

Their food is abundant and well cooked, and the meals are carefully planned. They have meat, coffee and rolls, and oatmeal for the children, for breakfast; for lunch, cold meat and tea; for dinner, meat, potatoes, some kind of vegetable, and dessert. Their meals are served in a dining-room, with a white cloth on the table, and Mrs. W. has some wedding silver which she uses constantly. Mr. W. turns over all his wages to his wife, except $2. a week which he keeps for spending-money. His wife knows that he spends $.40 of that regularly on beer, so it has been deducted and put in the expenditure for drink. In addition, they have a case of beer each week which costs $.60, so their total expenditure for drink is $1. a week. The woman does not drink. Mr. W. spends $1.60 a week for shaving, tobacco, and laundry, and buys some of his clothing. The expenditure of $85. for clothing is very reasonable for their standard. Mrs. W. is very economical in her shopping and makes all her own and the children's clothes. Their recreation in the summer does not amount to more than $25. They all go together, and take a good many little trips. The insurance is very moderate, only 20 cents for the man, 10 cents for the woman, and 20 cents for the children—50 cents in all. In addition to the daily penny paper, they take two magazines at a dollar a year each. They paid $8. for a private physician during the year, and about $2. for household medicines.

This family was able to put $300. in the bank during the year, and it is an excellent example of the typical hard-working, economical, and prosperous family of the middle class, who live very comfortably and save money regularly.

CHAPTER VII

FAMILY BUDGETS

In order to obtain an accurate account of the daily expenditures, little account-books were given to the more intelligent housewives. Many women who willingly promised to keep such a budget of expenses were unable to do so because of illness, irregular income, or inability to be so systematic. If the mother could not write readily, a son or daughter often kept the account for her. Fifty families succeeded in keeping the budgets for periods of from one week to one year. These families were visited frequently by the investigators and the importance of accuracy emphasized. The usual daily expenditures are for food, light and fuel, or clothing, and these expenses have accordingly been called the "budget expenses". The cost of food was always entered, even if other expenses were not, hence these budgets are the most valuable in showing the actual daily cost of food and the dietary standards of the families. Expenditures for clothing and light and fuel were estimated most carefully for the entire year, in addition to the period during which the account was kept, and entered in the budget by the investigators. The cost of light and fuel has already been discussed, and it is the purpose of this chapter to give the results of the budgets in regard to the expenditures for food and clothing. The cost of food is the most important,

202

and the most difficult to estimate accurately without an itemized account.

These fifty budgets were kept from one week to one year:

8 were kept for 1 week

Length of Time Kept.

12 " " " 2 consecutive weeks
4 " " " 3 " "
18 " " " 4 " " or one month
1 was " " 5 " "
2 were " " 6 " . "
1 was " " 7 " "
1 was " " 9 weeks
3 were " " one year
—
50

That is, 24 budgets were kept from one week to one month, 23 from one month to nine weeks, and 3 for one year. The entries began and ended on a pay-day night, if possible, when the stock of food on hand was at its lowest, and when frequently the groceries for the week were bought.

During the spring of 1904, the members of the Greenwich House Cooking Class made out a list of current prices for the principal food commodities bought in the neighborhood. This list was verified by the writer by visits to the markets, and by the prices given in the budgets.

Meats (per pound): Beef—Chuck steak. . . . . . . .10 and .12

Round steak. . . . . . . .10 to .16

Sirloin steak } .16 to .20
Porterhouse steak }

Corned beef (navel). .05 to .06

Prices of Food.

Pork—Shoulder 09

Chops and steak . . . .14 to .16

Sausage. 12

Headcheese. 12

Mutton. . . . . .09 to .14

Veal—Cutlets and chops. . . .20

Breast. 08

Lamb. . . . . .14 to .18

Bread, per loaf. . . . . .05 to .08

```
Wheat flour, 3½ lbs.........................10 to .12
        24 lbs........................80 to .95
Cornmeal, per lb. ........................03½
Coffee, per lb ...........................20 to .30
Tea, per lb...............................30
Sugar, per lb.. ..........................05 to .06
        3½ lbs..............................16 to .20
Fish (per pound). Fresh cod... .............10 to .14
        Smelts...................18
        Weak fish.................08
        Flounders................05
        Canned salmon, per can. ....10 to .20
        Oysters, per quart.........40
American cheese, per pound .................15
Eggs.......................... 6 for .25 to 13 for .25
Milk, per quart...........................04 to .08
Butter, per pound.........................21 to .30
Vegetables. Potatoes, per quart..............10 to .15
        Red onions, per quart............10
        White onions, per quart..........15
        Turnips, white, per quart........10
        yellow, each............05
        Cabbage, per head..............15 to .20
        Spinach, per quart..............10 to .25
        Parsnips, each..................02 to .04
        Sprouts, per quart..............15
        Cauliflower, per head. ...........12 to .18
Canned vegetables: Tomatoes.................07 to .12
        Corn and beans...........10 to .15
        Peas....................10 to .15
        Asparagus...............25
```

The budgets show most interestingly the small quantities bought at each purchase—potatoes and vegetables by the Quantities Bought quart, sugar and flour by the pound or 3½-lb. at a Purchase. bag, tea and coffee frequently by the quarter pound, a single carrot, turnip, or onion, and one cent's worth of salt, pepper, vinegar, etc. There are several reasons for this; the most general are limited storage facilities and a limited purse which must be stretched to cover not only the food each week, but perhaps the rent, the insurance, a pair of shoes, several pairs of stockings, or coal and gas. The food-purchases must be cut down to meet these other necessary demands. It is frequently said by persons who little understand the situation that "the poor man's extravagance is his habit of living from hand to mouth at extravagant retail prices". This "habit" is the result of circumstances, and is deplored by the more intelligent women. Careful managers who have steady incomes buy their groceries in quantities at large department stores, where they watch sales, and buy 20 lbs. of sugar, a dozen or two dozen cans of vegetables, etc. Others buy their "dry groceries" (coffee, tea, sugar, cereals), for a week, on Saturday night. Some housekeepers claim that the extra cost of ice in summer for keeping food in larger quantities more than offsets the higher price paid for smaller quantities.

The budgets further illustrate what English and foreign economic writers have recognized, i.e., that the ordinary diet of the American workingman's family, Quality. compared with that of other countries, is abundant and varied. While foreigners bring their "macaroni", "bologna", or "potato and tea" standards to this country, the different conditions of labor and climate soon modify and enlarge this diet. This is shown in the budgets of foreign-born families that have become Americanized. Unfortunately there is a disp sition among the more prosperous families to buy the "best of food", meaning the highest-priced meat, butter, and flour. They are ignorant of the fact that the "best food" is that which supplies the most nutriment for the least money. Those who try to economize and buy judiciously consult carefully the prices they pay, with only vague ideas of nutritive values. One of the objects of the cooking class was to discuss the relative value and importance of various food products.

As this was primarily a study of the *cost of living* in a given neighborhood, the cost of food was noted without

Nutrition of Food. special attention to the adequacy of the diet or the amount of nutriment in the food eaten. The question "is the food adequate and wholesome?" was in every case answered by the investigator's knowledge of the amount spent for food, the character and selection of the foods, and the general healthy appearance of all the members of the family. A dietary study based on the standards of Voit or of Atwater to determine the nutritive and fuel value of the food consumed would be most interesting, but outside the limits of this study. For the purpose of comparison, the expenditure for food in the budgets selected for description in this chapter has been reduced to a common basis, i.e., *the cost per man per day*, and the amount and percentage spent for animal and vegetable foods has also been noted. Undoubtedly a pecuniary saving would be made if more were spent for vegetable foods carefully chosen for their protein, such as beans and peas. The poorer families seem naturally to select the foods which chemical analysis shows to supply the most nutrients at the lowest cost, but unfortunately the proper proportions of nutrients in their dietaries are often lacking. On the whole, however, the selection of foods in these families does not seem unwise when it is done by the mother, but when the children do the marketing, as is frequently the case, there is more waste and extravagance.

The "cost per man per day" of food in the following budgets is based on the standard commonly accepted by

Method of Computing Cost per Man per Day. scientists, which gives the dietary requirements of women and children as follows.*

* See Bulletin No. 46, Dept. of Agriculture. " Dietary Studies in N. Y. City in 1895 and 1896 " by W. O. Atwater.

FACTORS USED IN CALCULATING MEALS CONSUMED IN DIETARY STUDIES

One meal of woman equivalent to 0.8 meal of man at moderate muscular labor.

One meal of boy 14 to 16 years of age equivalent to 0.8 meal of man
"   "   " girl 14 " 16   "   "   "   "   " 0.7 "   "   "
"   "   " child 10 " 13 "   "   "   "   " 0.6 "   "   "
"   "   "   "   6 " 9   "   "   "   "   " 0.5 "   "   "
"   "   "   "   2 " 5   "   "   "   "   " 0.4 "   "   "
"   "   "   "   under 2 years of age   "   " 0.3 "   "   "

For example, in a study of a family of five persons, father, mother, girl 12 years, boy 7 years, and a girl 3 years, continued for one week:

The man is expressed as........................ 1.0
The woman is expressed as. .... .8 of a man
The girl (12 years) is expressed as.............. .6 "   "
The boy (7 years) is expressed as............... .5 "   "
The girl (3 years) is expressed as............... .4 "   "
                                                   ———
Whole family is equal to. .... 3.3 men

The number of meals taken was as follows:

Man (away for lunch 6 days)............ 15   meals
Woman (21 meals×.8 meal of a man).... 16.8 "
Girl (21 meals×.6 meal of a man)........ 12.6 "
Boy (21 meals×.5 meal of a man)........ 10.5 "
Girl (21 meals×.4 meal of a man) .... 8.4 "

Total number of meals equivalent to.. 63.3 meals of a man
Equivalent to one man 21.1 days.

The total cost of food was $6. a week for this family, which is therefore equal to .28 "per man per day".

All except the poorest of these families had three meals a day. The diet consisted of meat, vegetables, milk, bread, and coffee or tea daily. Meat was always
Menus. eaten once, and sometimes twice, a day. The budgets show a pitiful lack of variety in food to make the meals interesting and appetizing. The women were often eager to learn new ways of preparing food, but very ignorant

of any but the simplest kind of menus. Some typical menus
are as follows:

1. Family of five "well nourished", $5.50 a week for food
   carefully bought.
   Breakfast—Bread, butter, coffee.
   Lunch—Eggs, rice, bread, often soup or meat stew.
   Dinner—Meat or ham and eggs, bread and butter, potatoes
   and beans, or other vegetable.

2. Family of five (three small children), $6. a week for food.
   Breakfast—For man, 2 eggs, bread, and coffee; for
   children, only bread and coffee or oatmeal.
   Lunch—What is left from dinner.
   Dinner—Beef or pork, potatoes, tomatoes or corn, sometimes a salad, baker's bread, apple sauce or prunes, or
   pie or cake.

3. Family of nine, $4.50 a week for food.
   Breakfast—Oatmeal and milk, sugar for younger children;
   or bread and coffee.
   Lunch—Bread and milk, or "left-overs".
   Dinner—Cheap stew or chuck steak, bread, tea, potatoes,
   and sometimes butter.
       This family was manifestly underfed from the appear-
   ance of the children: the food was wholesome but
   insufficient.

4. In an Italian family of ten, the food cost less than $8. a
   week, including lunch-money, but the children looked
   well nourished. There was plenty of soup and salad
   and cheese. They baked their own bread, and the
   flour cost almost $1. a week.

5. In contrast to this was an Irish family of seven who spent
   $13. a week for food. This included $2. to $2.50 for
   meat for Sunday and Monday, and at least .50 a day
   on other days; 3 lbs. butter, 9 lbs. sugar, 1 lb. coffee,

1 lb. tea, and 6 or 7 qts. of potatoes a week were also purchased, as well as 2 loaves of bread, .10, rolls, .10, and cake, .10, every day.

6. Another allowance, generous to extravagance for the income, was $8. a week for a family of four.

Breakfast—Hash, or eggs and bacon, coffee, bread.

Lunch—Cold meat, salads, tea, cake.

Dinner—Chicken or roast or steak, potatoes, fresh vegetables, hot biscuits, dessert.

This family lived well for any neighborhood.

The principal articles of food in the account-books are meat, milk (fresh and condensed), baker's bread, butter, potatoes, and tea. The meat is usually beef, with occasionally pork or a cheap cut of lamb. The meat for Sunday, often a roast, costs from $1. to $2.50 and lasts for Monday, and sometimes for lunch on Tuesday. An average-sized family spends from .15 to .40 a day for meat. Potatoes are used freely, often a quart for a meal in large families. The vegetables are mostly canned corn or tomatoes, turnips, carrots, and cabbage. Macaroni, beans, bread, vegetables, and soup are the main food of the Italians. The poorer families live on bread, tea, soup or stew, and oatmeal. Few women bake their own bread, and some of those who do so feel that it is as expensive as buying baker's bread when flour is so high, but that it is more wholesome. Bread costs .05 and .08 a loaf. A careful manager buys bread a day old, and then gets an .08 loaf for .05. Bread costs from .15 to .40 a day in a family of six or eight. Cakes and pastry are very seldom baked at home. Milk in the bulk costs .04 a quart in summer and .05 in winter, and very few families recognize the desirability of paying .08 a quart for bottled milk. Sweetened condensed milk is used almost entirely for tea and coffee, and as a "spread" on bread for

Kinds of Food.

the children in place of butter. The tea and coffee habit is universal; even little children drink strong tea and coffee several times a day. Wise mothers buy two or three quarts of milk a day for the children to drink, but generally the children do not like it as well as tea or coffee.

An interesting fact illustrated by the budgets is that while the amount and steadiness of the income depend largely on the character and often the nationality of the husbands, the expenditures, especially for food and clothing, depend upon the character of the wife and mother. An Italian husband brings in the income, but an Irish wife spends it, or a thrifty English wife tries to make the best of the irregular income that her Irish husband earns.

Ten of the budgets which were kept for four weeks or longer have been selected as representative of all the budgets. The averages per week are more accurate than where the budget was kept for a shorter time. None of these families has been previously described in the chapter on "Typical Families". The items have been uniformly arranged to show the kind of food bought, the amount (wherever it was given), the proportion of animal and vegetable foods, the total cost of food, the average cost per week for the whole family, and the average cost "per man per day".

Selected Budgets.

I. *Budget of a Housekeeper's Family.* Family of a widow (Irish) and four children, all girls, 15, 13, 11, and 9 years old. They were formerly helped by charitable societies, but at this time were trying to be independent and pay off their debts. The woman was housekeeper or janitor of a tenement-house and received her rent free and $4. a month for her services. The daughter earned $4. a week in a dressmaker's shop. The two rooms they occupied were in the basement, and dark and damp. The budget was kept for the month of February,

1904. Income for the month, including rent, $35. Expenditures $35.12. Deficit $0.12.

EXPENDITURES FOR MONTH (4 WEEKS)

Food.	$16.00
Rent.	10.00
Coal.	3.64
Oil.	1.96
Wood.	.54
Chimney.	.10
Broom.	.28
Medicine and doctor.	2.60
Total.	$35.12

EXPENDITURE FOR FOOD FOR 4 WEEKS

Kind of Food Material.	Amount.	Cost.	Amount per Week.	Cost per Week.	Per Cent.
Beef, veal, mutton.	Not given	$4.26	Not given	$1.07	
Ham and bacon.	" "	.25	" "	.06	
Fish, fresh.	" "	.30	" "	.08	
Sardines, canned.	3 cans	.32	¾ can	.08	
Eggs.	14	.37	3½	.09	
Butter.	1¼ lbs.	.37	5/16 lb.	.09	
Milk.	28 qts.	1.40	7 qts.	.35	
Total animal food.	......	$7.27	......	$1.82	45.5
Vegetables, fresh.	......	$0.53	......	$0.13	
" canned.	12 cans	1.21	3 cans	.30	
Potatoes.	14½ qts.	1.29	3.6 qts.	.32	
Bread.	53 loaves	2.65	13 loaves	.66	
Cake.	......	.10	......	.03	
Fruit.	......	.20	......	.05	
Sugar.	13½ lbs.	.81	3.4 lbs.	.20	
Tea.	¾ lb.	.27	3/16 lb.	.06	
Coffee.	1 "	.19	¼ "	.05	
Crackers.	1 "	.10		.03	
"Noodles".	......	.68	......	.17	
Sundries.	......	.70	......	.18	
Total vegetable food.	......	$8.73	......	$2.18	54.5
Total all food.	......	$16.00	......	$4.00	100.

Cost "per man per day". .18

The most characteristic feature of this budget is the small quantities in which food was bought, sugar regularly ½ lb. a day, potatoes by the half-quart, 2 eggs, 1 onion, a turnip or carrot at a time. The meals consisted generally of tea and bread and soup. They had meat only two or three times a week. No cereal was used. Tomatoes costing from .07 to .12 a can were the usual vegetable. Very little butter was used—probably sugar took its place. The woman did not know how to cook, and hence the diet was monotonous as well as inadequate. She said she ought to spend $1. a day for food for her family of five, but they never had that much. The animal foods were 45.5 per cent and vegetable foods 54.5 per cent of the total expenditure.

II. *Budget of Watchman's Family.* This family consisted of father (Irish), mother (English), and two children, little girls 5 and 2 years of age. The man earned $12. a week, and out of that kept $1. for spending-money. The total income for the year was $606. Rent was $10. a month. The three rooms were neat and attractive, and the table had a white cloth. The woman was a good cook and a careful manager. Having a steady income, she could buy groceries for two weeks at a time. The budget was kept during the month of March, 1905. There was a great variety in the food, including various kinds of meat, fish, and vegetables. Milk and fruit were freely used.

The most striking item was the large amount of meat and fish. Compared with the previous diet, this shows a larger amount spent for meat, butter, and fruit, and a smaller amount for bread, sugar, and canned vegetables. This diet was abundant and wholesome, but extravagant in that equally nourishing food could have been bought much cheaper. The animal foods were 58 per cent and the vegetable foods were 42 per cent of the whole. This family had some luxuries, in the expenditures for cake, pie, ice-cream, and fruit, which were impossible with the diet costing .18 per man per day.

EXPENDITURES FOR FOOD FOR 4 WEEKS.

Kind of Food Material.	Amount.	Cost	Amount per Week.	Cost per Week.	Per Cent.
Beef, veal, mutton.	29½ lbs.	$3.23	7.4 lbs.	$0.81	
Pork, ham, bacon.	23 "	2.86	5.7 "	.71	
Fish, fresh.	12 "	1.27	3 "	.32	
Sardines and herring. ...	......	.31	......	.08	
Clams.	2 dozen	.30	½ dozen	.07	
Cheese.	2¼ lbs.	.24	5/16 lb.	.06	
Eggs.	19	.35	5	.09	
Butter.	3 lbs.	.90	¾ lb.	.22	
Milk (bottled).	28 qts.	1.68	7 qts.	.42	
Condensed cream.	1 can	.10	¼ can	.03	
Total animal food.	......	$11.24	......	$2.81	58.
Vegetables, fresh.	......	$1.07	......	$0.27	
" canned.	3 cans	.18	¾ can	.05	
Potatoes.	10½ qts.	1.05	2.6 qts.	.26	
Bread.	31 loaves	1.41	8 loaves	.35	
Cake and pie.	......	1.00	......	.25	
Coffee.	½ lb.	.15	⅛ lb.	.04	
Tea.	1 "	.35	¼ "	.09	
Sugar.	3½ lbs.	.22	⅞ lb.	.05	
Cereals: Rolled oats.....	7 "	......	1.7 "		
Rice.	2 "	.36	½ "	.09	
Fruit (oranges, apples, prunes).	......	.76	......	.19	
Ice-cream.	......	.70	......	.17	
Sundries.	......	.90	......	.23	
Total vegetable food. .	......	$8.15	......	$2.04	42.
Total for all food.	......	$19.39	......	$4.85	100.

Cost per man per day. .... .27

III. *Budget of Porter's Family.* Family consisted of father (American), mother (English), and three children, two boys, 9 and 8 years old, and a little girl, 4 years old. The budget was kept for four weeks in January and February and five weeks in May and June, 1904, in order to see whether there was more expense for food at one season than at another. There was found to be little difference in the average week's expense. A very thrifty, intelligent couple. Their home consisted of three light, well-ventilated rooms in a rear house, which were neat and homelike. The rent was only $9. a month, because it was a rear house. The meals were well cooked and nicely served at a table covered with white oil-cloth. The woman bought her food carefully and watched all special sales of groceries. She also made all her own and the children's clothes. The man earned $11. a week, and the woman did a washing for .75 a week. As the man worked occasionally overtime, the total income for the year amounted to $670., or an average of about $12.88 a week.

During the winter weeks the food cost .26 per man per day, and during the summer weeks .24. In the latter period a boy 16 years old had 78 meals with the family. The man was always away at lunch, which reduced the number of his meals a week. A comparison of the diets in the summer and winter weeks shows that about the same average amount was spent for meat each season, but more was spent in winter for butter, eggs, milk, and canned vegetables; and more for fresh vegetables, bread, tea, and fruit in summer, when fresh vegetables, such as cucumbers, radishes, string-beans, lettuce, and green peas, were frequently bought. The expenditures for food in this budget might well be taken as a standard for careful selection of foods on a limited income for a family of like character. The average amount per week for food was $5.67 for five, and sometimes six, in the family. The usual daily menu was: Breakfast—Eggs, bread, butter, tea, cereal, and milk. Lunch—Soup, bread, and cocoa. Dinner—Chops, steak, etc., potatoes, a fresh vegetable, fruit, and sometimes pie or cake. The difference between the percentage spent for animal foods in this and the preceding budget is striking.

Both women bought cheaper and more nourishing cuts of meat, but the other family had much more than was necessary, while this family used 2½ times as much milk and spent almost twice as much for fresh vegetables.

EXPENDITURES FOR FOOD FOR 9 WEEKS

Kind of Food Material.	Amount.	Cost.	Amount per Week.	Cost per Week.	Per Cent.
Beef, veal, mutton......	Not given	$8.09	Not given	$0.90	
Pork, ham, bacon......	" "	1.95	" "	.22	
Chicken..............	" "	.63	......	.07	
Fish.................	" "	.96	......	.11	
Oysters..............	" "	.13	......	.01	
Butter...............	13 lbs.	3.34	1.4 lbs.	.37	
Cottolene............	......	.10	......	.01	
Eggs................	104	2.01	12	.22	
Milk................	149 qts	7.45	18 qts.	.83	
Cheese..............	1½ lbs.	.30	......	.03	
Total animal food.....	......	$24.96	......	$2.77	49.
Vegetables, fresh.......	......	$4.37	......	$0.49	
" canned.....	12 cans	1.14	1.3 cans	.13	
Potatoes.............	21 qts.	2.27	2.3 qts.	.25	
Bread and rolls........	......	5.20	......	.57	
Cake and pie..........	......	1.53	......	.17	
Coffee...............	½ lb.	.14	......	.02	
Tea	3½ lbs.	1.59	.4 lb.	.17	
Cocoa...............	......	.40	......	.04	
Sugar...............	32 lbs.	1.69	3½ lbs.	.19	
Graham and wheat flour.	9½ "	.38	1.1 "	.05	
Cereals (oatmeal, cornmeal, rice)...........	Not given	.51	......	.06	
Crackers.............	10½ lbs.	1.15	1.2 lbs.	.13	
Fruit................	......	2.49	......	.27	
Sundries *...........	......	3.23	......	.36	
Total vegetable food..	......	$26.09	......	$2.90	51.
Total for all food.....	......	$51.05	......	$5.67	100.

Cost per man per day.............................25

IV. *Budget of Truckman's Family.* This budget was kept for the month of May, 1904. The family consisted of father

* Sundries include ice for five weeks in summer, .75.

and mother (American) and three children, girl 6 years, boy 4 years, and baby 1 year. Their four rooms were light, and the sanitary conditions were fair, but the rooms were very untidy and overcrowded. Dirty dishes and left-over food were always on the table. The man's wages were from $10. to $12. a week, and a lodger brought the total income up to $686. a year, or about $13.20 a week. The income for the month the budget was kept was $60.75, expenses $60.69. Rent was $15. a month.

FOOD EXPENDITURE FOR 4 WEEKS

Kind of Food Material.	Amount.	Cost.	Amount per Week.	Cost per Week.	Per Cent.
Beef, veal, mutton......	Not given	$4.67	......	$1.17	
Ham, pork, bacon......	" "	.92	......	.23	
Fish.................	" "	.54	......	.13	
Butter...............	4¼ lbs.	1.16	1 1/16 lbs.	.29	
Cheese..............	½ lb.	.10	1/16 lb.	.03	
Eggs................	43	.70	11	.17	
Milk................	44 qts.	2.64	11 qts.	.66	
Total animal food....	......	$10.73	......	$2.68	57.
Vegetables, fresh........	......	.68	......	.17	
" canned......	4 cans	.36	1 can	.09	
Pota'oes..............	13 qts.	1.38	3¼ qts.	.35	
Bread and rolls........	......	2.32	......	.58	
Flour................	3½ lbs.	.12	.9 lb.	.03	
Sugar................	14 "	.68	3½ lbs.	.17	
Coffee...............	5 "	1.00	1¼ "	.25	
Tea.................	2 "	.70	½ lb.	.18	
Cocoa...............	......	.18	......	.04	
Cake................	......	.35	......	.09	
Cereal (oatflakes, rice, and barley)..........	5½ "	.24	1.4 lbs.	.06	
Fruit................	......	.12	......	.03	
Catsup..............	......	.05	......	.01	
Total vegetable food..	......	$8.18	......	$2.05	43.
Total for all food......	......	$18.91	......	$4.73	100.

Cost per man per day............................... .25

It must be remembered that here and in all these budgets the lunch-money, where there is any, is not included in the actual cost of food to the housewife, but it is included in the statistical tables, where the expenditure given for food is accordingly somewhat higher. This diet was plain and good, but monotonous. It consisted chiefly of bread and milk, corned beef and cabbage, potatoes, and eggs. There was no variety in the vegetables. The food was not well cooked, nor attractively served. The woman was a methodical manager in dividing her income every week, but was ignorant of food values and lazy about cooking. The food also suffered because the expenditure for insurance was so high— $1.70 a week. The cost per man per day, .25, is the same as in the preceding budget, but in this family this expenditure is very high for the nutritive value of the food.

V. *Budget of Stone-cutter's Family.* The man and woman were born in Italy, but the four children (two girls, 13 and 7 years, and two boys, 11 and 9 years) were born in New York. The budget was kept for the month of February, 1904. It illustrates the diet and food-expenditures of an Americanized Italian family. The mother kept the accounts in Italian and they were afterwards translated by the girl 13 years old. The rooms were very untidy, dark, and damp. There was no furniture of any value, except a sewing-machine. Rent was $9. a month. The woman was a stupid peasant, but she was ambitious for her children, who were pretty and bright. The man was an artificial-brownstone-cutter in summer, but his work was irregular. He was always out of employment two or three months a year, and in the winter worked in an artificial-flower factory, where he earned $9. to $10. a week. The woman sometimes made collars and artificial flowers at home. The total income for the year was $690., and the expenditures were $730. The family pays off in summer the debts made in winter. As this investigation ended April 1, 1904, the indebtedness of $40. for the winter would undoubtedly be paid off during the summer. This is an exceptional Italian family where there is apparently neither thrift nor saving.

FOOD EXPENDITURES FOR 4 WEEKS

Kind of Food Material.	Amount.	Cost.	Amount per Week.	Cost per Week.	Per Cent.
Beef, veal, mutton......	Not given	$5.36	Not given	$1.34	
Ham, pork, bacon.	" "	1.77	" "	.44	
Fish..................	" "	.80	" "	.20	
Chicken...............	" "	2.45	" "	.61	
Butter................	" "	1.26	" "	.31	
Cheese................	" "	.95	" "	.24	
Eggs..................	" "	1.00	" "	.25	
Milk..................	28½ qts.	1.43	7 qts.	.36	
Total animal food.....	......	$15.02	......	$3.75	55.
Vegetables, fresh.......	Not given	$2.21	......	$0.55	
" canned.....	" "	.56	......	.14	
" dried.......	" "	.67	......	.17	
Potatoes..............	" "	.90	......	.22	
Bread................	" "	2.81	......	.70	
Sugar................	13½ lbs.	.67	3⅜ lbs.	.17	
Coffee...............	1½ "	.35	⅜ lb.	.09	
Macaroni.............	......	2.07	......	.52	
Cereal (rice, barley).....	Not given	.69	Not given	.17	
Fruit................	" "	.10	......	.03	
Olive-oil.............	" "	.70	......	.18	
Sundries.............	" "	.65	......	.16	
Total vegetable food..	......	$12.38	......	$3.10	45.
Total for all food.....	......	$27.40	......	$6.85	100.

Cost per man per day..............................26

The striking thing about this diet is the abundance of fresh and dried vegetables, and macaroni and cheese. The "fresh vegetables" were salad, mushrooms, onions, cabbage, or greens for soup, while the dried vegetables were beans and chestnuts (used as a vegetable). The meat was generally soup-meat or veal, though bologna and ham were frequently used. During the month a case of macaroni was bought for $1.60; previous to that about .25 a week was spent for macaroni. The amount spent for drink was carefully put down in the accounts, and was undoubtedly considered a part of their food. It has not been included in the food expenditures here for the sake of uniformity with other budgets. During these four weeks this family spent $7.40 for drinks for family use, exclusive of what the man spent on himself. This included $2.20 for beer, $4. for wine, .65 for brandy, and .55 for sarsaparilla, making an average of $1.85 a week, in addition to the regular food expenditures.

VI. *Budget of Oysterman's Family.* This was an Irish family of nine—the father, mother, mother's sister, and six children, four boys aged 15, 13, 5, and 3 years, and two girls aged 10 and 8 years. The sister paid $4. a week for her board when she was working. The man was steady and industrious. He worked on the oyster-boats in winter and was a tent-maker in summer, with long periods of unemployment between. He usually earned from $12. to $14. a week. The oldest boy earned $94. in the year. The total income was $744. a year, with expenditures of $784. This deficit was owed to the landlord and friends. The family have always been poor in spite of all their efforts to get ahead, because of sickness and unemployment. The mother and little girl suffer greatly with rheumatism, and the little boy (5 years) has infant paralysis. The sanitary conditions of the house were very bad. The four rooms were kept as neat as possible, but they were bare and unattractive. The woman tried to buy nourishing food, but she was ignorant of food values. The entire family could not sit at the table at once, so the food was served piecemeal and unattractively. This is a typical family of its class. The budget was kept for the month of

February, 1904. The income during that time was $45.50, the expenditures $49.39, leaving a deficit of $3.89, which is proportionate to the total deficit for the year ($40.).

FOOD EXPENDITURES FOR 4 WEEKS

Kind of Food Material.	Amount.	Cost.	Amount per Week.	Cost per Week.	Per Cent.
Beef, veal, mutton, and bacon...............	Not given	$9.64	......	$2.41	
Fish..................	......	1.48	......	.37	
Butter.... .:..........	11¼ lbs.	2.98	2.8 lbs.	.75	
Milk, fresh.............	35 qts.	1.75	9 qts.	.44	
" condensed........	14 cans	1.40	3½ cans	.35	
Cheese.................	½ lb.	.10	⅛ lb.	.02	
Eggs..................	......	.12	......	.03	
Total animal food.....	......	$17.47	......	$4.37	68.
Vegetables, fresh.......	......	$0.59	......	$0.15	
" canned.....	6 cans	.60	1½ cans	.15	
Potatoes..............	16 qts.	1.70	4 qts.	.42	
Bread................	43 loaves	2.34	11 loaves	.59	
Sugar.................	14 lbs.	.76	3½ lbs.	.19	
Tea...................	3 "	.75	¾ lb.	.19	
Coffee................	2 "	.45	½ "	.11	
Flour and macaroni.	......	.44	......	.11	
Crackers and sundries. . .	......	.37	......	.09	
Oatmeal...............	......	.20	......	.05	
Total vegetable food. .	......	$8.20	......	$2.05	32.
Total for all food.....	......	$25.67	......	$6.42	100.

Cost per man per day.............................. .17

In reckoning the cost per man per day, the actual number of meals eaten during the week by each member of the family was taken. This low average allowance was supplemented for the working members of the family by their lunch-money at noon.

The most unusual expenditure here is the amount for animal food (68 per cent of the whole), and especially for meat. This is undoubtedly one of the causes for the rheumatism in the family. A large amount was also spent for butter, and little for the vegetables, which were only turnips, cabbage, and canned tomatoes. The diet is the regulation Irish one of "meat, potatoes, and tea". The food was neither adequate nor contained the proper proportions of nutriment. Condensed milk is not so economical nor so good a food as fresh milk. The mother said the children were all "delicate and not hearty eaters". The lack of variety and of proper nourishment in the diet may account for this. At the prices paid for food, this family needed $8. a week for food more carefully selected, in order to be adequately nourished.

VII. *Budget of Longshoreman's Family.* This family consisted of the father (Irish), mother (English), and eight children (six boys and two girls) from 1 to 18 years. The man had the attractive personal qualities of his race, was not a drinking man, but lacked perseverance and steadiness of purpose. He was constantly changing his "job". During the year of investigation he worked only thirty weeks. His large family had received so much aid from charitable societies and churches that he had become completely pauperized. The son 18 had the unsteadiness of the father, and a boy 16 was very wild, and in a reformatory part of the time. The mother was English and had been well educated. She was a careful manager and an intelligent buyer, and put much care and thought on her marketing. With such a variable income, she never could save for a future season of unemployment, in spite of her economy. As she said, "It takes so much to go around." The total income for the year amounted to $810., including $91. in gifts and charity. The average weekly income was therefore $15.58, but it varied from a few dollars to $30. a week. A careful budget was kept during the month of February, 1904. The income this month was below the average, $39.40; the expenditures were

$53.05, leaving a deficit of $13.65. This was a chronic condition with them, but the next month may have brought
them out of debt and the following one plunged them back
again. The deficit for the whole year was $75.—for groceries,
rent, doctor, butcher, and clothing.

Food Expenditures for 4 Weeks

Kind of Food Material.	Amount.	Cost.	Amount per Week.	Cost per Week.	Per Cent.
Beef, veal, mutton......	Not given	$5.90	......	$1.48	
Pork, ham, bacon......	" "	3.13	......	.78	
Fish, clams............	" "	1.93	......	.48	
Butter................	9½ lbs.	2.86	2.4 lbs.	.72	
Cheese................	......	.15	......	.04	
Eggs..................	Not given	.15	......	.04	
Condensed milk........	24 cans	3.60	6 cans	.90	
Fresh milk............	26 qts.	1.30	6½ qts.	.32	
Buttermilk............	......	.05	......	.01	
Total animal food.....	......	$19.07	......	$4.77	51.
Vegetables, fresh.......	......	$1.29	......	$0.32	
" canned.....	......	.20	......	.05	
" dried.......	......	.70	......	.18	
Potatoes.............	22 qts.	2.79	......	.70	
Bread and rolls........	......	8.09	......	2.02	
Sugar.................	......	.90	......	.23	
Tea..................	4 lbs.	1.40	......	.35	
Coffee................	......	.05	......	.01	
Cereals (oatmeal, rice)...	......	.54	......	.14	
Cake.................	......	.63	......	.16	
Fruit.................	......	.20	......	.05	
Sundries..............	......	.53	......	.13	
Flour and macaroni.	......	.74	......	.18	
Total vegetable food ..	......	$18.06	......	$4.52	49.
Total for all food.....	......	$37.13	......	$9.29	100.

Cost per man per day................................ .22

It is interesting to contrast this distribution of food
materials with that of the preceding budget. Much less was

here spent for meat and more for bread. This family almost lived on bread and soups or stews. An attempt was made to give variety to the food, as the following menus show, but the amount was always inadequate. Soups were frequently made of dried beans or peas and a little bacon, and occasionally they had clam-soup, ox-tail soup, kidney-stew, or a cheap cut of lamb with peas, and other deviations from the ordinary diet of the neighborhood. It is difficult to see, without a strict dietary analysis, in what ways more nourishing food could be had for the money, yet the cost per man per day, .22, is higher than usual.

As the food-supply for this large family is unique in some respects, it has seemed worth while to copy from the budget the purchases for one week. The week ending February 20 has been chosen as a typical week.

Saturday, February 13: Rolls .10, milk .08, pork-chops .48, rice .06, codfish .20, bread .08, butter .30, condensed milk .90, tea .35, sugar .20, flour .10, soap .10, soapine .10, gas .25, 1 pair rubbers .35, stockings .50, saffron and gin .15.

Purchases for One Week.

Sunday: Coffee-cake .20, bread .11, papers .10, lamb .64, peas .10, potatoes .15, bread .08, sauce .03, bread .16.

Monday: Stew-meat .34, bread .08, beer .10, rolls .15, bacon .10, pancakes .20, bread .08.

Tuesday: Bacon .10, bread .16, milk .05, meat for stew .28, greens .07, onions .02, potatoes .10, hash .12, butter .15, bread .08, stamps .02, papers .06, wood .05.

Wednesday: Rolls .15, milk .13, bread .26, bacon .10, beans .10, potatoes .10, fish (bloaters) .15, tobacco .05, starch .05, talcum .10.

Thursday: Bread and rolls .39, milk .05, pork-chops .35, gas .25, potatoes .15, turnips .10, pepper .05, salt .05, butter .15.

Friday: Milk .15, bread .29, potatoes .20, soup-meat .30, greens .05, onions .03, rice .04. Total $11.97. Food $9.84.

MENU OF MEALS DURING WEEK ENDING FEB. 20

Day.	Breakfast.	Dinner.	Supper.
Saturday....	Oatmeal, milk-rolls	Pork-chops, rice	Codfish, bread, butter, milk
Sunday.....	Coffee-cake, bread, butter, tea	Lamb, peas, potatoes, bread, and butter	Left-overs from dinner, bread
Monday.....	Rolls, bacon	Meat-stew, bread, beer	Pancakes, bread, butter, tea
Tuesday.....	Bacon, bread, and milk	Meat-soup, potatoes	Hash, bread, and butter
Wednesday..	Rolls, bread, and milk	Bacon and beans, potatoes, bread	Bloaters, bread, and milk
Thursday....	Rolls, bread, tea, and milk	Pork-chops, potatoes, turnips, bread	Bread, butter, and tea
Friday......	Oatmeal, milk, bread	Soup (with rice) and potatoes	Bread and milk

This diet is wholesome, but entirely inadequate in the amounts purchased for a family of 10 persons. There is nothing in this list that could be called a luxury! The family were underfed all the year, except the man, who was given the largest share, in order to keep up his working power.

VIII. *Budget of Scrubwoman's Family.* The family consisted of eight: the mother (German), three boys, aged 15, 11, and 7 years, and three girls, 16, 13, and 4 years, and the woman's brother, who paid $6. a week board. The woman was left a widow with six small children, and was forced to place some of them in institutions for a few years. The church aided her with work at that time, but the family were never dependent upon charity. The mother went out cleaning and washing five days in the week and did sewing at home. The oldest daughter was a cripple, but had learned pasting at a trade school, and earned $2.75 a week. The oldest boy could earn $5. a week as an electrician's apprentice, but he worked only part of the year. They lived in three very crowded rooms, always littered with piles of clothing. The rent was $11. The budget was kept for six weeks in March and April, 1904, by the oldest daughter. The food was good and abundant and quite varied, and German in character.

EXPENDITURES FOR FOOD FOR 4 WEEKS

Kind of Food Material.	Amount.	Cost.	Amount per Week.	Cost per Week.	Per Cent.
Beef, veal, mutton......	Not given	$5.70	......	$1.42	
Ham, pork, bacon......	" "	1.07	......	.27	
Fish and clams........	" "	2.57	......	.64	
Butter...............	10 lbs.	2.10	2½ lbs.	.52	
Eggs.................	Not given	1.40	......	.35	
Cheese..............	" "	1.75	......	.44	
Milk, condensed.......	22 cans	2.20	5½ cans	.55	
" fresh...........	30 qts.	1.50	7½ qts.	.38	
Total animal food....	......	$18.29	......	$4.57	46.
Vegetables, fresh......	......	$1.13	......	$0.28	
" canned.....	13 cans	1.30	......	.33	
" dried.......	......	.15	......	.04	
Potatoes.............	Not given	2.35	......	.59	
Bread and rolls........	" "	9.25	......	2.31	
Sugar................	" "	1.30	......	.32	
Tea..................	" "	.30	......	.08	
Coffee...............	" "	1.45	......	.36	
Fruit................	" "	.73	......	.18	
Cereals (oatmeal, rice, barley).............	" "	.91	......	.23	
Flour and macaroni....	" "	.50	......	.12	
Pie and cake.........	" "	1.15	......	.29	
Sundries.............	" "	1.31	......	.33	
Total vegetable food ..	......	$21.83	......	$15.46	54.
Total all food........	......	$40.12	......	$10.03	100.

Cost per man per day............................ .27

During this time neither the girl (16) nor the boy (15) were working, and the brother came home for lunch, so that all the family had all their meals at home, except the mother, who was away for lunch five days a week. The most striking feature of this budget is the large amount of delicatessen food which was bought—cooked ham, pickles, sardines, pickled fish and canned fish, potted tongue, etc. This was because the mother was not at home to do the marketing or cooking. An unusual quantity of bread was eaten: generally .40 a day was spent for bread and rolls. Cake and pie and coffee and condensed milk were also largely used. Condensed milk was used as a "spread" on bread by the children. The expenditure for cheese and cereals was higher than in any other family. On the whole, the food was adequate and wholesome and the family all appeared well nourished, but it was probably more expensive than necessary if it had been more intelligently selected and prepared.

IX. *Budget of Housekeeper's Family.* The mother of this family, a widow, was housekeeper or janitor of the tenement-house in which she lived, and received her rent free for her services, an equivalent of $15. a month. A son away from home sent $70. during the year. The family living at home consisted of five: the mother (Irish), a son 19, daughter 17, girl 10, and boy 8 years. The daughter earned $7. a week in an office, and kept $2. to clothe herself and for spending-money. The son was a longshoreman, whose work was irregular. When working he paid $5. a week for his board. The total income for the year was $956., including $100. which the woman was compelled to draw from the bank (from her husband's insurance) in addition to the contributions of the children. They lived in four small rooms, which were neat and clean and in good sanitary condition. The budget was kept very accurately for the month of February, 1904. The mother was faithful and conscientious and ambitious for her children. The family lived comfortably, by careful economy, but were unable to save anything, because of their heavy insurance ($86.94 a year).

FOOD EXPENDITURES FOR 4 WEEKS

Kind of Food Material.	Amount	Cost.	Amount per Week.	Cost per Week.	Per Cent.
Beef, veal, mutton......	Not given	$6.58	......	$1.65	
Pork, ham............	" "	.52	......	.13	
Fish, oysters..........	" "	1.02	......	.25	
Butter...............	" "	1.40	......	.35	
Eggs.................	" "	1.20	......	.30	
Cheese...............	" "	.63	......	.16	
Milk, condensed........	5 cans	.50	1¼ cans	.13	
" fresh.............	25 qts.	1.25	6¼ qts.	.31	
Total animal food.....	......	$13.10	......	$3.28	49.
Vegetables, fresh........	Not given	$1.04	Not given	$0.26	
" canned.....	" "	.45	" "	.11	
" dried.......	" "	.21	" "	.05	
Potatoes..............	" "	.85	" "	.21	
Bread................	" "	4.96	" "	1.24	
Coffee...............	1 lb.	.35	¼ lb.	.09	
Tea.................	3½ lbs.	.92	.9 "	.23	
Cocoa...............	Not given	.30	Not given	.08	
Sugar...............	" "	2.29	" "	.57	
Flour and crackers......	" "	.83	" "	.21	
Fruit (apples and oranges).............	" "	1.14	" "	.28	
Cereal (barley, rice).....	" "	.16	" "	.04	
Cake and sundries......	" "	.34	" "	.09	
Total vegetable food ..	......	$13.84	......	$3.46	51.
Total all food........	......	$26.94	......	$6.74	100.

Cost per man per day.............................. .28

The daughter was the only one away from home at noon. The total average per week for food for the year was estimated at $8. a week, including the daughter's lunch-money. The month the budget was kept was an unusually hard one for them. The family had enough food, but a depressing lack of variety. Tea and bread, meat, and potatoes were the staple articles, though the amount spent for sugar, apples, oranges, and eggs was quite unusual. The woman occasionally baked pies and puddings. The children were generally sent to the store, and everything was bought in very small quantities—5 cents' worth of potatoes, half a pound of sugar, etc.; hence they failed to make the most economical use of this allowance for food.

X. *Budget of Steamfitter's Family.* This family consists of a young man (33 years old) and his wife (32) without children. Both were native-born and are a typical young American couple of this class. A budget of all expenditures was kept for eleven weeks from March to June, 1904, and later for a complete year, July, 1904, to July, 1905. The woman has been known to the investigator for three years. She is bright, ambitious, and reliable. The husband is a good workman, but not always steady, and formerly drank considerably. They had four rooms in a new tenement (including a separate dining-room) which were small and dark, but neat, home-like, and attractively furnished in refined taste. There were some good old-fashioned pieces of furniture. The man was a steamfitter's helper, and earned from $2.65 to $2.75 a day when he worked. The woman was a careful manager, and watched all the sales in the department stores for bargains in food and groceries. The man was extravagant and improvident and would pawn his jewelry or clothes to obtain ready money. The itemized income and expenditures given in the budget for the year are as follows:

Income

Man's wages...............................	$625.00
Gift from his mother.......................	40.00
Boarder, 8 weeks..........................	24.00
Total................................	$689.00

Expenditures

Rent......................................	$144.00
Food.....................................	179.40
Clothing..................................	64.75
Insurance.................................	23.16
Fuel and light............................	36.95
Recreation (woman).......................	5.11
Union dues...............................	15.00
Gifts.....................................	1.88
Church...................................	8.40
Books and papers..........................	7.02
Furniture.................................	11.93
Car-fares.................................	27.58
Medical attendance........................	7.69
Spending-money, man......................	86.61
Gas-meter deposit.........................	5.00
Seat in coach to funeral...................	2.00
Fire-insurance............................	2.00
Watch from pawn..........................	3.90
Sundries, including ice, moving, New Year's entertaining, etc...........................	25.62
Balance in bank...........................	31.00
Total................................	$689.00

These expenditures are typical of the standard of young couples of this class. Nothing would be saved, were it not for the thrift of the wife.

The average amount per week, during the year, which was spent for food was $3.45, exclusive of lunch-money. Four weeks in March and April have been selected, which are near the general average for food expense.

Kind of Food Material.	Amount.	Cost.	Amount per Week.	Cost per Week.	Per Cent.
Beef, lamb, and mutton.	Not given	$2.41	Not given	$0.60	
Pork and ham.	" "	1.64	" "	.41	
Chicken.	6½ lbs.	.82	1.6 lbs.	.20	
Fish.	. . . . .	.93	. . . . . .	.23	
Butter.	1½ lbs.	.39	⅜ lb.	.10	
Eggs.	42	.90	10	.23	
Cheese.	¼ lb.	.04	⅛ lb.	.01	
Milk, condensed.	5 cans	.44	1¼ cans	.11	
" fresh.	6½ qts.	.32	1½ qts.	.08	
Total animal food.	. . . . . .	$7.89	. . . . . .	$1.97	60.
Vegetables, fresh.	Not given	$0.43	Not given	$0.11	
" canned.	3 cans	.30	¾ can	.08	
Potatoes.	4 qts.	.40	1 qt.	.10	
Bread and rolls.	. . . . .	1.13	. . . . . .	.28	
Sugar.	10½ lbs.	.50	2.6 lbs.	.13	
Coffee.	2 "	.50	½ lb.	.12	
Tea.	1 lb.	.26	¼ lb.	.07	
Cereal (oatmeal).	3½ lbs.	.12	. . . . . .	.03	
Fruit (bananas).	. . . . .	.17	. . . . . .	.04	
Cake and pie.	. . . . .	.34	. . . . . .	.08	
Sundries.	. . . . .	1.18	. . . . . .	.29	
Total vegetable food. .	. . . . . .	$5.33	. . . . . .	$1.33	40.
Total all food.	. . . . . .	$13.22	. . . . . .	$3.30	100.

Cost per man per day. 31

The man paid for his noon lunch out of his spending-money. He was at home for only 15 meals a week. Meat was eaten every day, sometimes twice a day, but only the cheaper cuts of beef and mutton were bought. Smoked ham and pork-chops were frequently used. A considerable amount of fish was eaten—sturgeon, flounders, and fresh codfish, which is unusually cheap in the down-town New York markets. Butter and fresh milk were used sparingly, but more than a can of condensed milk a week for coffee. The only fresh vegetables were onions and cabbage; the only canned goods were tomatoes and peas. At least one 5-cent loaf of bread was eaten a day. One quart of potatoes and about a dozen eggs were used each week, "sundries" were largely sweets—bottles of honey, molasses, jam, fruit crackers, etc. The diet consisted largely of bread and meat or fish, but it was wholesome and adequate, and in no way extravagant. The woman was an enthusiastic member of the Settlement Cooking Class and was eager to try new ways of preparing food. Both of them seemed well nourished.

The man's work did not demand the diet of a man at hard muscular labor.

Budget XI. For the purpose of contrast and comparison, the budget of a family of two living in a different neighborhood and in comfortable financial circumstances is here inserted. The neighborhood was a typical New York suburb, where prices for food were considerably higher than in Greenwich Village. The woman kept no maid and endeavored to market carefully and economically, but also desired to have an abundance and variety of good food. The diet was bountiful but not extravagant; the most expensive foods in the market were not bought. The man was in the city at noon and Sunday dinners were taken at a boarding-house; hence the expenditure for food was for 14 meals a week for the man and 20 for the woman, making the average cost "per man per day" about .65.

A typical four weeks' expenditure for food follows (for the month of October, 1905):

Kind of Food Material.	Amount.	Cost.	Amount per Week.	Cost per Week.	Per Cent.
Beef and lamb.........	Not given	$4.31	......	$1.08	
Ham, pork, sausage.....	" "	1.52	......	.38	
Chicken...............	" "	.35	......	.09	
Butter................	7 lbs.	1.83	1.8 lbs.	.46	
Eggs.....,...........	99	2.55	25	.64	
Milk..................	26 qts. }	4.12	{ 6½ qts. }	1.03	
Cream................	20 bot. }		{ 5 bot. }		
Cheese................	......	.06	......	.01	
Total animal food.....	......	$14.74	......	$3.69	56.
Vegetables, fresh.......	......	$2.53	......	$0.63	
" canned.....	4 cans	.54	1 can	.14	
Potatoes (white, sweet)..	......	.73	......	.18	
Sugar.................	20 lbs.	1.20	5 lbs.	.30	
Coffee................	3 "	.84	¾ lb.	.21	
Cereals...............	......	.45	......	.11	
Fruit.................	......	2.08	......	.52	
Bread.................	5 loaves	.25	1¼ loaves	.06	
Small cakes...........	......	.30	......	.08	
Sundries..............	......	2.56	......	.64	
Total vegetable food ..	......	$11.48	......	$2.87	44.
Total all food........	......	$26.22	......	$6.56	100.

Cost per man per day.............................. .65

The daily menus consisted of fruit, cereal, eggs and bacon or sausage, coffee, hot muffins or bread and butter for breakfast; luncheon for the woman—fruit, milk, salad, or "leftovers" from dinner; and for dinner three courses—soup, a roast, steak, lamb-chops, or chicken, potatoes, fresh vegetables, dessert, small cakes, coffee. Frequently soup was omitted and a salad course substituted. Milk, butter, and eggs were used very freely. Meat was eaten only once a day, and a roast often lasted two or three days, served in different ways. Granulated, loaf, and pulverized sugar were used—about 3½ lbs. of the granulated a week. The fruit expenditure was high, for melons, grapes, apples, and prunes were constantly used. Cereals were oatmeal, cream of wheat, rice, and corn-meal. The expenditure for baker's bread was very low, because home-made corn and graham bread was preferred. Fresh vegetables were almost entirely used (canned vegetables very seldom), and included green corn, onions, tomatoes, beets, cauliflower, lettuce, and celery.

A comparison of prices paid for the different foodstuffs in Budget X and this budget, as well as the amount and character of the food expenditure for a typical week, is interesting, and strikingly illustrates the difference in the cost of living in a workingman's neighborhood and in a residential suburb.

Kind of Food.	Budget X, Price.	Budget XI, Price.
Beef: Round steak................	.16 a lb.	None
Porterhouse steak.........	None	.25 a lb.
Chuck steak................	.10 a lb.	None
Rib-roast.................	None	.18 a lb.
Pot-roast.................	"	.16 "
Corned beef................	.05 a lb.	.08–.12 a lb.
Smoked ham.....................	.14 "	.25 a lb.
Pork-chops....................	.10 "	.15 "
Chicken........................	.12½ "	.18 "
Codfish........................	.10 "	.15–.18 a lb.
Butter.........................	.26 "	.25–.30 "
Eggs...........................	.25 a dozen	.30 a dozen
Fresh milk.....................	.05 a quart	.08 a quart
Condensed milk.................	.08–.10 a can	None
Cream.........................	None	.10 half-pint bot.
Cabbage.......................	.08–.10	.15
Potatoes......................	.10 a quart	.20 a small 3-qt. measure
Canned tomatoes...............	.08	.15
" corn....................	.10	.12–.15
Sugar.........................	.16 for 3½ lbs.	.20 for 3½ lbs.
Tea...........................	.26 a lb.	None
Coffee........................	.25 "	.26–.30 a lb.

A typical week's expenditure for food for these two couples is as follows:

Budget X, April 2-9.		Budget XI, Oct. 23-30.	
3½ lbs. granulated sugar. ...	$0.17	10 eggs.	$0.25
½ lb. butter...............	.13	1 lb. butter...............	.27
Eggs....................	.13	Sweet potatoes............	.15
1 can condensed milk......	.09	Measure of tomatoes.......	.15
½ lb. mixed tea............	.13	Head of lettuce...........	.05
1 can peas................	.10	6 ears of corn.	.15
4½ lbs. smoked ham........	.60	Salt.....................	.05
1 head cabbage............	.10	Grapes....................	.15
Bananas..................	.10	1 lb. butter...............	.25
Bread....................	.05	10 eggs..................	.25
Soda.....................	.05	Tomatoes and lettuce......	.15
Pork-chops...............	.10	Crackers, cakes, olives......	.30
Bologna..................	.06	1½ lbs. steak..............	.38
Cooked corned beef........	.10	Lard.....................	.38
Meat.....................	.15	Cream of tartar...........	.08
Pickles...................	.01	Concord grapes............	.15
Pie......................	.05	3 lamb-chops.............	.18
Quart potatoes............	.10	Measure of tomatoes.......	.15
Onions...................	.02	Cream of wheat...........	.15
3½ lbs. oatmeal	.12	¼ lb. cheese..............	.06
2 qts. milk................	.10	6 lbs. rib-roast of beef......	1.08
2 lbs. flounders............	.10	Quart onions..............	.15
Rolls.....................	.05	Potatoes (measure)........	.20
Bananas..................	.05	Box gelatine..............	.13
Sturgeon..................	.06	Deerfoot Farm sausages....	.25
Round steak..............	.09	Concord grapes............	.15
Rolls.....................	.05	Cauliflower...............	.15
1¼ lbs. steak..............	.20	Milk for week, 6 qts.......	.48
¼ lb. cheese..............	.04	Cream for week, 5 bottles...	.50
Bread....................	.10		
Eggs.....................	.13		
Sundries.................	.10		
	$3.43		$6.79

These ten selected workingmen's budgets show a "cost per man per day" ranging from .17 to .31, with an average of 24.6 cents. Of this the average amount spent for animal food was 13.2 cents, or 54 per cent, and for vegetable food 11.4 cents, or 46 per cent of the expenditure. Mr. Atwater, who made dietary studies of 22 New York families in 1895 and 1896 for the United States Department of Agriculture, found the average cost per man per day in those families to be 21.5 cents, of which 14 cents, or 65 per cent, was spent for animal food, and 7.5 cents, or 35 per cent, for vegetable food. He estimated that a family could have the proper nourishing food per man per day at .15 to .17. It must be remembered that this was the year of lowest prices (1896). Mr. Carroll D. Wright, United States Commissioner of Labor, says: "It is a safe and conservative conclusion that the increase in the cost of living from 1896 to 1902 was not over 16.1 per cent." At that rate, assuming that Mr. Atwater's estimate is correct, these selected families could have lived on an average cost "per man per day" of from .17 to .20 in 1904. They were therefore extravagant through ignorance of dietary values and the nourishing qualities of different foods.

CLOTHING

The cost of clothing for the year was itemized in the budgets, with the assistance of the investigator. This was obviously the most difficult expense to estimate, and in most cases the total expense could only be approximated. Each article worn, or probably purchased by each member of the family was itemized, if possible, and entered in the budget. The many difficulties in the way of accuracy have already been explained, but Table I shows, for every family, the number of persons clothed by the given amount. The three families who kept budgets for the year had an accurate account of the clothing expenditure, but unfortunately this was not always itemized, giving the cost of each article, for the benefit of the investigator. The results in these families were:

1. Family of three—two adults and baby. Income $489. Expenditure for clothing $32. Per cent of total expenditure 6.6.

2. Family of two adults. Income $689. Expenditure for clothing $64.75. Per cent of total expenditure 9.8.

3. Family of four—two adults and two young children. Income $1600. Total expenditure $11.50. Expenditure for clothing $87.60. Per cent of total expenditure 7.6.

For those families who kept budgets only a few weeks or a month, and for all those who kept no budgets, the expenditure for the entire year had to be carefully estimated.

The expenditure for clothing varied from $10. a year for an old couple who had an income of $380., to $560. for a family ot nine who had an income of $1500. The subject of the cost of clothing has already been discussed under the "Standard of Living," and also in detail for some of the "Typical Families". It is accordingly unnecessary to give here more than a list of the prices paid for the commonest articles of clothing, as they are given in the budgets. Ordinarily these expenditures cover merely decent working clothes, perhaps a Sunday outfit, and a small allowance for ribbons, collars, and other ornamental articles of apparel. Naturally some families are very extravagant in their purchases of clothing, especially where they are bought ready-made, but on the whole the amount spent is neither disproportionate to the total expenditure nor extravagant. The average in this investigation was $88.45 a year for a family of 5.6 on an income of $851.38, or 10.6 per cent of the total expenditure. The cost of clothing for all members of the family could not always be included in making this average, as part of the clothing expense was entered under "spending-money"; in all probability an average of about $100. a year was spent by all the family for clothing.

The prices paid for clothing and the amount and variety purchased depended of course on the quality of the goods Prices Paid for and the purse of the buyer. Usually there was Clothing. only enough money on hand each week to buy the cheapest ready-made clothing, which wears out quickly and is not worth repairing. Indeed, there is very little mending done, which is an extravagant trait.

The budgets show that the prices usually paid for common articles of clothing were as follows:

PRICES PAID FOR CLOTHING (READY-MADE)

MEN'S CLOTHING

Suits	$5.00–$19.00
(Usually	$7.00–$10.00)
Overcoats	$6.00–$13.00
"Pants"	$1.00– $3.00
Shoes (pair)	$1.25– $5.00
Socks (pair)	.10– .25
Hats	$1.00– $2.00
Shirts	.25– $1.00
Flannel shirts	$1.50– $2.50
Overalls	.50– .75
Underwear (set) from	.50– $2.98
Neckties	.15– .25
Collars	.10– .15
Gloves	.98– $1.25

WOMEN'S CLOTHING

Suits	$5.00–$15.00
Coats	$4.00–$18.50
Dress skirts	$2.00–$14.00
Dresses	$2.00– $7.50
Shirt-waists	.25– $2.95
Capes	$2.00– $5.00
Hats	.49– $5.00
Shoes (pair)	$1.00– $3.50
Stockings (pair)	.10– .25
Calico wrappers	.98– $1.25
Underwear (set) ...	.50– $1.50
Petticoats	.50– $2.00
Nightgowns	.25– $1.25
Gloves	.50– .75

BOYS' CLOTHING

Suits	$1.50–$10.00
Overcoats	$1.50– $8.00
"Pants"	.25– $1.00
Caps and hats	.15– .50
Shoes (pair)	$1.00– $1.75
Shirt-waists	.20– .49
Stockings (pair)	.10– .15
Flannel waists	.50
Sweaters	.49– $1.25
Underwear (set)	.50– $1.00
Neckties	.15– .25

GIRLS' CLOTHING

Suits	$5.00–$15.00
Coats	$1.50– $7.00
Dresses	$1.00– $7.50
Dress skirts	.90– $3.98
Petticoats	.25– .49
Underwaists	.25– .50
Shirt-waists	.50– .98
Flannel waists	.50– $2.98
Shoes (pair)	$1.00– $2.00
Stockings (pair)	.10– .15
Aprons	.25– .49
Underwear	.12– .50
Hats	.49– $5.00

CHILDREN'S CLOTHING

Dresses	.25–$2.98
Boys' "pants"	.10– .15
Caps	.10– .25
Baby shoes (pair) ...	.49– .98
Stockings (pair)	.10

Waists	.25
Aprons	.10
Hats	.25–$2.79
Coats	$1.00–$4.98
Under. hirts	.10– .20

In the average family the father and older boys and girls usually have two suits of clothes and from 2 to 12 pairs of shoes, 6 to 24 pairs of stockings, and 2 to 4 hats each, a year.

The clothing budgets of three typical families will give a fair idea of the management and cost in different families.

I. *Clothing Budget of Porter's Family.* Four in family— father, mother, and two children, girl 8 and boy 6 years. Total income and expenditure was $652., and the expenditure for clothing was $49., or 7.5 per cent of the whole. They were all neatly and the children attractively dressed on this amount, because the woman had a sewing-machine and could make pretty and durable things on very little. She watched the sales at department stores and had very good ideas on economy in clothing. The amount spent by this family might be taken to represent the minimum necessary to clothe a family of this size and age distribution comfortably and neatly in this neighborhood. Everything was neatly mended and made over, if possible. A very pretty little Easter dress for the little girl was made of 4 yards of red albatross, at .28 a yard, and enough all-over white lace for the yoke and vest cost .25. Total cost about $1.50. Her winter dress cost .60—four yards of material at .15 a yard. The man had had his best suit for three years.

EXPENDITURE FOR CLOTHING

MAN		WOMAN	
Hat	$1.50	2 wrappers	$2.50
Underwear	2.00	Underwear	2.00
Flannel shirt	1.35	Dress material	.80
1 shirt	.50	3 pairs stockings	.75
2 pairs shoes	5.00	2 pairs shoes	3.00
6 handkerchiefs	.50	Slippers	.50
Necktie	.25	Thread, etc.	.57
	$11.10		$10.12

GIRL (8)		BOY (6)	
Coat	$1.69	Suit	$2.50
Hats	2.59	2 pairs "pants"	.50
Shaker flannel	.25	6 pairs shoes	6.00
Material for 3 petticoats	.35	6 pairs stockings	.60
Dress material	1.50	Overcoat	1.98
Dress material	.60	3 caps	.60
Coat-collar	.49	Material for blouses	.54
2 aprons	.18	Underwear	1.15
Underwear	1.15		
Muslin	.21		$13.87
4 pairs shoes	4.00		
Mending "	.50		
4 pairs stockings	.40		
	$13.91		

Total.................................... $49.00

II. *Clothing Budget of Longshoreman's Family.* Another family of four—father, mother, daughter 15, son 14 years. Total income and expenditures $675. In this family $100., or 14.8 per cent, was spent for clothing, all bought ready-made, as neither the mother nor the daughter could sew. They were dressed neatly, the mother always in black and the daughter rather showily. The man had no overcoat, and the boy's suit was cheap and shabby. They made no better appearance on the street or on Sunday than the previous family who spent only half as much. That family, however, bought no suit for the man during the year, and the children were younger.

The expenditures for this family were as follows:

MAN		WOMAN	
2 suits at $5	$10.00	Dress	$4.00
Winter underwear	5.00	Hat	2.00
Summer underwear	2.00	2 pairs shoes	4.00
2 flannel shirts	4.00	Underwear	3.00
Hat	1.00	5 pairs stockings	.50
2 pairs "pants"	4.00		
2 pairs shoes	4.00		$13.50
	$30.00		

GIRL 15

Suit	$15.00
Hat	5.00
2 pairs shoes	4.50
3 waists	3.00
White waist	.50
Underwear	1.00
4 pairs stockings	.40
Hats	2.00
Skirt	1.50
Ribbons, gloves, etc.	2.50

$35.40

BOY 14

Suit	$5.00
2 pairs "pants"	3.00
6 pairs shoes	7.50
Mending "	2.00
6 pairs socks	.60
Underwear	1.00
3 shirts	1.50
2 caps	.50

$21.10

Total $100.00

III. *Clothing Budget of Post-office Clerk's Family.* A better-dressed family of six—father, mother, two boys, 16 and 8 years, and two girls, 17 and 13 years. This is a typical Irish family of the more prosperous class, fond of showy clothes and appearing well dressed on the street. The father was a local politician and had a "job" in the post-office for $100. a month, and an older son (who clothed himself and paid $5. a month board, hence is not included in this budget), the son of 16, and the daughter of 17 all had steady work. The total income was about $1500. and nothing was saved. The expenditures for clothing for six were $275., or 18.3 per cent of the whole expenditure. The standard of dress was high for the neighborhood, the young people were "stylishly" dressed and in good taste, but not as extravagantly as their neighbors, a family of nine who spent $560. on clothes. Everything was purchased "ready-made" or was made by a dressmaker. The clothes were thrown away when worn out; very little mending was done. The woman would not darn stockings, she said.

EXPENDITURES FOR CLOTHING

MAN

2 suits	$24.00
2 hats	3.00
4 shirts	2.00
3 pairs shoes	6.00
Mending shoes	1.80
24 pairs socks	3.00
2 white shirts	1.00
Collars and cuffs	1.00
Winter underwear	3.00
Summer underwear	3.00
Ties, gloves	3.00
	$50.80

WOMAN

3 wrappers	$3.75
2 hats	2.00
4 dress waists	5.00
Shoes	6.00
Underwear	1.00
24 pairs stockings	2.40
	$20.15

DAUGHTER (17)

Suit	$18.00
Voile skirt	7.00
White dress	8.00
Working skirt	3.00
Winter suit	10.00
3 hats	11.00
3 white waists	4.00
Shoes	6.50
24 pairs stockings (.15–.25 a pair)	5.00
Ribbons, gloves, extra waists, etc., out of "spending-money"	20.00
	$92.50

SON (16)

2 suits	$24.00
2 hats	3.00
Caps	.50
6 pairs shoes	12.00
24 pairs socks	3.60
Underwear	4.00
3 wash-shirts	1.50
2 flannel shirts...........	2.50
Collars, ties	2.00
	$53.10

GIRL (13)

3 dresses	$7.50
Hat.....................	2.50
5 pairs shoes	10.00
2 summer dresses	1.38
Underwear	2.00
24 pairs stockings........	3.60
Caps	.75
3 aprons	.45
Mittens, ribbons, etc.	1.00
	$29.18

BOY (8)

3 suits (av. $2.50)	$7.50
3 summer suits	2.25
12 pairs shoes	12.00
Caps.....................	.75
Underwear	1.00
24 pairs stockings	3.60
7 shirt-waists	1.75
Ties and collars	.42
	$29.27

Total	$275.00

The expenditures in these budgets were entirely for new clothing, either clothes bought ready-made, or the materials for making them, or, as in the last budget, including sometimes the cost of making by a dressmaker. Some housewives feel it is better economy to buy second-hand clothing, especially shoes and suits of clothes, as they are often of better quality of material than new clothes for the same price. Others, however, resent the suggestion that they would buy "cast-off garments". The clothing sales at the settlements and churches are viewed in a different light, and many of these families' expense for clothing was greatly reduced by these opportunities for buying warm and durable clothing very cheaply.

CHAPTER VIII

COMPARISON WITH PREVIOUS INVESTIGATIONS

ALL investigations on the standard or cost of living are
the outgrowth of the work of Engel and Le Play, who were
"Extensive" and the first to realize the value and importance of
"Intensive" such information. Engel was the father of
Methods of Ob-
servation. the "extensive" and Le Play of the "intensive"
method of observation. The "extensive" method is to
collect rapidly many facts and observations and then reduce
them as far as possible to statistical form. The "intensive"
method is to study in detail a few carefully chosen families
in order that an intimate knowledge of the life of those
families may be gained. This is considered the more valuable
method at its best, but it requires tact and judgment in
selecting cases, and insight and sympathy in interpreting
them. Both methods are valuable in arriving at the truth,
and their results tend to confirm and supplement each other.
The most important investigations on the cost of living have
been the work of Engel, Booth, Rowntree, and the United
States Department of Labor by the extensive method, and
those of Le Play and Rowntree by the intensive method. A
brief comparison of the work of these great investigators
with the results of this small neighborhood study is both
instructive and interesting.

Frederic Le Play, the great French economist, was the
pioneer in this sort of investigation. He was born in 1806

and died in 1882. As early as 1829 he began his study of
the lives of workingmen and their families. He
Work of Le Play.
first selected a family as a fair type of its class
and then lived in this family from eight days to one month.
As he was a man of rare social tact and was able to speak five
languages, he was generally able to gain the information
he desired. In 1835 he first published his great work "Les
Ouvriers Européens", which contained the monographs of
36 representative families, compiled between 1829 and 1855.
A second edition appeared in 1877–79, in six volumes, with
the monographs extended to 57. His observations, therefore, continued over fifty years. All grades, trades, and
nationalities are included. The monographs are of families
in England, France, Germany, Hungary, Spain, various parts
of Russia, and even in European Turkey. These families
were studied for various periods of time. All trades in city
or country life are represented, including peasant farmers,
miners, blacksmiths, carpenters, weavers, printers, factory
workers, mechanics, etc. "These studies", he says in his
introduction, "are upon the labor, domestic life, and the
moral condition of the European workman". His outline
for a family monograph has been accepted as a model for
all later intensive investigations.

FAMILY MONOGRAPH OF LE PLAY

I. *Description of Locality.* List of members of family—
Religion and Morality—Hygiene—Rank or So-
cial Condition of the family.

II. *Means of Existence of the Family.*
1. Immovable property.
Money on hand, working tools, interest in benefit
society, etc.
2. Subventions (such as pig, cow, or kitchen-garden).
3. Family enterprises.

III. *Mode of Existence.*
  1. Food and meals, menus.
  2. Dwelling, furniture, clothing.
  3. Recreations.
IV. *History of the Family.*
  Budgets of receipts and expenses.

Each group of monographs was prefaced by a review and analysis of the social organization and customs of that district. Le Play made no compilations or tabulations of the results of his studies. His aim was to give a vivid and accurate description of the lives of individual workingmen's families, living in different parts of Europe, rather than to draw any conclusions or deductions.

Dr. Engel, the German statistician, was the next to make an investigation of the cost of living. His tables of expenditures in proportion to incomes of varying size, made in 1857, after extensive investigations in Saxony, have become classical, and a guide for comparison ever since.

Work of Engel.

ENGEL'S TABLE

Items of Expenditure	Income $225–$300.[1] Per Cent.	Income $450–$600.[2] Per Cent.	Income $750–$1100.[3] Per Cent.
1. Subsistence	62. ⎫	55. ⎫	50. ⎫
2. Clothing	16. ⎪ 95.	18. ⎪ 90.	18. ⎪ 85.
3. Lodging	12. ⎪	12. ⎪	12. ⎪
4. Firing and lighting	5. ⎭	5. ⎭	5. ⎭
5. Education, church, etc	2. ⎫	3.5 ⎫	5.5 ⎫
6. Legal protection	1. ⎪ 5.	2. ⎪ 10.	3. ⎪ 15.
7. Care of health	1. ⎪	2. ⎪	3. ⎪
8. Comfort (mental and bodily recreation)	1. ⎭	2.5 ⎭	3.5 ⎭
Total	100.0	100.0	100.0

[1] A workingman. [2] A man of the intermediate class (" Mittelstandes ").
[3] A person in easy circumstances (" Wohlstandes ").

From these results Dr. Engel propounded an economic
law. The four distinct propositions are:

Engel's Law

First: That the greater the income the
smaller the relative percentage of outlay for subsistence.

Second: That the percentage for clothing is approximately
the same whatever the income.

Third: That the percentage of outlay for lodging or rent,
and for fuel and light, is invariably the same whatever the
income.

Fourth: That as the income increases in amount, the
percentage of outlay for sundries becomes greater.

This investigation confirms propositions I and IV, but
neither the results from these 200 families nor from the
11,146 "normal" families investigated by the United States
Department of Labor agree with propositions II and III
(as will be shown later). In the 200 New York families the
percentage expended for rent and for light and fuel tends
to decrease, while for clothing it tends steadily to increase the
greater the income.[1] A possible explanation of this difference
may be the conditions under which the New York workingman lives and his higher standard in some respects. There
could scarcely be a greater contrast than the conditions
under which a Prussian family lived in 1857, and under which
a New York workingman's family lived in 1904.

Selecting families in this investigation having incomes

Table of Com-
parison.

within the groups classified by Engel, we have
the following table of comparison (see p. 247.)

It is quite remarkable that the percentage of expenditures
compare even as closely as they do under such different
social and industrial conditions. The difference in expenditure for food may be partially explained by the fact that
Engel undoubtedly included an allowance for intoxicating

[1] See Chapter IV.

liquors (including beer) in his percentage for "subsistence", which is included under "sundries" in this investigation. The percentage expended for clothing by the New York family did not dress the entire family, as has already been explained, but part of it is included under "spending-money", which swells the average for "sundries". It is natural that there should be a much larger percentage for rent in New York City. In general, however, there is enough harmony in the expenditures for different purposes to be extremely interesting, if due allowance is made for the difference in the standard of living in the two countries at different periods of time.

Items of Expenditure.	Income $225. to $300. a Year.		Income $450. to $600. a Year.		Income $750. to $1100. a Year.	
	N. Y. City, 1904.	Engel's Table, 1857.	N. Y. City, 1904.	Engel's Table, 1857.	N. Y. City, 1904.	Engel's Table, 1857.
	Per Ct.	Per Ct.	Per Ct.	Per Ct.	Per Ct.	Per Ct.
Subsistence................	44.[1]	62.	47.	55.	45.	50.
Clothing..................	7.	16.	9.	18.	10.	18.
Rent......................	30.5	12.	24.	12.	18.	12.
Fuel and light	6.5	5.	6.	5.	5.	5.
Sundries (including insurance)	12.	5.	14.	10.	22.	15.
Total.................	100.0	100.0	100.0	100.0	100.0	100.0

[1] Low percentage for food due to unusually small families in this group.

Mr. Charles Booth of London followed this extensive method of observation in his study of London, and after an investigation lasting three years (1886–89) published his great work "The Life and Labor of the People of London". The second edition, published in nine volumes in 1895, includes many chapters of special investigation. Mr. Booth and his assistants studied the wage-earning classes of London in their family, social, and industrial life, and classified the population first by income

Mr. Charles Booth's Work.

and later by trades. In his own words, he endeavored to
"show the numerical relation which poverty, misery, and
depravity bear to regular earnings, and to describe the
general conditions under which each class lives". For this
purpose he divided the population of London into eight classes,
according to the earnings of the head of the family, as follows:

Class A. Lowest class of occasional laborers, loafers, and
            semi-criminals.

Class B. Casual earnings—"very poor".

Class C. Intermittent earnings ⎱
Class D. Small regular earnings ⎰ —"the poor".

Class E. Regular standard earnings—unskilled labor.

Class F. Higher-class labor—foremen and skilled artisans.

Class G. Lower middle class.

Class H. Upper middle or "servant-keeping" class.

Class.	Rate of Earnings.	Per Cent of To-tal Population.
A.........................	} Below 18s. a week	{ .7
B.........................		7.5
C.........................	} 18s. to 21s. a week........	22.5
D.........................		
E.........................	22s. to 30s. a week.........	{ 51.5
F.........................	30s. to 50s. a week.........	
G and H and above	....	17.8
		100.0

Classes A to D are the classes of "poverty sinking into
want", and are 30.7 per cent of the population; Classes E to
H and over are the classes in "comfort rising to affluence", and
are 69.3 per cent of the population of all London. He
accordingly puts "the poverty line" roughly at 21s. a week;
families having less than this income are living in poverty.
Mr. Booth accepts Classes E and F together as truly repre-

senting the *standard of life* in England. The general standard of living in these New York workingmen's families corresponds most closely to Classes E and F in London, though the average weekly income is much higher.

It is impossible to make any comparison by classes between the investigations in New York and London, because of the different aims and character of the investigations, and also because Mr. Booth's classifications are based on the earnings of the head of the family merely, instead of the total yearly income from all sources. The methods of tabulation in the two studies are also dissimilar.

The greatest difference is in the rate of wages in New York and London. Mr. Booth gives 21s. ($5.25) a week for a small family and 26s. ($6.50) a week for one of larger size as the rate of earnings which puts a man's family above the poverty line, and estimates that ⅓ of the population of London are on or below this line. This would be considered an entirely inadequate income in New York City. Mr. Booth adds: "21s. a week or 3s. 6d. a day is the bottom level for an adult laborer in London for regular work, up to 30s. for all unskilled labor", depending on a man's strength, experience, or the demand for labor. In New York $1.50 a day or $9.50 a week is the bottom level for unskilled street-laborers, while most unskilled laborers can earn from $10. to $12. or $14 a week. For skilled work in London 8d. to 1s. an hour is paid, and 40s. ($10.) is the usual remuneration for work by the week. In New York a skilled worker in almost any trade earns from $15. to $25. a week or even more. Boys in London begin work at 14 years for 4s. a week, and the largest proportion receive from 6s. to 10s. a week; boys in New York begin work on $2. to $2.50 a week (1904–1905), and

Rate of Wages in New York and London.

For Adult Male Workers.

For Boys.

boys between 15 and 18 years, in this investigation, were
earning from $3. to $6. a week. Girls, in
London, earn from 5s. to 15s.; here they earn
from $2. to $6., usually from $3.50 to $5. in factories, stores,
etc. Women there earn from 10s. to 20s. a week
for regular work, while here they easily earn
from $5. to $10. a week.

For Girls.

For Women.

These figures for New York are conservative and the
result of an extended observation and acquaintance with
working people, but are not based on any available statistics.
Of 75,000 adult male wage-earners in London, for whom Mr.
Booth had the actual figures, 5 per cent earned under 20s.,
40.5 per cent from 20s. to 30s. a week, 46.5 per cent from 30s.
to 45s. a week, and *only 8 per cent earned over 45s. a week*.
The New York workingman considers $11.25 (45s.) a week
a very low rate of wage, but it must be remembered that in
both New York and London the earnings of supplementary
earners are often greater than those of the head of the family.
The average weekly income from all sources throughout the
year, rather than the nominal wage per week, determines the
standard of living.

Mr. Booth also made a detailed study of 30 families in
East London, who kept "household budgets" for five weeks.
As the total income for these families is given
they may be compared with some New York
families of similar income. He reduced all their expenditures
to those of a "moderate family" in each class; i.e., a family
consisting of father, mother, and three children aged about 11,
8, and 6 years. Of these families 6 were "very poor", 10
"poor", and 14 above the "line of poverty". Reckoning
the average annual income and expenditure on the basis
of the average weekly ones for a "moderate family" as given
by Mr. Booth, and contrasting the average expenditures for

30 Household
Budgets.

these 30 families with those of the 11 families in this
Comparison of 30 investigation who had an annual income near-
London Families est to the London averages, the results are as
with 11 New York
Families. follows:

Items of Expenditure.	30 London Families, Average Income $315.12.		11 New York Families, Incomes $200–$400.	
	Amount.	Per Cent.	Amount.	Per Cent.
Food	$181.48	55.6	$158.14	44.2
Rent	64.48	19.7	109.07	30.5
Clothing	20.80	6.4	26.10	7.3
Light and fuel	26.00	8.	23.45	6.5
Insurance	11.44	3.5	17.14	4.8
Sundries	22.36	6.8	23.83	6.7
Total	$326.56	100.0	$357.73	100.0

Size of London family 5, average size of New York family
in this group 4.2. This partly explains the higher percentage
spent for food by the London families. Rents are much
higher in New York. There is no material difference in the
percentages spent for other purposes. The number in both
groups is too small for an accurate basis of comparison, but
the averages are interesting.

Estimated Ex- Mr. Booth makes an estimate of the expen-
penditures for ditures for a young family in London, consist-
Young Family in
London. ing of father, mother, and two small children,
on an average weekly income (for the year) of 24s. (the man's
wages):

EXPENDITURES PER WEEK

For food and firing .... 14s. ($3.50) or 58. per cent
For rent, lighting, and furniture .... 6s. ($1.50) or 25. "   "
For clothes, tobacco, recreation, and doctor.. 4s. ($1.00) or 17. "   "

24s.   or   100. per cent

Such a family, independent, thrifty, and industrious, would be similar to a young family in New York on an average weekly income of $10. Taking, for example, schedule No. 145,[1] consisting of father, mother, and three children, 6 and 4 years and 9 months, and grouping the expenditures in the same way, we have as an actual result:

	Per Week.	Per Cent.
Expenditures for food and firing............	$5.45	54.5
Rent and furniture and lighting............	3.10	31.
Clothes (.75), insurance (.25), doctor (.25), recreation, etc. (.20)..................	1.45	14.5
	$10.00	100.0

This shows the harmony in the percentage of expenditures in a London family living on about the same standard with one in New York, making due allowance for difference in wages, in rent, etc.

The next extensive investigation of the cost of living was that of Mr. B. Seebohm Rowntree, of York, England, who in 1899 undertook an investigation of the wage-earning classes of the town of York, below the "servant-keeping" class. His agents made a house-to-house inquiry, extending to the whole of the working-class population of the city, regarding the housing, occupation, earnings, and size of every family. This covered 11,560 families with a population of 46,754, or two-thirds of the total population of the city. This very extensive method of observation was supplemented by an intensive study of 18 families who kept family budgets. The results of this investigation Mr. Rowntree gives in his book "Poverty: A Study of Town Life". Mr. Rowntree grouped the working-

Work of Mr. B. Seebohm Rowntree.

[1] See Table I, p. 20.

class population into four classes, A, B, C, D, according to income, in much the same way as did Mr. Booth for London, but based on the total weekly family income instead of the wages of the head of the household. This was the method of classification in the present investigation. Class D had the highest incomes, from 30s. to £5 a week, or an average income of 41s. 9¼d. ($10.43½) for a moderate family, and was also the largest in size—one third of the total population of the city. This class corresponds to Mr. Booth's Classes E and F,—and most nearly in its social and industrial characteristics to the average family in this investigation. The average weekly income of the New York families was, however, $16.37. This illustrates our higher rate of wages. Mr. Rowntree considers £5 a "very high" income for a wage-earner's family in York, while this is frequently the income

Comparison of Rent in New York and York, England. in New York: 29 families or 14.5 per cent of those included in this investigation had total incomes of $1200. a year or over.

	Average Size of Family.	Average Weekly Income.	Average Weekly Rent.	Percentage of Rent to Income.
"Class D" in York	4.03	$10.43	$1.33	12.8
200 families in New York City	5.6	16.37	3.12	19.1
Av. New York family income $500–$600......................	5.2	$10.57	$2.41	22.8

Comparing Class D with an average family in New York having about the same income ($10.57), this table shows also that the rent paid by families of similar income was 10 per cent higher in New York than in York.

In regard to the average amount and proportion of income **Of Sources of Income.** from various sources, the average York and New York workingman's families compare as follows:

Source of Income.	York.		New York.	
	Amount.	Per Cent of Income.	Amount	Per Cent of Income.
Male head of household	$6.10	74.3	$10.40	63.5
Female head of household	.39½	5.	1.53	9.4
Male supplementary earners	1.06	13.2	} 1.88	} 11.5
Female supplementary earners	.35	4.5		
Lodgers........................	.26	3.	1.51	9.2
Other sources...................	0	....	1.05	6.4
Total average income	$8.16½	100.0	$16.37	100.0

In York it is comparatively unusual for a wife to go out to work if her husband is living or in employment; in New York it is very common.

Mr. Rowntree very carefully and scientifically made an estimate of a "minimum standard necessary to maintain merely physical efficiency" based on chemical analyses and food values.[1] His figures are given in the following table, where they are compared with what was actually spent by an average family in New York, whose income was the lowest (between $200. and $400. a year).

Items of Expenditure.	Minimum Standard for Necessary Expenditures in York, England. Five in Family.			Actual Av. Expenditures for Three Families in New York, Income $200–$400 a Year. Five in Family.[2]	
	Amount per Week.		Per Cent.	Amount per Week.	Per Cent.
Food	$3.18	12s. 9d.	58.8	$2.75	39.4
Rent	$1.00	4s.	18.5	2.17	31.2
Clothing	.56	2s. 3d.	10.4	.64	9.2
Light and fuel	.52	2s. 1d.	9.7	.40	5.8
Sundries	.14	7d.	2.6	.47	6.8
Insurance	.0			.54	7.6
Total	$5.41	21s. 8d.	100.0	$6.97	100.0

[1] See "Poverty", Chapter IV, pp. 105–110.   [2] See Table II D, p. 51.

In this "minimum standard" *no allowance* is made for any expenditure other than that absolutely required for the "maintenance of merely physical efficiency"—no newspaper, no recreation, no church or charity gifts, no tobacco or beer, no allowance for sickness or death (must have a charity doctor and be buried in a pauper's grave)—and nothing can be saved. The second column shows that the poorest family in New York, of the same size, made allowance for some of these things, probably at the expense of their health, for the percentage spent for sundries and insurance was 14.4, while only 2.6 per cent was allowed by Mr. Rowntree's estimate. This difference is undoubtedly at the expense of the food, which should be about 58.8 per cent, and was only 39.4 per cent. These families were, therefore, greatly underfed.

Rent is naturally a much higher expenditure in New York than in York, and after this was paid less than the minimum proportion could be spent on clothing, light and fuel. Allowing for the higher rate of wage in New York, and the higher cost of living, the average weekly income in the two groups would be about the same. Mr. Rowntree found that the average wage for a laborer in York, 18s. to 21s., was therefore *insufficient* to provide even this minimum standard.

In York the average weekly rent for the entire working-class population was 14.88 per cent of the income; in New York, for 200 families, it was 18 per cent of the income. In York 10.1 per cent of the working-class population were living in overcrowded quarters (more than two to a room); while in the 200 families in this study there were 37, or 18.5 per cent. Mr. Rowntree's statistics in regard to rent [1] agree with the results of this investigation, showing that the percentage expended for rent diminishes as the income increases, contrary to Engel's law.

[1] "Poverty", Chapter VI, p. 165.

Mr. Rowntree's analysis and description of 18 Family
Budgets is very interesting, but a direct comparison with
the Family Budgets in this study is impossible, because the
methods of tabulating the results are not the same, nor is
the material given by these 18 families in sufficient detail to
enable parallel tabulations to be made from it. In 14 families
(average income $4.91 a week) the average cost for food "per
man per day" was about 12 cents, and those families "had
only about three-fourths of the food necessary for physical
efficiency"; in the 4 more prosperous families (average income $9.52 a week) it was 20 cents, and those families are
described as "adequately fed".

Comparing the percentage of expenditures of the 14
budget families (for whom the details are given) whose
average income was $4.91, with the 11 poorest families in
this study whose incomes were between $200. and $400.
a year (average $6.62 a week), we have the following table:

Expenditure for	14 Families in York.	11 Families in New York.
	Per Cent.	Per Cent.
Food....................................	51.	44.2
Rent....................................	18.	30.5
Clothing................................	6.3	7.3
Fuel and light..........................	9.	6.5
Insurance..............................	3.9	4.8
Sundries [1]...........................	11.8	6.7
Total.............................	100.0	100.0

[1] "Sundries" for the York families include 3 per cent on repayment of debt and
1.3 per cent balance saved.

The eighteenth annual report of the United States Department of Labor (1903) is a study of the "Cost of Living" for
one year in 25,440 workingmen's families, throughout the
United States, generally having less than $1200. a year

income. The average income for that number was $749.40
for the year investigated (1901). A more detailed study was
made of 2567 families, who were willing to give
the information desired, and their average income was $827.19. A study was also made of
11,156 families, who were called "normal", i.e., families
which had the husband at work, a wife, not more than five
children and none over 14 years of age, no dependent, lodger
or servant, and expenditures for rent, fuel, lighting, food,
clothing, and sundries. The general results depend upon
which group of families is being considered.

Work of U. S. Department of Labor.

This vast amount of information was collected by the
agents of the department, without usually any previous
acquaintance with the families investigated. A comparison
of the results of the Department of Labor investigation with
those of this small and intensive study of 200 families illustrates forcibly the fact that the averages and percentages
drawn from a very large number of cases studied in a very
general way correspond very closely to the results of a
smaller number of cases very carefully and intimately
observed. Many striking comparisons of the results of these
two investigations might be made, but for the purpose of this
brief summary only a few have been selected. A more
extended study may be made by comparing the ten statistical tables of this report with the Department of Labor
report. The methods of tabulating the results of this study
were frequently based on the tables given in that report,
modified, however, to suit the purposes and needs of this
investigation. The prices paid for food and the conditions
under which these families lived were also more similar than
those in York and London, compared with New York.

First, as to general results in the two
investigations:

Comparison I.

Average expenditure	200 Families in N. Y. City.		U. S. Dept. of Labor for 2567 Families.[1]		U. S. Dept. of Labor for 175 "Normal" Families.[2]	
Average income.....	$851.38		$827.19		$800–$900	
Size of family	5.6		5.31		5	
	Amount.	Per cent.	Amount.	Per cent.	Amount.	Per cent.
Food...........	$363.42	43.4	$326.90	42.54	$338.13	42.8
Rent	162.26	19.4	99.49	12.95	131.61	16.66
Clothing	88.45	10.6	107.84	14.04	106.20	13.45
Fuel and light....	42.46	5.1	40.38	5.25	38.28	4.84
Insurance (life)...	32.35	3.9	19.44	2.53	} 175.78	22.25
Sundries........	147.31	17.6	174.49	22.69		
Total expenditures	$836.25	100.0	$768.54	100.0	$790.00	100.0

[1] 18th Annual Report of U. S. Commissioner of Labor, p. 648.
[2] Ibid., Table V, L and M, pp. 582–584.

The conclusions are evident. It is obvious that the New York family would spend a slightly higher percentage for food (owing to city prices) and a considerably larger percentage for rent than the general average for the United States. These larger necessary expenditures had to be offset by a smaller amount spent for clothing.

Comparison II. Concerning the "Sources of Income" the comparison is as follows:

A. PER CENT OF FAMILIES HAVING AN INCOME FROM VARIOUS SOURCES

	200 New York Families.[1]			25,440 Families in the United States.[2]		
	Native.	Foreign.	Native and Foreign.	Native.	Foreign.	Native and Foreign.
Income from husband.	89.5	81.1	85.5	96.2	95.4	95.9
" " wife....	52.4	40.	46.5	8.8	8.1	8.5
" " children .	32.4	42.1	37.	18.65	27.4	22.2
" " boarders and lodgers.......	27.6	34.7	31.	21.81	25.4	23.3
Income from other sources	64.8	51.6	58.5	14.08	14.75	14.35

[1] Chapter IV, Table V B, p. 84.
[2] 18th Annual Report of Commissioner of Labor, Table III F, p. 363.

B. Average Amount of Income in Families having an Income from

Occupation of	200 New York Families.[1]			25,440 Families in the United States.[2]		
	Native.	Foreign.	Native and Foreign.	Native.	Foreign.	Native and Foreign.
Husband	$630.57	$634.51	$632.34	$637.22	$597.19	$621.12
Wife.................	154.39	203.75	171.33	122.43	138.32	128.52
Children	178.13	336.38	263.67	296.24	345.13	320.63
Boarders and lodgers..	187.19	312.02	253.63	230.21	276.81	250.77
Other sources	95.51	91.45	93.81	88.65	97.89	92.49
Av. total income	$816.61	$889.81	$851.38	$742.00	$760.57	$749.50
Av. size of family	5.3	6.	5.6	4.67	5.18	4.88

[1] Chapter IV, Table V E, p. 86.
[2] 18th Annual Report of Commissioner of Labor, Table III G, p. 368.

C. Percentage of Total Income from Various Sources for
All Families Investigated

Source.	200 New York Families.[1]			25,440 Families in the United States.[2]		
	Native.	Foreign.	Native and Foreign.	Native.	Foreign.	Native and Foreign.
Husband	69.1	57.8	63.5	82.64	74.95	79.49
Wife	9.9	8.8	9.4	1.46	1.47	1.47
Children	7.1	15.9	11.5	7.45	12.43	9.49
Boarders and lodgers..	6.3	12.2	9.2	6.77	9.25	7.78
Other sources	7.6	5.3	6.4	1.68	1.90	1.77
Total	100.0	100.0	100.0	100.0	100.0	100.0

[1] Chap. IV, Table V D, p. 85.
[2] 18th Annual Report of Commissioner of Labor, p. 63.

Some interesting deductions may be drawn from these
tables in regard to the domestic and industrial conditions of
our native and foreign-born families in New York City, and
in the country at large.

The average expenditures for 2567 selected families in
the United States compared in detail with 200
Comparison III. families in New York City in this investigation,
with their percentage to the total average expenditures, are
as follows:

EXPENDITURES FOR VARIOUS PURPOSES OF ALL FAMILIES INVESTIGATED

Expenditures for	200 New York Families.[1]		2567 United States Families.[2]	
	Amount.	Per Cent.	Amount.	Per Cent.
Food	$363.42	43.4	$326.90	42.54
Rent	162.26	19.4	99.49	12.95
Fuel and light	42.46	5.1	40.38	5.25
Clothing	88.45	10.6	107.84	14.04
Insurance (life)	32.35	3.9	19.44	2.53
Mortgage..................	0	0	12.13	1.58
"Spending-money"	27.52	3.3	0	0
Taxes.....................	0	0	5.79	.75
Recreation.................	13.17	1.6	12.28	1.60
Union	1.37	.2	3.87	.50
Gifts or loans	6.18	.7	2.39	.31
Intoxicating liquors	20.76	2.5	12.44	1.62
Church	3.72	.4	7.62	.99
Books and papers	4.93	.6	8.35	1.09
Furniture, etc..............	13.78	1.6	26.31	3.42
Car-fares	6.97	.8	0	0
Sickness and death	26.85	3.2	20.54	2.67
Other purposes	22.06	2.7	62.77	8.16
Total	$836.25	100.0	$768.54	100.0

[1] See Chap. IV, Table VII, p. 103.
[2] Dept. of Labor Report, p. 648.

Readers may readily compare these results. The average
size of the family was 5.6 in the New York families and 5.31
in the 2567 families throughout the United States. If the
expenditures for "car-fares" and "spending-money", which
were given separately in the New York families, were taken
from the amount for "other purposes" in the United States

families, the general amounts and proportions of expenditures would not vary greatly.

The percentage expended for various purposes by the 11,156 "normal" families in the United States, compared with 200 New York families, *by size of family* (including both native and foreign families), is shown in the following table:[1]

Comparison IV.

Size of Family.	Food.		Rent.		Clothing.†		Light and Fuel.		Sundries.‡		Per Cent of Income Expended.	
	N. Y.	U. S.	N. Y.	U. S.	N. Y.	U. S.	N. Y.	U. S.	N. Y.	U. S.	N. Y.	U. S.
2 in fam.*	36.5	40.3	21.1	20.2	10.2	12.4	4.3	5.9	27.9	21.1	90.	90.4
3 " "	38.4	41.7	19.8	18.5	11.4	12.6	5.5	5.8	24.9	21.3	95.2	93.4
4 " "	41.6	43.2	21.9	17.8	10.7	13.	5.4	5.7	20.4	20.2	97.2	95.3
5 " "	45.5	44.6	21.6	17.4	8.1	13.2	5.5	5.5	19.3	19.3	98.9	97.
6 " "	41.2	45.7	19.1	16.8	11.1	13.4	5.1	5.3	23.5	18.9	97.7	98.2
7 " "	47.	47.2	18.1	16.6	9.5	13.8	4.5	5.6	20.9	16.8	99.9	100.1

* Generally no children.
† Partial clothing for New York families.
‡ Including insurance.

The comparison cannot be carried farther, since the largest "normal" family had only five children.

The percentage of expenditures for various purposes in the 200 New York families and 11,156 "normal" families in the United States, *by classified incomes*, is given in the table on page 262.[2]

Comparison V.

[1] See Table IV (Summary), p. 79, and Dept. of Labor Report, Table V F.

[2] See Table II, Summary B, p. 55, and Dept. of Labor Report, Table V R.

PERCENTAGE OF EXPENDITURES FOR VARIOUS PURPOSES IN 200 NEW YORK FAMILIES AND 11,156 "NORMAL" FAMILIES IN THE UNITED STATES.

Income.	Food.		Rent.		Clothing.[1]		Light and Fuel.		Sundries.[2]		Total for Each.
	N.Y.	U.S.	N.Y.	U.S.	N.Y.	U.S.	N.Y.	U.S.	N.Y.	U.S.	
Under $200	......	50.85	......	16.93	......	8.68	......	7.96	......	15.58	100.
$200–$300	44.2	47.33	30.5	18.02	7.3	8.66	6.5	7.22	11.5	18.77	100.
300– 400	44.4	48.09	25.9	18.69	9.3	10.02	6.2	7.11	14.2	16.09	100.
400– 500	50.1	46.88	22.4	18.57	8.5	11.39	6.	6.66	13.	16.50	100.
500– 600	45.5	46.16	21.7	18.43	9.	11.98	5.7	6.21	18.1	17.22	100.
600– 700	44.2	43.48	21.2	18.48	9.2	12.88	6.4	5.77	19.	19.39	100.
700– 800	45.8	41.44	18.6	18.17	10.3	13.50	5.4	5.26	19.9	21.63	100.
800– 900	45.8	41.37	17.6	17.07	9.4	13.57	5.4	4.97	22.4	23.02	100.
900– 1000	45.8	39.90	17.6	17.58	9.4	14.35	4.8	4.96	23.8	23.21	100.
1000– 1100	43.6	38.79	17.3	17.53	10.8	15.06	4.5	4.93	23.8	23.69	100.
1100– 1200	43.6	37.68	17.3	16.59	10.8	14.89	4.5	4.71	23.8	26.13	100.
1200– 1500	39.5	36.45	18.	17.40	11.3	15.72	4.5	5.03	26.7	25.40	100.
1500 or over	35.8	36.45	16.2	17.40	16.6	15.72	3.2	5.03	28.2	25.40	100.
Total	43.4	43.13	19.4	18.12	10.6	12.95	5.1	5.69	21.5	20.11	100.

[1] Partial clothing for New York families. [2] "Sundries", including Insurance.

The New York families are not all "normal" according to the Department of Labor use of that term, nor are the percentages for clothing in all cases for the **Results.** total amount expended by the entire family; but making allowance for these small differences, the results of the two investigations are strikingly similar. They both fully confirm propositions I and IV of Engel's Economic Law, namely, that the greater the income the smaller the percentage of outlay for food, and that as the income increases in amount the percentage of outlay for sundries becomes greater. They also agree in not conforming to his two other propositions. The percentage of outlay for clothing is *not* approximately the same whatever the income (as Engel stated), for in both these investigations it increases as the size of income increases (from 7.3 and 8.68 per cent for incomes under $200. to 16.6 and 15.72 per cent for incomes of $1500. and over). In regard to Engel's other proposition, i.e., "that the percentage for rent and for fuel and light is invariably the same whatever the income", these figures show that the percentage spent for rent by the United States families does not change materially with the income, but for the New York families it decreases steadily as the income increases. The percentage expended for light and fuel does not vary greatly for either.

In conclusion, it is not too much to say that, on the whole, there is a remarkable harmony in the results of all of the investigations just described, notwithstanding great differences in social and industrial conditions and periods of time and whether they were obtained by the extensive or the intensive method. Especially is this true of the results of the extended investigations of the Department of Labor for the United States, and of this neighborhood study for New York City.

CHAPTER IX

CONCLUSION AND SUMMARY

ANY statement of facts, even for a limited number of families, is of value in throwing light on social questions.

Value of this Investigation. Mere figures are, however, colorless and cold without a personal descriptive touch to give them life and warmth. It is difficult for those not living in the midst of the conditions which cause them, to comprehend what some social and industrial problems mean. To know "how the other half lives" broadens the interest and sympathy of the educated, cultured, "leisure class". An ability to put one's self in the other man's place is impossible without an intelligent understanding of the daily lives and needs of the great bulk of our population, the wage-earners. This investigation has aimed to give a true picture of the social, economic, and industrial life of the wage-earners of a city neighborhood.

The 200 families selected for study because of their friendship or acquaintance with the investigators are believed to be typical of different classes of workingmen. Character of the Families. They represent the leading trades and occupations of city workingmen. The neighborhood is a cosmopolitan, representative workingmen's district under city conditions.

264

The social condition of these families varies from the very poor, who are underfed, poorly clothed, wretchedly housed, and who have only the barest necessities of life, to the well-to-do families, who are well fed, well dressed, and whose homes are light, pleasant, and comfortable. The incomes given for one year may be greater or less the next year, but the expenditures will vary proportionately. Food is the most elementary necessity of life, but under city conditions it has been shown to be of secondary importance to rent, and often to insurance. Food and clothing expenditures vary greatly with the income, but rent and insurance are considered by the average family to be the invariable and necessary expenditures. It has also been shown that as the income increases the family's needs and desires expand, and many comforts and even luxuries of life enter into the family budget under the head of "Sundries".

The importance of the character of the wife in the household economy has been emphasized. She is the manager and dispenser of the family income. What **Relation of the Wife to the Standard of Living.** is done with the weekly income and the amount of comfort it yields depends almost entirely upon her character and ability. The average wife and mother in a workingman's family manages surprisingly well. With no domestic training the average working girl goes straight from the factory, store, or office to start a new home. Sometimes the results are deplorable, but generally, though extravagant and wasteful at first through ignorance, an intelligent and honest woman soon works out a system of household economy that is surprising. If this native intelligence could be supplemented by systematic instruction in marketing, food values, cooking, and sewing, the results would be most encouraging. Often the wits of the housekeeper have been sharpened by necessity. There is

frequently "no margin for thrift; money saved means necessary food foregone", as Mr. Rowntree says. At the same
time thrift and good management have been shown to go
far toward making adequate an income generally believed
insufficient for the necessities of life. The attitude of the
wife and mother toward what is a necessity and what is a
luxury, what is desirable and what is to be endured, reflects
the real standard of living of the family. To show this, as
well as the moral and ethical standards of each family, has
been one aim of this investigation.

Another purpose has been to collect reliable and accurate
data on actual living conditions and then to present these
Deductions from facts as far as possible in statistical tables.
Statistical Tables. The remarkable harmony between the results
of this and other investigations has been pointed out. The
most interesting deductions from these statistical tables may
be briefly summarized as follows:

(1) There is a constant interdependence between the
size of the family and the income, and also the resulting
surplus or deficit. As the family increases in size the income
increases, though not proportionately, and all expenditures
tend to increase also. This means that the per cent of
income expended increases, and the average surplus decreases,
until it becomes a deficit in the largest families.

(2) As the income increases the percentage expended
for food, rent, light and fuel tends to decrease, but for clothing and sundries it increases.

(3) The foreign-born families had a larger average family
and a larger average income than the native families.

(4) More than four-fifths of the families had some income
from the husband, almost one-half had some income from
the wives, and more than one-third had some from the
children.

(5) In families where there was any income from any of these sources the husband contributed an average of $632.24, the wives $171.33, the children $263.67, boarders and lodgers $253.63, and "other sources" $93.81.

(6) Thrift seems to be found in nations in which the preponderance of the income is from the husband.

(7) As the income increases more is spent for the luxuries of life, i.e., drink (alcoholic liquors), spending-money, newspapers, recreation, church, and gifts or loans to friends.[1] The native families spent more for recreation, newspapers, spending-money, and trade-unions; the foreign families spent more for drink, church and education, as the income increased.

(8) More native families reported a surplus, but the average surplus in the foreign families was larger.

(9) The chief causes of dependency in these families were (1) large families on small incomes, with few children of wage-earning age; (2) illness or death of principal wage-earner, and (3) irregularity of work due to drink, incapacity, or industrial conditions.

(10) The 23 families who were independent of organized charity, and whose incomes were less than $600. a year, were underfed, poorly clad, and usually wretchedly housed.

Though the average income and expenditures of 200 families so different in their social and industrial condition Average Income do not give authoritative results for any one and Expenditures. class or for the working people as a whole, yet the total averages are interesting. The average income for the 200 families was $851.38. The average size of family was 5.6. The average expenditures for different purposes were:

[1] See Table VI, p. 95.

		Per Cent of Total Expenditure.
Food	$363.42	43.4
Rent	162.26	19.4
Clothing	88.45	10.6
Light and fuel	42.46	5.1
Insurance	32.35	3.9
Sundries	147.31	17.6
Total	$836.25	100.0
Average surplus	$15.13	

The writer believes this to be a representative allowance for a typical independent and industrious workingman's family in a city neighborhood. The small surplus shows that a family of this character is constantly on the verge of dependence—if not on a charitable society, then on their relatives and friends, in case of any long period of unemployment or industrial depression. One hundred and fifty-three out of the 200 families had a deficit or just came out even at the end of the year. Most families live from week to week. The mother, even though she is provident and thrifty, can make very little financial provision for the future and maintain her family in health and comfort. It is indispensable that the income be not only of moderate amount, but that it be steady, in order to keep up a fair degree of comfort and prosperity.

What, then, is a "fair living wage" for an average family? A number of careful estimates have been made in answer to this question. The Massachusetts Bureau of Statistics puts it at $724. a year for a family of five; the New York Bureau of Labor at $520.; Mr. John Mitchell, President of the United Mine Workers of America, at $600.; Mr. Robert Hunter, author of "Poverty", says $460. (for actual and necessary expenses); and Dr. Edward T. Devine, Secretary of the Charity Organization Society of New York City, estimates $600. as a minimum. These

A "Fair Living Wage".

estimates were all made at periods of lower prices and cost of living than the present (1906).

A "fair living wage" should be large enough not only to cover expenses which Mr. Rowntree calls "necessary for maintaining merely physical efficiency", but it should allow for some recreation and a few pleasures, for sickness, short periods of unemployment, and some provision for the future in the form of savings, insurance, or membership in benefit societies.

The whole question of a fair wage depends primarily on the amount and cost of food necessary for proper nutrition. If a man is underfed, he must underwork, as Mr. Rowntree says; his children are stunted in growth and intellect, and when a man is unfit for work he fails to get it or works for the lowest wages. Mr. Rowntree adds: "The most hopeless condition of the poor, as every social worker knows, is unfitness for work. Unfitness for work means low wages, low wages mean insufficient food, insufficient food means unfitness for labor, and so the vicious circle is complete".[1]

This investigation has shown that a well-nourished family of five in a city neighborhood needed at least $6. a week for food. The average for 39 families, having five in the family, was $327.24 a year for food.[2] If we consider $6. a week (or $312. a year) as 43.4 per cent of the total expenditure (which was the average percentage expended for food in these 200 families, and very near the average for the workingmen's families in the extensive investigation of the Department of Labor), the total expenditures would be about $720. a year. It therefore seems a conservative conclusion to draw from this study that a "fair living wage" for a workingman's family of average size in New York City should be *at least* $728. a year, or a steady income of $14. a week. Making

[1] Rowntree, "Poverty", p. 46.   [2] Table II D, p. 51.

allowance for a larger proportion of surplus than was found in these families, which is necessary to provide adequately for the future, the income should be somewhat larger than this—that is, from $800. to $900. a year.

In conclusion, the fact that the "plane" or condition of living which is sometimes forced upon a family by stress of economic circumstances does not necessarily reflect the standard of living of that family, should be emphasized. The "standard of living" is a relative phrase, depending not only upon the amount of income, price of commodities, rent, and other *facts*, but also upon the attitude of each family toward life. This standard also varies greatly according to extravagance or thrift, wasteful expenditures or intelligent household economy. From an economic standpoint, however, the amount of income is the most important factor in determining the standard of comfort attainable in an average workingman's family.

INDEX

INDEX

273

POVERTY, U. S. A.

THE HISTORICAL RECORD

An Arno Press/New York Times Collection

Adams, Grace. **Workers on Relief.** 1939.

The Almshouse Experience: Collected Reports. 1821-1827.

Armstrong, Louise V. **We Too Are The People.** 1938.

Bloodworth, Jessie A. and Elizabeth J. Greenwood.
The Personal Side. 1939.

Brunner, Edmund de S. and Irving Lorge.
**Rural Trends in Depression Years: A Survey of
Village-Centered Agricultural Communities, 1930-1936.**
1937.

Calkins, Raymond.
**Substitutes for the Saloon: An Investigation Originally
made for The Committee of Fifty.** 1919.

Cavan, Ruth Shonle and Katherine Howland Ranck.
**The Family and the Depression: A Study of
One Hundred Chicago Families.** 1938.

Chapin, Robert Coit.
**The Standard of Living Among Workingmen's Families
in New York City.** 1909.

**The Charitable Impulse in Eighteenth Century America:
Collected Papers.** 1711-1797.

Children's Aid Society.
Children's Aid Society Annual Reports, 1-10.
February 1854-February 1863.

Conference on the Care of Dependent Children.
**Proceedings of the Conference on the Care
of Dependent Children.** 1909.

Conyngton, Mary.
How to Help: A Manual of Practical Charity. 1909.

Devine, Edward T. **Misery and its Causes.** 1909.

Devine, Edward T. **Principles of Relief.** 1904.

Dix, Dorothea L.
On Behalf of the Insane Poor: Selected Reports. 1843-1852.

Douglas, Paul H.
**Social Security in the United States: An Analysis and
Appraisal of the Federal Social Security Act.** 1936.

Farm Tenancy: Black and White. Two Reports. 1935, 1937.

Feder, Leah Hannah.
**Unemployment Relief in Periods of Depression:
A Study of Measures Adopted in Certain American
Cities, 1857 through 1922.** 1936.

Folks, Homer.
**The Care of Destitute, Neglected, and
Delinquent Children.** 1900.

Guardians of the Poor.
**A Compilation of the Poor Laws of the State of
Pennsylvania from the Year 1700 to 1788, Inclusive.** 1788.

Hart, Hastings, H.
Preventive Treatment of Neglected Children.
(Correction and Prevention, Vol. 4) 1910.

Herring, Harriet L.
**Welfare Work in Mill Villages: The Story of Extra-Mill
Activities in North Carolina.** 1929.

The Jacksonians on the Poor: Collected Pamphlets.
1822-1844.

Karpf, Maurice J.
Jewish Community Organization in the United States.
1938.

Kellor, Frances A.
Out of Work: A Study of Unemployment. 1915.

Kirkpatrick, Ellis Lore.
The Farmer's Standard of Living. 1929.

Komarovsky, Mirra.
The Unemployed Man and His Family: The Effect of Unemployment Upon the Status of the Man in Fifty-Nine Families. 1940.

Leupp, Francis E. **The Indian and His Problem.** 1910.

Lowell, Josephine Shaw.
Public Relief and Private Charity. 1884.

More, Louise Bolard.
Wage Earners' Budgets: A Study of Standards and Cost of Living in New York City. 1907.

New York Association for Improving the Condition of the Poor.
AICP First Annual Reports Investigating Poverty. 1845-1853.

O'Grady, John.
Catholic Charities in the United States: History and Problems. 1930.

Raper, Arthur F.
Preface to Peasantry: A Tale of Two Black Belt Counties. 1936.

Raper, Arthur F. **Tenants of The Almighty.** 1943.

Richmond, Mary E.
What is Social Case Work? An Introductory Description. 1922.

Riis, Jacob A. **The Children of the Poor.** 1892.

Rural Poor in the Great Depression: Three Studies. 1938.

Sedgwick, Theodore.
Public and Private Economy: Part I. 1836.

Smith, Reginald Heber. **Justice and the Poor.** 1919.

Sutherland, Edwin H. and Harvey J. Locke.
Twenty Thousand Homeless Men: A Study of Unemployed Men in the Chicago Shelters. 1936.

Tuckerman, Joseph.
On the Elevation of the Poor: A Selection From His Reports as Minister at Large in Boston. 1874.

Warner, Amos G. **American Charities.** 1894.

Watson, Frank Dekker.
The Charity Organization Movement in the United States: A Study in American Philanthropy. 1922.

Woods, Robert A., et al. **The Poor in Great Cities.** 1895.